LAWYERS, COURTS, AND PROFESSIONALISM

**Recent Titles in
Contributions in Legal Studies**

LAWYERS, COURTS, AND PROFESSIONALISM

The Agenda for Reform

Rudolph J. Gerber

Forewords by

SANDRA DAY O'CONNOR
Justice, United States Supreme Court

DANIEL J. MEADOR
James Monroe Professor of Law,
University of Virginia

Contributions in Legal Studies, Number 50
PAUL L. MURPHY, *Series Editor*

GREENWOOD PRESS
New York • Westport, Connecticut • London

Library of Congress Cataloging-in-Publication Data

Gerber, Rudolph Joseph, 1938–
  Lawyers, courts, and professionalism : the agenda for reform /
Rudolph J. Gerber.
      p.   cm. — (Contributions in legal studies, ISSN 0147–1074 ;
  no. 50)
    Bibliography: p.
    Includes index.
    ISBN 0–313–26567–4 (lib. bdg. : alk. paper)
    1. Lawyers—United States.   2. Justice, Administration of—United
  States.   I. Title.   II. Series.
  KF297.G47 1989
  349.73'092'2—dc19
  [347.300922]   88–7703

British Library Cataloguing in Publication Data is available.

Library of Congress Catalog Card Number: 88–7703
ISBN: 0–313–26567–4
ISSN: 0147–1074

First published in 1989

Greenwood Press, Inc.
88 Post Road West, Westport, Connecticut 06881

Printed in the United States of America

The paper used in this book complies with the
Permanent Paper Standard issued by the National
Information Standards Organization (Z39.48–1984).

10 9 8 7 6 5 4 3 2 1

Copyright Acknowledgments

Portions of this book have originally appeared in "Legal Education and
Combat Preparedness," *American Journal of Jurisprudence*, Vol. 34, by
permission; and "Moral Character: Inquiries Without Character," *The Bar
Examiner*, Vol. 57, No. 2, by permission; letter to author by Carolyn D.
Nyhus, Committee on Character and Fitness, Committee on Examinations,
1986, by permission.

Dedicated to My Parents
Rudolph Vogt and Isabel Bauer Gerber
on the occasion of
their Fiftieth Wedding Anniversary
Ad Multos Annos!

Nihil est tam populare quam bonitas;
nulla de virtutibus tuis plurimas nec
admirabilior nec gratior misericordia
est. Homines enim ad deos nulla re
proprius accedunt quam salutem
hominibus dando.
　　—Cicero, *In Defense of Ligarius* XII, 37–38.

CONTENTS

FOREWORD

Self-examination is important in all walks of life, but nowhere is it more essential than in the legal profession. Membership in our profession entails an ethical responsibility to temper narrow self-interest in pursuit of the more fundamental goal of public service. A public-spirited attorney will strive to serve the interests of his or her clients in a fair and balanced manner while also serving as a responsible participant in the larger system of justice. But because of the tremendous power lawyers wield in our political system, and the relentless pull of economic self-interest, the temptation to manipulate the system of justice for personal gain is ever present. Lawyers can and often do advocate the interests of their clients overzealously without considering the effects on the legal system which strives, however imperfectly, to provide justice for all. Lawyers can also abuse their position of trust by taking advantage of clients for personal economic gain. This may take the form of solicitation and advertising that fails to acknowledge that lawyers do not provide a standardized consumer product but rather a unique service that must be tailored to the needs and circumstances of the particular client.

In this provocative book, Judge Rudolph J. Gerber challenges our profession to engage in some soul-searching reflection and self-criticism. Drawing on his own diverse experiences as a lawyer, public servant, law professor, philosopher, and state trial judge, he argues that lawyers too often fail to meet their professional responsibilities in a number of ways. For too many attorneys, the accumulation of wealth has become the dominant focus of professional life, with little energy or commitment remaining for public service or pro bono work on behalf of those in need. The law schools have overemphasized adversarial approaches to problems, training litigators for combat; but they have paid too little attention to the humane arts of negotiation, counseling, and nonadversarial modes of conflict resolution so vital to solving modern legal problems. In the courtroom, it is thus no surprise that lawyers too often pursue victory for their clients at all costs. Abuse of the discovery process during litigation is a prime example. Overzealous advocacy often prolongs disputes and uses scarce judicial resources to the detriment of both the client and the larger society.

The solutions advocated by Judge Gerber to the challenges facing the legal profession range from the practical to the visionary. While I may not agree with all his ideas, I share his basic concern to rekindle a spirit of professional responsibility and a commitment to public service within the legal profession. The importance of our law schools in this effort cannot be overemphasized. Judge Gerber sensibly urges law schools to seek students with a commitment to public service and to encourage them to pursue a life in the law that places public service above the private pursuit of wealth. Our law schools should, he urges, attempt to educate "public trustees"—lawyers trained to serve the public as able counselors, negotiators, legislators, administrators, civil servants, judges, conciliators. Our law students must also be educated to appreciate the high ethical standards that their profession requires and to recognize the inevitable tensions they will face between the pursuit of economic gain and their duties to their clients, between bold advocacy on the part of their clients and their obligation to the larger system of justice.

Our litigators must be reminded that they are "officers of the court"—a role they shirk if they stridently pursue victory at the expense of the fair and efficient operation of the legal system. As Judge Gerber urges, trial judges must play a more effective role as case managers and case settlers and must exercise firmer control over excessive litigation tactics. All the participants in the legal profession—lawyers, scholars, bar associations, judges—have a vital role to play if we are to nurture and sustain the high ethical standards required of the profession.

I commend Judge Gerber for his compelling vision of a legal profession in which the pursuit of wealth and personal power is subordinated to the nobler pursuit of justice. His criticisms of the legal profession today are far-reaching, and the self-reflection in which he asks us to engage is difficult, even uncomfortable. But it is a necessary step in the continuing efforts we all must make to ensure that our profession upholds the highest ideals of professional responsibility.

Sandra Day O'Connor
Associate Justice
Supreme Court of the United States

FOREWORD

In the United States, as the end of the twentieth century nears, there is a growing perception that the American legal profession is taking on a radically different character from that which it has had traditionally. Many lawyers, judges, and law professors sense that something has gone wrong; there is an unease summed up in the often-heard lamentation over the "loss of professionalism." This book states the matter in unequivocal and unsparing terms. Here there are no euphemisms, no pulling of punches, and no effort to put a good face on a bad situation.

This description of the state of affairs within the legal profession—and a diagnosis of some of the causes—is not written from the calm detachment of the academy. Rather, it comes from the pen of a firsthand expert witness and participant. The author, Rudolph Gerber, writes from years of experience as a judge on the Superior Court of Maricopa County, Arizona, a busy and well-run metropolitan trial court. Although the book reflects much scholarly insight and draws on the thoughts of some of the best legal minds, it is primarily a report directly from the front-line trenches, where the give and take of litigation unfolds daily in the presence of the author who presides over these adversarial battles. It is rare in legal literature that we get such a direct, candid, and thoughtful analysis of the legal profession and the law in action from one who is so positioned.

Some lawyers and judges may disagree with Judge Gerber's observations and analyses. Some may even be offended. I myself do not necessarily agree with all that is said here. However, much that is said is surely accurate and, in any event, deserves serious consideration by all who are concerned with the administration of justice in this country. Without a legal profession of integrity, dedicated to the public service, and a court system that functions effectively and fairly, our entire system of law is in danger. That something has gone awry is reasonably clear. Whether Judge Gerber has the right diagnosis and solutions is a matter that readers can judge for themselves.

Justice Oliver Wendell Holmes said long ago that one may live greatly in the law as well as elsewhere. This book provides evidence, in vivid language, that brings into question such a vision of the high calling of the law. That is a sad turn of events. The maintenance of a healthy American legal order is ultimately at stake. Perhaps it is not too late to turn the situation around. This book should stimulate heightened interest in these problems and in ideas for dealing with them.

Daniel J. Meador
James Monroe Professor of Law and Director,
Graduate Program for Judges
University of Virginia

PREFACE

Cursed as a nonacademic to labor without teaching or research assistants, I have had to write this book myself. I have been blessed with devoted editing and library help from Charles Jennings, Judy Bickert, Susan Armstrong, Kathy Harsha, and Fran Hood. Judges John Noonen and Joseph Livermore, and lawyers Mark Kennedy and Robert Myers critiqued and disagreed with parts of the manuscript. Their reward, great as it deserves to be, waits in the next world. Professors Deborah Rhode, Phil Gaffney, Stephen Gillers, Daniel Meador, Calvin Woodard, and Albert Turnbull served as unsuspecting guides and cheerleaders. Much as I would like these and others to shoulder my errors and exaggerations, responsibility, like charity, begins at home with me—a home, I am proud to say, that permits scholarship and solace, thanks to my devoted family—Jo, Jennifer, Krissy, and Joseph. For them I pray that justice be a reality rather than a mere word and that its devotees have the willingness to reject its counterfeits.

LAWYERS, COURTS,
AND
PROFESSIONALISM

INTRODUCTION

They have no lawyers among them, for they consider them as a sort of people whose profession it is to disguise matters.

— Thomas More, *Utopia*

... the owls were bearing the barn away.

— Dylan Thomas, "Fern Hill"

Lawyers use the law as shoemakers use leather; rubbing it, pressing it, and stretching it with their teeth. . . .

— King Louis XII of France

These troubled pages find their origin in a three-way intersection: the reading anew of Jeremy Bentham's criticism of the English law of a century ago; the stimulation of the University of Virginia's LLM program for appellate judges; and the provocations experienced after nine years on an excellent general jurisdiction trial bench.[1]

When in a prior incarnation as a philosophy student I first essayed into Bentham, he appeared only as a muddled utilitarian. Re-read as a critic of Anglo-American legal institutions, Bentham shows an insight that springs forth, as Gerald Manley Hopkins would say, as "shining from shook foil." Bentham described the disarray of British justice a century ago as "desperate." The time had come, he argued, "when the scalpel must be set to work" on the legal system in a manner "much rougher than the anatomist could have wished." Blackstone himself would have to be put on the table for radical surgery. Were Bentham alive today in the United States, his scalpel—and candor—would be sorely needed. Indeed, the scalpel might not be sufficiently sharp to excise the tumors now growing on our justice system

The University of Virginia's pioneering program to stimulate appellate judges to rethink our judicial process invites some disturbing reflections on our justice system, how it has become weighed down with lawyers, costs, and improprieties to the point where, as the philosopher Heidegger might have said, instead of truth or justice, it reveals an everyday collage of veils, masks, games, smoke, gymnastics, and at times legal extortion.[2]

The experience of nine years on the bench of an excellent major metropolitan court offers a view of Lady Justice that does not match her noble statue outside our courthouses. She has become a lady immobilized under crushing paperwork, with litigious flies buzzing about her face. Her plight is ignored by her courtesans—judges and lawyers, many of whom seem to have surrendered even lip service to her. Indeed, instead of courting her, part of the legal profession now practices a kind of paper and economic artillery bordering on the oppressive. As they line their pockets, lawyers often empty those of their clients and in the process bear the courts away from her ideals. A fellow judge recently found in our legal system signs of the same decay that eventually ended the glory of ancient Greece:

There seem to be some definite and ominous signs that modern day America is on the same contentious path as Athens. Historians say that Athens went to pieces largely because its free citizens turned into the most quarrelsome and litigious people ever known to man.[3]

Lost virtue is part of this sordid picture. When Oliver Wendell Holmes, Jr., announced his decision to enter law school, his distinguished father asked, "What is the use of that, Wendell? A lawyer can't be a great man."[4] Whether a legal career generates glory or ignominy, one real question today is whether it is possible at once to be a lawyer and a good person, or, in an institutional context, whether it is possible to emerge from our justice system with an improved rather than degraded sense of justice. Perhaps the involvement of lawyers in Watergate and Philadelphia's and Chicago's judicial scandals are the natural, unavoidable consequence of today's legal culture. One may wonder why so many on John Dean's Watergate list were, lawyers. Here, well after Watergate, is a business-man experienced in legalities reflecting on a recent deposition with an officer of the court:

When I review the personalities of the thousands I have known in my 60-plus years, I conclude that I genuinely enjoy most and, at worst, am neutral about the remainder. The rare exception is the gold-plated son-of-a-bitch who engenders one of basest emotions, that of unadulterated hate and contempt. I have had the unfortunate experience of having been exposed to such an individual recently—a member of the legal profession, a litigator.[5]

Commenting on the "consistently rude, coercive, threatening, abusive and insulting" litigator, the writer comes up with a fitting name for the litigator: "The Junk Yard Dog."

A chasm now opens between the law's rhetoric and its realities. Focus for a moment on law professors as representative guides through the labyrinth. Some law teachers now describe the legal system as a value-free enterprise of totally arbitrary rules; at the same time, and without seeing any contradiction, they seek to inculcate in future lawyers the nonarbitrary rules of professional ethics. In the criminal arena, law professors extol the Bill of Rights, Fifth Amendment right to counsel, and Fourteenth Amendment due process, ignoring the fact that only 5 percent of criminal defendants at best ever go to trial and most cannot afford a lawyer.

In tort law, professors elaborate the grand theories of proximate cause, strict liability, and comparative negligence but rarely mention that today's tort litigation is so quixotic that trial is rarely to anyone's benefit except lawyers paid by the hour. In contract classes, students learn about "freedom of contract" and "unconscionability," while in the real world most insured accident victims have little alternative to accepting settlements from insurance companies aware that most such victims cannot afford litigation. Professors expound on the glories of the adversary trial but rarely mention the questionable strategies that decorate it. When they write about law, too often they publish such titles as "Recent Developments in the Rule in Shelley's Case," to be dutifully digested, if at all, only by law librarians. Judges, meanwhile, passively watch this charade with sleepy equanimity, fiddling while Rome burns.

In recent years, federal and state courts have become congested to the point where collapse faces many urban civil court systems. Annually, more than 8 million lawsuits are filed in state and federal courts with 8 million plaintiffs and 8 million defendants. When class action and multiple party suits are included, a minimum of 20 million people are suing one another each year. Every year taxpayers foot a 2-billion-dollar bill to process legal papers. In many states, it now takes five or more years to get a dispute to trial. Ironically, in 1987, lawyers in Connecticut and California sued both states over the backlog they helped cause. In California, the average minimum cost to the taxpayers of a public jury trial exceeds $8,300; at least one-fourth of all jury awards are less than that amount. In Wisconsin, the median amount sued for is $4,500. In sum, processing lawsuits often costs more than the value of their verdicts.

A 1984 Rand Corporation study of thousands of asbestos-related lawsuits shows that cases took an average two years and eight months to close, with 11 percent taking six years. Asbestos victims received only 37 percent of the compensation paid by defendants; the other 63 percent went to pay litigation costs, principally attorney fees. Not only is the process more costly than the amount at issue; the consistent winners are not the litigants but their counsel.

In the face of such criticism, the legal profession often invokes a celebration of imagined past glories:

Our profession in its highest walks afforded the best employment in which any man could engage . . . to be a priest, and possibly a high priest in the Temple of Justice; to serve at her altar and aid in her administration; to maintain and defend the inalienable rights of life, liberty and property upon which the safety of society depends.[6]

And, lest spirits flag:

I say—and I say no longer with any doubt—that a man may live greatly in the law as well as elsewhere; that there as well as elsewhere his thought may find its unity in an infinite perspective; that there as well as elsewhere he may wreak himself upon life, may drink the bitter cup of heroism, may wear his heart out after the unattainable.[7]

This clubbish chauvinism and hyperbole conjure up another Nero, more lost in fiddling while Rome burns all the hotter.

One of the things most lacking in the legal establishment of lawyer-judges is internal critique. A story about Lord Balfour is instructive. He visited America in 1917. After business in Washington, having five days free before sailing home, he asked Colonel Edward House how he could most profitably spend those days to acquire insight into American public opinion for his use as a member of the British Cabinet. The Colonel purportedly replied:

You have, I know, friends in the upper classes in Long Island, New York. Spend all your five days with them and listen to all their views. Then you will know what the great mass of American men and women think, for they will think just the opposite of your Long Island friends.

The point of the story as applied to our legal establishment is that the using public has acquired a radically different attitude toward our justice system, and it is hidden from the very group that needs most to hear it.

Here is one taste of the public's attitude toward lawyers and courts:

In 1974, an ABA poll showed that 68% of the public believed lawyers overcharged; 60% believed lawyers work harder for the wealthy than for the non-wealthy; 82% believed that legal matters could be handled as well or more cheaply by accountants, bankers, or insurance agents, and 42% believed lawyers did nothing about the bad apples in the profession. In 1977, a Gallup poll showed only 26% rated it as low or very low—lower than doctors, engineers, teachers, bankers, police, journalists, undertakers, builders and barely above politicians and car salesmen. Lawyers themselves believe that 20% of their members perform unsatisfactory work for clients.[8]

Public distrust has prompted the organized bar at state and federal levels to launch ambitious programs to counter this poor public image. In some states, lawyer associations have hired public relations firms to improve lawyers' image, run TV commercials on lawyers' public service, and encouraged more pro bono work. In the rarely painful examination of its unprofessional image, various lawyer groups have pecked away at these public relations puzzles while ignoring the soft ground opening beneath their scratchings. These groups regularly locate the sources of dissatisfaction over lawyers and courts outside the legal system. It is variously attributed to Watergate, Iranscam, insurers, politicians, a heartless public, a vindictive press, or other ignorant bodies apart from the bar and the courts.

One of the legal establishment's typical responses is that the profession always has been derided throughout history and these insults are the expected daily fare in a difficult profession working with an ignorant public. Plato, we are thus reminded, spoke of the "small and unrighteous" souls of lawyers. Bentham, himself a lawyer, remarked that "lawyers are harpies of the law who poison the language to fleece their clients." Keats, too, we are made to recall, bragged that "we may class the lawyers in the natural history of monsters." Shakespeare, in his classic, misinterpreted line from *Henry VI*, suggested as the first thing to do, "let's kill all the lawyers." Today's criticism of lawyers and courts, the legal establishment shrugs, fits comfortably into this same merry tradition of jocular overstatement.[9]

Consistent with this complacent view, the legal establishment's recommendations for improving its diseased image not surprisingly focus on externalities— the need for better PR, more TV commercials and billboards, more participation in public affairs, more real understanding from an uninformed public, and pabulum similar to much of what appears in the 1986 American Bar Association exhortation on professionalism.

For the most part, lawyers and judges have shown an awesome ability to look deeply at evil outside, but this same profession—which prides itself on unmasking deception—fails to look deeply and critically at itself. The enemy is made to appear entirely outside the city walls.

In reality, the enemy is within the wall, all the greater an enemy because unacknowledged. It is the bar, and its reluctant ally, the courts, that rightly provoke much of the public's criticism. Lawyers and judges have taken the commoner's sense of justice, elevated it to an inaccessible institution, clothed it in arcane language, and practiced its mysteries in secret like a mercenary priesthood. Legalities have become to some a professional game like football, with legal rights tossed high over the heads of litigants who watch the moves from the sidelines as they suffer repeated injury in the sporting name of justice, a game they watch but cannot play.

Like Atticus in *To Kill a Mockingbird*, lawyers once were admired and imitated. The public's criticism is no longer disguised envy. One striking aspect of the modern image of the lawyer is its intense hostility. It shows up in bitter jokes about the profession's ethics:

Question: Why did the research scientist substitute lawyers for rats in his laboratory experiments?

Answer: Lawyers breed more rapidly, scientists became less attached to them, and there are some things that rats just won't do.

A recent *National Law Journal* poll asked the most negative aspects of lawyers. By far the largest proportion, 32 percent, disapproved of lawyers because "[t]hey are too interested in money."[10] Obviously avarice alone does not distinguish lawyers from businesspeople or architects or doctors. However, the second and third reasons given in the poll for thinking ill of lawyers are unique: lawyers "manipulate the legal system without any concern for right or wrong" (22 percent), and "file too many unnecessary lawsuits" (20 percent).[11]

The thrust of these two accusations is something different from mere avarice: it is not merely that lawyers are money-oriented but that they have undermined the communal values residing in law. The result is ambiguity. Law, on the whole beneficial to the public, can almost always be circumvented, as in the old adage, "A coach and four may be driven through any Act of Parliament." Lawyers may obey the community's law, but as we have seen in the Iran-Contra scandal, they also escape through its loopholes.[12] Lawyers thereby break the law embodying our values as a community, the kind of law that Heraclitus says people should fight for as for their own city wall.[13]

Lawyering of the 1980s and 1990s is increasingly severed from the bonds that unite citizens within the city wall. The legal establishment has transformed justice into an image of war, a sort of cockfight, in which it is the lawyers' business to get a game bird with the best pluck and the strongest spurs.[14] To the public, lawyers become shock troops threatening to undermine common values and doing so before the eyes of a potted-plant judge. Much law, the public says, but little justice.

The present system needs more than an occasional Band-Aid. The major surgery needed will not occur, nor will the disease be fully diagnosed, as long as public justice resides in their unrestrained hands. Most lawyers and judges are too immersed in the system to reflect on its inadequacies. The problems have become systemic, organizational, and theoretical, not resolvable simply by adding more judges or rules or exams or PR. Bentham again is illustrative of the need for sweeping changes in theory: in his first book, *Elements of Critical Jurisprudence*, an enthusiastic outburst celebrating his principles of utility, he expanded on things Bacon had said:

Between us two, might the philosopher and the lawyers say, there is a great gulph. I have endeavoured to throw a bridge over this gulph: so that on it, as on Jacob's Ladder, if not Angels, man, however, may continually be henceforth seen ascending and descending.[15]

Undoubtedly, solutions to these justice problems are as varied as the problems. The ensuing pages do not suggest all of them. Indeed, their aim is the more modest one to show that some problems exist and that they are within the city wall, indeed, within the legal system's wall. Many, perhaps most, lawyers and courts escape these criticisms. Most of my acquaintances do. But there remain enough smoke and mirrors in the trenches and on the benches to justify inquiry into how litigators become warriorlike, how they manifest battle skills, what, if anything, warfare has to do with justice, how courtroom winners are often losers, and how these officers of the court and the courts themselves often behave well short of courtly.

A word on method. In lieu of any formal methodology, I have drawn at times on some discrete Continental movements. Phenomenology, structuralist analysis, and language analysis as developed respectively in the works of Edmund Husserl, Claude Levi-Strauss, and Jacques Derrida have provided some extracurricular insights.

In its original philosophical context, phenomenology refers to an analytic descriptive method developed in the early twentieth century by the German philosopher Husserl, who saw western philosophy and psychology overlaid with layer upon layer of interpretations that progressively hid rather than illumined the reality being interpreted. His call of *zu den Sachen selbst*—"back to the things themselves"—and his colleague Heidegger's analysis of truth as "unveiling" of what is concealed ($\dot{\alpha}\lambda\dot{\eta}\theta\epsilon\iota\alpha$) meant a step-by-step peeling away of centuries of dead tradition to reveal original data anew. Husserl's *epoché* ($\dot{\epsilon}\pi o\chi\dot{\eta}$) required holding in abeyance any confidence in established ways of seeing and doing in preference for going back to the "thing itself," denuded of any interpretative layers and fresh in its originality. Despite its foreign origin, phenomenology shows some relevance to an incipient effort to uncover the original inspiration beneath our layered legal traditions.

French anthropologist Claude Levi-Strauss, a member of a loose movement called structuralism, sees social structures—including legal institutions—as reflecting basic needs for a psychological homeostasis between human beings and chaos. Language and law illustrate an unconscious classification process that is nonreflective, nonhistorical, and often irrational. Levi-Strauss sees structuralism as "the search for unsuspected harmonies." It seeks to present a system of relations latent in a series of objects. The significant structures are beneath the surface, or *synchronie*, with a series of quite differing embodiments at the individual level, or *diachronie*. The latter, however, is only intelligible in light of the former, and it is this *synchronique* system that, in turn, defines the mind. Levi-Strauss compares two types of organized society to two types of machines, specifically to clocks and steam engines. Like clocks, primitive societies use a constant input of energy: they maintain themselves indefinitely in their initial state, appearing to be antihistorical and nonprogressive. Modern legal institutions, on the other hand, are like thermodynamic machines: they operate by virtue of a difference of temperature between their parts, and, although they produce more than earlier ones, they progressively destroy their sources of energy.

From this structural viewpoint, the American legal system may not be superior to any other epoch but only "hotter," more cumulative, and more consumptive. Characteristic of all legal organizations is the effort to establish an energy equilibrium, a *homologie*, between natural and social conditions, a "law of equivalence," to effect social balance. What the twentieth century has created, instead, is a complex attempt at homeostasis that is too energy-intensive to accomplish that goal, a system devouring itself.

Jacques Derrida, the French literary critic associated with deconstruction, has shown how language in official institutions is figurative and slippery and often doesn't mean what it says. Deconstruction is a source for identifying either/or dichotomies common in ideological language such as the guilt/innocence, winner/loser pairs necessitated by our binary legal language.

These foreign influences constitute in these pages a seasoning or, at most, a salad. Though Husserl, Heidegger, Levi-Strauss, and Derrida dominate Continental philosophy, anthropology, and linguistics, some of their insights are useful as a pollinizing propaedeutic to our legal institutions. For example, suspended confidence via Husserl's *epoché* means an initial abandonment of the establishment's defensive instinct of braggadocio, the reflexive attitude that "it's always been done this way." While confidence is held in abeyance, one can try to peel back the diapered layers of convention one at a time to regain origins concealed and distorted under the traditions. Complexity by itself, as Levi-Strauss points out, is not a necessary mark of perfection; simple structures may be more efficient, longer-lasting, and ultimately more effective than complex ones.

These insights help recall the simple origins of law, lawyers, and courts: the purpose of law is to regulate conduct, and the goal of public justice institutions, including courts and law firms, is to resolve conflicts by publicly accepted principles in a way that reduces rather than increases social friction. Disputants should come away from courts and law firms with at least enough satisfaction at the result to forgo personal revenge. An adequate system resolves disputes without such vendettas; both winner and loser rest peacefully with the judgment from institutions that have won their confidence. Shakespeare's *Romeo and Juliet*, like *West Side Story*, illustrates the historical spiral of revenge resulting from an inadequate delivery of justice. In the process of dispute resolution, the appearances of justice are as important as the reality. As phenomenologists like Husserl indicate, appearances alone convey an impression of either fairness or its absence. Appearances can generate confidence as much as the reality underlying them; they can promote confidence, still anger, repress the urge for self-help, and generate Levi-Strauss' social homeostasis—or their opposites.

The precise extent of public dissatisfaction with our legal system probably varies between urban and rural areas and congested and noncongested courts, but its vagaries are less important than that it is sizeable. Significant dissatisfaction by users exiting legal institutions produces social unrest at worst and, at least, an aversion to re-using these institutions and a breakdown in homeostasis as the public is tempted to take the law into its own hands, as in *West Side Story*. Aversion to existing legal institutions already appears in organized movements like alternative dispute resolution, "rent-a-judge" organizations, and various antilawyer do-it-yourself organizations like HALT. In some major urban areas, legal and judicial institutions have become places to avoid; their use produces more negative than positive results, less homeostasis and more social friction.

Although the following pages do not employ many question marks, they should be read as though they did. The suggestions may be wide of the mark, the viewpoint warped by years in the classroom and on the bench and service on a bar's board of governors. In any event, this essay hopes to suggest ideas for change from within the city walls. The criticism does not purport to abandon hope. The considerable good in the present system needs no praise; it is the limitations that need exorcism. I hope at least to escape Brendan Behan's remark that a critic is like a eunuch in a harem: "He's never done it himself and seldom seen it done but only has criticized others." The Spanish, too, have a proverb: "It is not the same to talk about the bulls as to be in the bullpen." These pages are written in the bullpen. No one should interpret them as the language of despair but rather in a Joycean spirit as a portrait of the jurist as a self-critic. Holmes' spirit reigns:

I trust that no one will understand me to be speaking with disrespect of the law because I criticize it so freely. I venerate the law and especially our system of law as one of the best products of the human mind. . . . But one may criticize even what one reveres. Law is the business to which my life is devoted, and I should show less than devotion if I did not do what lies to improve it.[16]

NOTES

1. As of 1987, the National Center for State Courts ranks the Superior Court of Arizona in Maricopa County as the most efficient in civil case processing in the United States.

2. M. Heidegger, *Von Wesen der Wahrheit (On the Essence of Truth)* (Frankfurt: Klostermann, 1954).

3. Robert D. Sunby, "Awarding Reasonable Attorney Fees Upon Frivolous Claims and Counterclaims Under § 14.025," 53:5 *Wisc. B. Bull.* 11, 19 (1980).

4. "When he was ninety Wendell Holmes would quote that phrase, adding that his father had kicked him upstairs into the law and he supposed he should be grateful." C. Bowen, *Yankee from Olympus*, 201 (Boston: Little, Brown, 1944).

5. M. Van Derveer, "Face to Face with an Abusive Attorney," *National Law Journal*, May 14, 1984, p. 13.

6. Theron George Strong, *Joseph H. Choate* 10 (New York: Dodd, Mead, 1917), from his "Farewell to the English Bar: Speech at a Dinner Given in His Honor," London, April 14, 1905.

7. Julius J. Marke, ed., *The Holmes Reader* 99 (New York: Oceana Publications, 1955).

8. *Washington Star*, August 28, 1978.

9. *Time*, April 10, 1978, p. 56.

10. "What America Really Thinks About Lawyers," *National Law Journal*, August 18, 1986, p. W–3.

11. Ibid. These attitudes also surfaced in a 1981 survey conducted by the American Bar Foundation. The ABA found that although members of the public scorn the image of the "shyster," they also "indicated that when they do seek a lawyer, they may want one who most fits the shyster image." See " 'Shyster' OK—if He's on Your Side," 67 *ABA J* 695 (1981). See also R. Post, "On the Popular Image of the Lawyer: Reflections in a Dark Glass," 75 *Cal.L.R.* 379 (1987).

12. Stephen Engelberg, "Contra Aid: Loose Law?" *New York Times*, January 15, 1987, p. A–12; see also Haynes Johnson, "The Arrogance of Power—Again," *Washington Post*, November 26, 1986, p. A–2.

13. C. Kahn, *The Art and Thought of Heraclitus: An Edition of the Fragments with Translation and Commentary*, 59 (Cambridge, Eng.: Cambridge Univ. Press, 1979). In his 1845 address to the Harvard Law School, Rufus Choate argued that lawyers "perform certain grand and difficult and indispensible duties of patriotism" because they serve a law that "is not the transient and arbitrary creation of the major will, nor of any will. It is not the offspring of will at all. It is the absolute justice of the State, enlightened by the perfect reason of the State. That is law. Enlightened justice assisting the social nature to perfect itself by the social life." R. Choate, "The Position and Functions of the American Bar, as an Element of Conservatism in the State: An Address Delivered Before the Law School in Cambridge," July 3, 1845, in *Addresses and Orations of Rufus Choate*, 135, 156 (4th ed. 1883). See R. Post, "On the Popular Image of the Lawyer: Reflections in a Dark Glass."

14. "What Pleasure Have Great Princes," in W. Byrd, *Psalmes, Sonets & Songs of Sadness and Pietie, Made into Musicke of Five Parts*, p. xix (1588).

15. Box 27, pp. 14–16, University College Collection, London.

16. Julius J. Marke, ed., *The Holmes Reader*.

1

The Aspiration and Expiration of Professionalism: Goals of Aspiring Lawyers

> The legal profession has become one of simple billings, and it's lost sight of its basic duty to the public.
> —Burlingame, California, attorney Joseph Cotchett on lawyers suing other lawyers for malpractice

> For [the associate] to come to any conclusion other than the fact that the dollar is what the practice is all about would require some sort of superhuman mental gyration on his part, because all of the stimuli to which he's exposed indicate the exact reverse. The buck is what it's about. Get it, get it now. . . .
> —J. Grady, "Commentary," in *The Lawyer's Professional Independence: An Ideal Revisited* 30 (J. B. Davidson, ed., 1985)

> My students today are much less socially conscious than my students were fifteen years ago. My students today are much more into themselves than the students were fifteen years ago. My students today care much less about poverty, suffering, the environment, and anything but getting the best job they can and making the most money they can.
> —Harold Berman, "Legal Education," 54 *UMKC L. Rev.* 396 (1986)

> All professions are in a conspiracy against the public.
> —Oscar Wilde

Since at least the days of Cicero, law has been considered a profession. Professions and business have traditionally been contrasted. The professional is seen as oriented not to personal profit but to disinterested tasks like the advancement of knowledge. Professionalism involves limitations on the aggressive pursuit of self-interest. Professionals subordinate their financial interests to the interests of the public, especially to people who need help.

When asked to define a profession, Roscoe Pound once said:

The term refers to a group . . . pursuing a learned art as a common calling in the spirit of public service—no less a public service because it may incidentally be a means of livelihood. Pursuit of the learned art in the spirit of a public service is the primary purpose.[1]

A profession differs from mere occupations. Eliot Freidson thus defines the legal profession as: An occupation whose members have special privileges, such as exclusive licensing, that are justified by the following assumptions:

1. That its practice requires substantial intellectual training and the use of complex judgments.

2. That since clients cannot adequately evaluate the quality of the service, they must trust those they consult.

3. That the client's trust presupposes that the practitioner's self-interest is overbalanced by devotion to serving both the client's interest and the public good.

4. That the occupation is self-regulating—that is, organized in such a way as to assure the public and the courts that its members are competent, do not violate their client's trust, and transcend their own self-interest.[2]

Lawyers repeatedly pride themselves on being professionals. Canon 12 of the American Bar Association code states that "it should never be forgotten that the profession is a branch of the administration of justice and not a mere money-getting trade."[3] The ABA's Professional Ethics Committee has also commented: "Personal sacrifice of financial rewards in cases such as this adds to professional honor and dignity and elevates the profession in public esteem. Such conduct marks a clear distinction between a trade or business and a profession."[4]

Professionalism also presupposes a substantial degree of public commitment and private autonomy.[5] Most bar discourse suggests an Olympian detachment from parochial concerns and institutional constraints. Over the last century, attorneys have thus variously described themselves as "sentinels," "ministers," and "high priests of justice," their eyes elevated "above the golden calf."[6] Legal practice is still idealized as a self-directed calling informed by "the spirit of public service."[7]

Such rhetoric increasingly wanders from the contemporary mercantile enterprise it purports to describe. As the legal profession's competitive ethos and partisan loyalties grow more pronounced, the pretense that the bar remains above mercantilism becomes more incredible. Observations from the bench on the kinds of persons who become lawyers suggest a different profile or, at least, a mixed one. The true picture of the aspiring lawyer is not as high-minded as the bar would like. The aspiring lawyer's traits are often narrow, the selection process misdirected, and career goals as narrow as a fat pocketbook.

LSAT TESTS

Law school admission tests (LSAT) provide one of the first and simplest clues about prospective lawyers: they are blessed with high IQs. The LSAT taken by applicants to leading law schools acts as the all-important selection device. It encourages undergraduates with a high score to believe they will do well in law school and in practice; it discourages those whose test performance is less good. Typically, law schools focus on this single, narrow score to determine admission. Sometimes they assign applicants a numerical figure that is a composite of undergraduate grade point average (UGPA) and LSAT score. Either procedure flattens applicants' qualities into a single decisive number.

Unfortunately, the predictive worth of a combined LSAT and UGPA for assessing law school success is not substantially greater than that of the LSAT alone. For Caucasian students, predictability of success in law school on the basis of LSAT combined with UGPA increases to 17 percent (from 14 percent for LSAT alone); for non-Caucasians, there is a rise to 20 percent (from 15 percent for LSAT alone). The proportion of cumulative law school grade accounted for by the LSAT is still modest.[8]

More crucially, the LSAT-UGPA numerical value, however derived, does not measure applicants' intangible qualities like leadership, integrity, motivation, and altruism. Admittedly these traits are difficult to assess quantitatively. A few schools, like the University of Virginia, try to discern character traits via personal interviews. Some other schools enlist local alumni to interview potential students. However, the vast majority of America's law schools use only either the LSAT score or a combined UGPA-LSAT figure as the single determinative factor in the admission decision.

This heavy reliance on the UGPA-LSAT scores gives nearly exclusive weight to intellectual prowess as the most important predictor of student and lawyer success. This narrowly intellectual criterion implies that the practice of law requires near-genius intelligence and little else. In fact, however, along with above-average intelligence, lawyering also requires unusual leadership, integrity, and ability to relate well to other human beings. These traits, at least as important as raw LSAT or IQ scores, appear nowhere on the UGPA-LSAT scores. They are ignored or downplayed by law school admission committees. On this purely quantitative scale, being a lawyer simply means being smarter than most others.

FAMILY AFFLUENCE

The family backgrounds of typical prelaw students also show a pattern. The bar has traditionally served wealthy interests more so than the contrary. Not surprisingly, one of the recurring sociological traits of prelaw student families is comfortable affluence. Although there are significant exceptions, particularly among minority ethnic groups, the traits appearing regularly in family backgrounds of prelaw students are above-average income and professional parents having a high degree of education and status.[9] This nurturing contact with affluence is not easily outgrown in mature years of lawyering.

Affluence will increasingly be the hallmark of future law students. A college graduate going to law school in 1989 would have to assess the cost by cumulating, for a three-year period, the following: average tuition ($7070 to $7720 for public law schools, $27,430 to $30,910 for private law schools), the median cost of living for three nine-month periods on a modest budget ($20,000), and the forgone economic opportunity ($21,000 to $35,000). The total cost will be as low as $48,070 for a working student attending a public law school and as high as $101,260 for a nonworking student attending an expensive private school.[10]

In this future law school, seats will be filled almost exclusively by the sons and daughters of rich and upper-middle-class white families, plus a handful of black and brown students from relatively impoverished backgrounds who receive substantial student aid. Even the sons and daughters of the well-to-do may have to work twenty hours a week during the semester and forty hours a week during summer vacations.[11] Financial concerns such as paying off tuition loans will dominate future lawyer attitudes.

AGGRESSION

In addition to these financial concerns, prelaw students show less attractive interests. Many exhibit psychological traits not found in any comparable extent in other preprofessionals. Particularly noteworthy in aspiring lawyer backgrounds are: (1) prominence of verbal aggression, (2) concern with human order and justice, and (3) a privileged curiosity into others' lives.[12] Many prelaw students seemingly choose law because of a desire to master an environment. As a group, law students tend to be intellectualized, prone to seeking mastery and competence, and concerned about aggression.[13]

Court behavior reveals significant aggression in prelaw students[14] and also in lawyers in practice.[15] "Aggression" refers not to anger or hostility but to a set of personality drives motivating an attack on the environment in order to master it. One of its courtroom manifestations appears as dogged persistence coupled with insensitivity to criticism and to ethics. The compulsive argumentation commonly seen in many law students and lawyers, which often flies in the face of open disapproval, may well be a manifestation of unusual aggression—unusual, at least, by nonlawyer standards. A person acting this aggressively ignores salvific social criticism.

Some students are drawn to law not only by the possibility of income rewards and comfortable social status but also by the opportunity for power, authority, and domination. These traits are also at odds with professionalism. The law's authoritative character is psychologically attractive to some personalities seeking a stable, invariant reference point:

Law has prospective meaning not only for the uncertainties and emotional discomforts of law-student personalities, but also for the relatively jaundiced outlook that appears to be another characteristic of our law-student group.[16]

Students laden with emotional discomfort may thrive on the adversary system.[17] Beginning law students do show a significantly higher degree of anxiety and cynicism than do medical students. They also rank as significantly less humanitarian in attitude than their nursing school student counterparts.[18] Even entering freshmen law students are generally more cynical and less humanistic than medical and nursing students. The law may provide structure for such insecurity:

[l]aw, by repute, is a certainty. It seems, to many and often intelligent laymen, known and knowable beyond a doubt. It is a completely stable and generally invariant reference point. To a person generally uncertain about himself, seeking the security of the clear and the definite, the apparent emotional benefit of absolute certainty and authority may be quite attractive. It may offer the prospect of relieving considerable anxiety and doubt.[19]

In such a skeptical orientation, humanitarian attitudes may become progressively submerged in a cynical, grinding personality.[20]

A high degree of interpersonal aggression also appears in many aspiring lawyers.[21] Those chosen to be lawyers tend to be more "toughminded" than other people.[22] Competitive and aggressive traits attract many in the first place.[23] A majority of prelaw students enjoy competitive situations and often "get a kick out of them," even to the point of wanting to "seek them out"; only about 25 percent report disliking competitive situations.[24] Student interest in the adversary system correlates positively with Machiavellian traits. Students with a strong belief in manipulative behavior have a high level of support for the adversary system, and vice versa.[25]

PRIORITIES AND VALUES

Student attitudes are the key to lawyer attitudes. Law student attitudes hardly match lofty pronouncements of public-spirited professionalism. If anything, prelaw student values show a trend toward self-interest and public indifference. In 1969, prelaw students throughout the country stated they were studying law for the following reasons:

1. to continue my intellectual growth (93 percent of the students gave this reason)
2. to increase my earning power (89 percent)
3. to obtain an occupation with high prestige (82 percent)
4. to better serve humankind (79 percent)
5. to satisfy job requirements (77 percent)
6. to contribute to my ability to change society (76 percent)

7. to engage in political activities (60 percent)

8. to study law for its intrinsic interest (53 percent)

9. to see whether I really like the law (34 percent)

10. to prepare for an academic career (24 percent)

11. to find myself (22 percent) and

12. to avoid the draft (12 percent).[26]

Surveys of prelaw students since 1969 show a continuing absorption in material values. "Prospects of above average income" appears a more influential goal in the decision to attend law school than such other factors as "freedom from supervision by others," "like to argue and debate," or "desire to work with people rather than with things." The low scores on prelaw students' interpersonal interest appear as far back as a 1961 study by the National Opinion Research Center. That study compared various professions according to three motivations: making a lot of money, opportunity to work with people rather than with things, and the opportunity to be creative. In these surveys, students planning law careers differed markedly from other professions: their highest interest was in making money, their lowest interest in originality.[27]

Recent studies yield similar results.[28] Contemporary students planning law careers are still particularly likely to value making money. More than half of those entering law school with other career goals have business in mind. These students evaluate their peers equally insightfully: 94 percent say that their fellow students' greatest desire is to make money.[29] Over 60 percent of students report that their peers are motivated by profit more than by service to others.[30]

Other top-ranking goals among prelaw students are "becoming an authority in one's field" and "keeping up to date with political events." Least likely to be important are goals such as achieving in the arts and sciences, participating in community action programs, and helping promote racial understanding. In a profession which provides direct services to people, it is surprising that almost one-third of its aspirants do not seem highly motivated toward helping others in difficulty. The value "people" shows little to no relationship to choice of a legal career. One might have surmised that wanting to work with people would be one of the attractions of legal work.[31]

Professor Alexander Astin, author of annual college student attitude surveys, has found that many students are attracted to law because of its supposed status.[32] Students defining themselves as "prelaw" who were asked their important life goals preferred such status-oriented goals as "becoming an authority in one's field" and "having administrative responsibility over the work of others."[33] Eighty-five percent of prelaw students favored the status of "being an authority in my field," compared with only 73 percent of nonprelaw students.[34]

When all prelaw students were asked to indicate which of fourteen life goals were important to them, the highest-ranked goals appear as "becoming an authority in my field," "keeping up-to-date with political affairs," and "being very well-off financially.'' The respective percentages are 85, 82, and 74 as compared with 73, 39, and 65 for nonprelaw freshmen.[35] Approximately one-third of prelaw students do not think the goal of "helping others in difficulty" is important.[36]

Financial incentives increasingly constitute the dominant attraction to a legal career. Three-fourths of recent prelaw students chose financial reasons as their prime reason to attend law school.[37] The proportion of prelaw students concerned with wealth has increased steadily in recent years, climbing from seventh to third place between 1969 and 1981. Simultaneously, the proportion of students concerned with developing a meaningful philosophy of life has declined. That value had been top ranked in Astin's 1969 study; it fell to eighth place in importance in 1981.

These data suggest that the goal of making a lot of money obviates the need for a meaningful philosophy of life—or, more likely, constitutes it. The high importance given to IQ, finances, and political matters, coupled with aggression studies, suggests that many bright students choose law because they want to reap profits as they change an environment.

Table 1 reveals Astin's most recent ranking of priorities of prelaw students. This survey shows a repetition of these same traits among prelaw candidates. Their first goal is "to become an authority." A great number place importance on finances: 74 percent of prelaw students compared with 65 percent of all other students.[38] To Astin's surprise, almost one-third of prelaw students do not endorse the goal of helping others as an important career value.[39]

These results conflict with the American Bar Association's claim of professionalism. Perhaps as a consequence, that agency in 1985 sponsored a telephone poll of four hundred law students.[40] That survey reveals the same disturbing traits: while the women in the poll were more motivated by altruistic motives, men were motivated by making money. Aspiring litigators, usually third-year students, were especially motivated by income and job security.[41] When questioners asked about specialization, almost three-quarters of law students wanted to work in corporate law, taxation, or litigation, "the most lucrative areas."[42]

Another probe into prelawyer and lawyer values comes in an ABA-sponsored poll of 615 practicing lawyers in 1986.[43] In that survey, almost one practicing lawyer in two chose a law career because of its appealing income potential. Nearly all the others (43 percent) revealed that the supposed prestige of a legal career drew them to law. Fewer than one-quarter of the 615 lawyers surveyed (21.6 percent) wanted to "see justice done" or wanted to "improve society."[44]

The bar's pursuit of wealth is poorly camouflaged. Law professors close to student attitudes now commonly assume that the desire to earn a law degree is driven mainly by economic benefits.[45] High income potential is even used as an incentive to increase law school enrollment.[46] The fifteen-year trend away from doctorates to law degrees and from law to investment banking indicates that the decision to become an attorney is now often triggered by the desire to have the most remunerative career possible.

Table 1
Values (Life Goals)

Life Goal	Percentage Checking Goal as "Essential" or "Very Important" among:		
	Pre-law Students	All Students	Difference
Being an authority in my field.	85	73	+12
Keeping up-to-date with political affairs.	82	39	+43
Being very well-off financially.	74	65	+ 9
Helping others who are in difficulty.	69	63	+ 6
Obtaining recognition from my colleagues for contributions to my special field.	68	55	+13
Raising a family.	68	67	+ 1
Being successful in a business of my own.	65	49	+16
Developing a meaningful philosophy of life.	61	49	+12
Influencing the political structure.	56	15	+41
Influencing social values.	47	32	+15
Having administrative responsibility for the work of others.	45	40	+ 5
Helping to promote racial understanding.	42	31	+11
Participating in a community action program.	35	24	+11
Writing original works (poems, novels, short stories, etc.).	15	12	+ 3
Becoming accomplished in one of the performing arts (acting, dancing, etc.).	11	12	- 1
Creating artistic work (painting, sculpture, decorating, etc.).	8	13	- 5
Making theoretical contribution to science.	6	14	- 8

SOURCE: A. Astin, "Pre-law Students—A National Profile," 34 *J. Legal Ed.* 73–85 (1984). Reprinted by permission.

EVALUATION

The adversary format that permeates a legal career beckons adversarial and avaricious temperaments. It nurtures aggression, competition, and role differentiation. It helps to subjugate social values to mercenary goals. Aspiring lawyers are strongly oriented toward material and power goals: making money, becoming an authority, winning recognition, succeeding in business. They are more interested in these goals than social issues.[47] These materialistic traits necessarily color the entire practicing bar. Not surprisingly, in their study of the Chicago bar, Edward Laumann and John Heinz find that practicing lawyers accord the most prestige to those specialties that are least altruistic rather than to those alleviating suffering or helping people, and that the least altruistic are most remunerative, and vice versa.[48]

Thus, over the last ten or fifteen years since the onslaught of automated accounting systems, hourly billing, and annual billable hour quotas, a disease has spread like a shadow over the profession's soul. Money has become the number one goal for many firms and individuals. Quality has become secondary, professional commitment has become a third priority, and public service and fun have been nearly eliminated. A managing partner of a large New York firm thus said recently that pro bono requests are

not our business. We're not in the business of providing public service or public good; we leave that to others. Pro bono activities are for others or for public institutions, public defender offices, legal services corporation offices. We're in the business of making money.[49]

Law is now "business as a business," performed according to the morals of the market place, whose traits appear in practicing lawyers' habits of churning cases to generate unnecessary fees, overbilling, obstructionism, filing useless motions, and protracting litigation. Some of this zeal is even counterproductive to lawyer goals; according to a recent *New York Times*, one reason companies lose jury trials is that lawyers appear to jurors as "obnoxious."[50]

THE AGENDA

Nothing in the studies discussed above diminishes the traditional tilt of the bar toward protecting its historical interests in money, power, and combat. Law still attracts those who like to control others to reap money, power, and prestige. Many incipient lawyers seem remarkably self-centered to the point of indifference to the welfare of others. Few traits of contemporary lawyers support their claim of professionalism.

If there is any optimism in this picture, it is only that the American Bar Association itself finds them disturbing:

Above all, we are profoundly disturbed by the mounting evidence, based on solid research, that the process of attracting, educating, and training young men and women for careers in law is often flawed by the invidious impact of money, prestige, and status. . . . Careers involving the legal problems of ordinary people . . . are variously but repeatedly disparaged and devalued.[51]

Daniel Webster long ago observed that a lawyer needs "accuracy and diligence" more than "greater comprehension of mind or brilliancy of talent." Lincoln, himself a lawyer, once counselled that "as a peacemaker the lawyer has a superior opportunity of being a good man."[52] Little exists in the recurring traits of aspiring attorneys to give comfort to Webster or Lincoln: law attracts few peacemakers and compromisers but many incipient warriors learning the weaponry needed to make money—an attitude epitomized by Weymouth Kirkland, a founding member of the large Chicago firm of Kirkland & Ellis, who once said to one of his partners, "A good lawyer is like a good prostitute: If the price is right, you warm up to your client."[53]

As values of mastery, aggression, money, and manipulation proliferate, lawyers who fit this pattern view their relationships with clients as one of controller-controlee or master-slave. They speak of possessing clients and "owning" lawsuits. No wonder, then, that the profession often discourages client participation and control of claims.[54] Author Ken Kesey recently told a law graduation class at the University of Washington that the new breed of lawyers has "a sort of hip cynicism, like painting your heart with lead."[55]

Aspiring lawyers who see the practice of law as primarily a vehicle for financial success rather than for helping others treat the courtroom as their private playpen. Many are overly aggressive, committed to winning over justice, willing to "churn" a case in order to generate fees. Many no longer regard the practice of law as a means of rendering service to the public but only as a business whose primary, if not sole, purpose is to generate revenue.[56] One would like to think, perhaps naively, that the law remains a place where people go to have their wounds healed, not a place to be injured still more.[57]

Altruistic personal traits, like those of Atticus in *To Kill a Mockingbird*, have receded. The values of healing and empathy, notably lacking in many student lawyers, remain the chief bulwark against a system hardening into cast iron, ruthless laws that, as Cardinal Newman once noted, make for an "arctic winter."[58] Despite the bar's proclamations of professionalism, there is little in the aspiring lawyer profile to thaw that winter or soften the heart of a litigator. Simply put, many mercenary persons are attracted to law, for which the bar pays a dear price in its claim to professionalism. Here is the American Bar Association's summary of how "professional" lawyers today appear:

The public views lawyers, at best, as being of uneven character and quality. In a survey conducted by this Commission, under the thoughtful direction of Commission member Gustave H. Shubert, only 6% of corporate users of legal service rated "all or most" lawyers as deserving to be called "professionals." Only 7% saw professionalism increasing among lawyers; 68% said it had decreased over time. Similarly, 55% of the state and federal judges questioned in a separate poll said lawyer professionalism was declining.[59]

These mercentile traits do not enhance the typical client-centered law practice involving most law graduates. Nor do they support the bar's claim on professionalism. Here are some necessary changes that need to be made by the bar and law schools to revive professionalism.

In the first place, the LSAT-UGPA domination in the law school admission decision needs to be relaxed. Too often admission committees rely heavily on LSAT and GPA figures (largely "masculine," left-brain measurements), quickly scan personal data and statements, and discourage personal interviews. This objective process reflects not so much a commitment to fairness as institutional apathy. The pendulum has swung too far toward anonymity and adulation of high IQ. Personal interviews should be available at least for the great middle range of applicants, particularly to assess commitment to representing the underserved and the public interest. Age and life experiences should also weigh more heavily in the selection process. While there is an arguable correlation between LSAT-GPA figures, law school grades and bar passage rates alone are unperceptive criteria for competent lawyering. Exposure to people problems rather than to mere academic tasks should also be a positive factor in the admission decision.

Second, law school administrators need to adopt relatively easily recognized personality criteria for part of an entering class, such as (1) experience in social or humanitarian endeavors, like nursing, Peace Corps, or volunteer work, or (2) a high altruism score on a required personality test such as the Minnesota Multiphasic Personality Inventory or Myers-Briggs. In any form, altruism should be an important entrance requirement, perhaps not as universally required as a high LSAT score but at least a desideratum for about half an entering class. Law schools should recruit altruistic students with the same fervor with which they now enroll minority students or high LSAT scorers; altruism is now less represented in the bar than women, blacks, and elevated LSAT scorers. The resulting lawyer universe would gradually show more public service and less money-anxiety.

Third, aspiring lawyers must be forced to accept that professionalism involves mandatory pro bono activity. The requirement was put forth in an early draft discussion of the Model Rules[60] and virtually hooted down,[61] in spite of the fact that ABA House of Delegates had gone on record in favor of the concept just five years earlier in 1975.[62] The ABA again rejected it in 1988. As an abstract ideal on paper, pro bono is desirable; as a specific disciplinary requirement to be enforced it is unacceptable. Model Rule 6.1 thus states the desirability of pro bono ("pro bono public service") but without obligation—and with nothing to ward off the smell of hyprocrisy.[63]

The official policy of the American Bar Association on pro bono since 1975 has been:

It is a basic professional responsibility of each lawyer engaged in the practice of law to provide public interest legal services without fee or at a substantially reduced fee in the following areas: poverty law, civil rights law, charitable organizations representation and administration of justice. It should always be provided in a manner consistent with the Model Rules of Professional Conduct. The organized bar should assist each lawyer in fulfilling his responsibilities in providing such services as long as there is need, and should assist, foster and encourage governmental, charitable, and other sources to provide public interest legal services.[64]

Certainly there is ample need for pro bono legal service. In Texas, a 1983 study found that 468,000 citizens have a civil legal problem and cannot afford an attorney. Fewer than 10 percent of these people obtained any legal assistance. In Colorado, a 1984 survey found that 61 percent of households below the poverty line—nearly 100,000—had a legal problem that year. But only 37 percent reported seeing an attorney in the previous five years. In Massachusetts, fewer than 15 percent of the civil legal needs of the poor are met. Only 15 percent of lawyers nationwide participate in organized pro bono programs for the poor, and few lawyers can be found to handle cases for groups such as Indians—unless, of course, lucrative land claims are involved.[65]

What pro bono work now exists is minimal and partisan. The most comprehensive survey of lawyers' pro bono activity reveals that about three-fifths of respondents devoted less than 5 percent of billable hours to such work, and that half of this group spent no time at all.[66] The investment for the bar as a whole averages 6.2 percent of billable hours. The vast bulk of these contributions did not redound to the advantage of chronically underrepresented interests; one-third of individual pro bono clients were relatives and friends. Of the organizations receiving assistance, 82 percent were churches, hospitals, and middle-class-oriented community groups, such as Boy Scouts, Jaycees, Masons, and garden clubs. Only 5 percent were legal aid and public defender organizations.

From some law schools, as few as 3 percent of graduating students are choosing to begin careers in the public sector. A declining number of lawyers is willing to stand for public office and there is a shrinking number of lawyer-legislators.

The organized bar's inability to come to real terms with a practical pro bono requirement serves as a significant guilt catharsis. By merely urging in Model Rule 6.1 the advancement of the public good, attorneys announce their special status as public servants. Yet it is still not in any individual lawyer's interest that this public service ideal have any teeth in an obligatory code.[67] The current code thus offers much admonition but no mandatory rule regarding pro bono. Nowhere is the disparity between rhetoric and reality more apparent than in the assertion of both the Model Rules and the Code that the basic responsibility for providing legal services for those unable to pay rests upon the individual lawyer.

The rhetorical posturing about pro bono achievements is at best rank hypocrisy. Pro bono publico, if it exists at all, has become a tithe lawyers pay as a quid pro quo for special privileges (e.g., exclusion of competitors, economic reward, high social status). It exists not as a fact but as sugary fiction. It recalls Jacques Derrida's observations about the meaninglessness of professional jargon that placates the public by claiming to serve it—while, in fact, keeping them separate from each other.

The most workable solution for pro bono is the rewriting of Model Rule 6.1 to make pro bono work obligatory, coupled with implementation by rule of mandatory stages of pro bono work. The obligation needs to become a prerequisite to licensing. Since repeated testing and licensing is also a necessity, the most practical way to implement pro bono is twofold: (1) a mandatory public "advocate" or "trusteeship" internship prior to bar admission, and (2) a recurring sabbatical year obligation on every lawyer to serve as a pro bono advocate at least half-time in that year as a precondition to license renewal. Pro bono advocates at each stage of their career would be required by rule to donate legal work for public interest agencies or for the poor, sick, and politically underrepresented, and to do so without full compensation.

CONCLUSION

True professionals combine the roles of healer, helper, defender, mediator, and teacher. Today we have lost the ability to distinguish between a calling and a station in life, to see differences between a profession and a trade. To the extent that law students and lawyers become absorbed in status and gain, law ceases to be a profession, and the law school becomes merely another training school like a transmission shop.

Until the bar reconsiders its narrow entrance requirements and public service rhetoric, its proclamations of professionalism ring hollow. Rather than support its repeated boasts of professionalism, lawyer attitudes reveal a progressive deprofessionalization of a once lofty calling, to the point where lawyering has become a mercantile business like any other. Only radical change can breathe altruism back into its soul.

Chief Justice Charles Evans Hughes once said:

The highest reward that can come to a lawyer is the esteem of his professional brethren. That esteem is won in unique conditions and proceeds from an impartial judgment of professional rivals. It cannot be artificially created. . . . It is not measured by pecuniary gains.[68]

NOTES

1. R. Pound, *The Lawyer from Antiquity to Modern Times* 5 (St. Paul: West Publishing, 1953).

2. "In the Spirit of Public Service," *ABA Report on Professionalism* 10 (1986).

3. The Canons may be found in Elliott E. Cheatham, *Cases and Other Materials on the Legal Profession* (Chicago: Foundations Press, 1938), pp. 519–534.

4. American Bar Association, *Opinions of the Committee on Professional Ethics and Grievances* (New York: American Bar Association, 1947), p. 191. Cases have reached similar results. For example: The New York State Court of Appeals held in 1910 that an attorney "is an officer of the court and is judged as such, and his technical contractual rights must yield to his duty as such officer" (*Matter of Friedman*, 136 App. Div. 750 and 199 N.Y. 537). Freund states that the legal profession, like others, "considers its function to be that of serving the public," and analyzes three standards that will best enable such service: independence, availability, and learning (Paul A. Freund, "The Legal Profession," *Daedalus*, Fall 1963, pp. 689–700). The most comprehensive discussions of lawyers' service ethic are to be found in casebooks on the legal profession for use in law school courses. Representatives among these are Cheatham, supra note 3; and George P. Costigan, Jr., *Cases and Other Authorities on the Legal Profession* (1980).

5. W. Moore, *The Professions: Roles and Rules* 5 (New York: Russell Sage, 1970); see also Becker, "The Nature of a Profession," in *Education for the Professions* 27, 38–39 (1962); Wilensky, "The Professionalization of Everyone?" 70 *Am. J. Soc.* 137 (1964).

6. J. Story, Address Delivered Before the Members of the Suffolk Bar (1821), excerpted in P. Miller, *The Legal Mind in America: From Independence to the Civil War* 63, 71 (Garden City: Doubleday, 1962) ("sentinels" and "ministers"); James Jackson, *Law and Lawyers*, in P. Miller, supra, at 274, 283 ("sentinel," "guardian of morality," and "conservator of right"); *People v. Beattie*, 137 Ill. 553, 574, 27 N.E, 1096, 1103 (1891) ("minister"); T. Strong, *Joseph H. Choate* 130 (New York: Dodd, Mead, 1917) ("high priest"); C. Brewer, "The Ideal Lawyer," 98 *Atl. Monthly* 487, 591 (1906) ("[h]e looks above the golden calf"); Report of the Committee on Code of Professional Ethics, 29 *A.B.A. Rep.* 600, 602 (1906) ("ministers"); Address of Chancellor Kent before the Law Association of the City of New York (Oct. 21, 1836), reprinted in 16 *Am. Jurist* 471, 472 (1836) ("sentinels").

7. R. Pound, *The Lawyer from Antiquity to Modern Times* 14.

8. Some law schools determine this "optimal combination" of LSAT score and UGPA by computing beta coefficient equations for each statistically significant subgroup of the applicant pool. The actual values for each candidate are then plugged into the appropriate equation: applicants are ranked in order of the magnitude of the resulting score. Different coefficients for the various applicant subgroups would minimize unfairness and maximize predictability. For details see *Mexican-American Legal Defense Fund* and also S. Brown and E. Marenco, *Law School Admission Study*, 39–46 (1980).

9. There is some evidence that scores on the Scholastic Aptitude Test vary directly with annual parental income. One might assume the same is true for LSAT tests. See *Test Scores and Family Income: A Response to Charges*, in Nader/Nairn, *Report in ETS*, Princeton, N.J., 1980.

10. J. Kramer, "Will Legal Education Remain Affordable, by Whom, and How?" 1987 *Duke L.J.* 240, 247 (1987).

11. Ibid., at 248.

12. A. Watson, "The Quest for Professional Competence: Psychological Aspects of Legal Education," 37 *U. Cinn. L. Rev.* 91, 95 (1968). See also B. Nachmann, "Childhood

Experience and Vocational Choice in Law, Dentistry, and Social Work," 7 *J. Counseling Psychology* 243 (1960).

13. Ibid. at 91. See also Paul Van R. Miller, "Personality Differences and Student Survival in Law School," 19 *J. Legal Ed.* 460 (1967).

14. W. Weyrauch, *The Personality of Lawyers* 27 (New Haven, Conn.: Yale Univ. Press, 1964).

15. C. Bruck, "How Ford Stalled the Pinto Litigation," 1 *Am. Law.*, June 1979, at 24. (Stating that "Ford has been cited in at least five appellate court decisions for having obstructed discovery by giving false answers to interrogatories, and by hiding damaging documents. Despite various attempts to get the manufacturer defaulted, the heaviest sanctions imposed on Ford so far have been a $500 fine and two new trials.")

16. R. Redmount, "A Conceptual View of Legal Education Process," 24 *J. Legal Ed.* 129 (1972).

17. Ibid.

18. Ibid.

19. Ibid. at 438.

20. Ibid. at 439.

21. Ibid. at 439.

22. Thomas L. Shaffer and Robert Redmount, *Lawyers, Law Students and People* 95 (Colorado Springs: Shephard's Inc., 1977).

23. Ibid. at 196.

24. W. Thielens, *The Socialization of Law Students* at 163 (New York: Arno Press, 1980). See also J. Stark, P. Tegeler, and N. Channels, "The Effect of Student Values on Lawyering Performance: An Empirical Response to Condlin," 37 *J. Legal Ed.* 409, 418 (1987).

25. See Stark et al., "The Effect of Student Values," at 418.

26. C. Auerbach, "Legal Education and Its Discontents," 34 *J. Legal Ed.* 43, 52 (1984).

27. J. Davis, *Undergraduate Career Decisions; Correlates of Occupational Choice*, 140 (Chicago: Aldine Publishing, 1965).

28. S. Warkov and J. Zelan, *Lawyers in the Making* (Chicago: Aldine Publishing, 1965); Robert Stevens, "Law Schools and Law Students," 59 *Va. L. Rev.* 551 (1973). Stevens found that women, blacks, and students with parents with relatively low family income were all more likely to cite service to the underprivileged as a motivation for entering law school than were other students.

29. R. Pipkin, "Law School Instruction in Professional Responsibility: A Curricular Paradox," 1979 *Am.B.F.R. J.* 247, 274 (1979). Cf. also F. Zemans and V. Rosenbaum, *The Making of a Public Profession*, 30 (Chicago: American Bar Foundation, 1981).

30. Audrey J. Schwartz, "Law, Lawyers and Law School: Perspectives from the First Year Class," 30 *J. Legal Ed.* 437, 439 (1980).

31. Davis, *Undergraduate Career Choices*, 140.

32. A. Astin, "Pre-law Students—A National Profile," 34 *J. Legal Ed.* 73 (1984).

33. Ibid. at 83.

34. Ibid. at 82.

35. Ibid. at 82.

36. Ibid.

37. Ibid.

38. A. Astin, "Pre-law Students," at 73, as quoted in 68 *ABA J.* 1359 (November

1982). Bernard Diamond has also observed, "today, law students tend to be more intelligent, more sophisticated, and more aware of what it means to be a lawyer. They are firmly driven toward a high social status, and they are well aware that a profession, rather than business, is the modern route to such status with its power and monetary rewards." S. Gillers, ed., *Looking at Law School*, 56 (New York: Taplinger, 1984).

39. Astin, supra, note 38.

40. "A Portrait of America's Law Students," 71 *ABA J.* at 43, 45 (May 1985).

41. Ibid. Social Justice as a goal ranked higher than finances in this poll, but the mechanics of the poll are not revealed in the article.

42. Ibid. at 45.

43. P. Reidinger, "It's 46.5 Hours a Week in Law," 72 *ABA J.*, Sept. 1, 1986 at 44.

44. Ibid.

45. J. Kramer, "Will Legal Education Remain Affordable?" ("This analysis assumes that the desire to earn a JD is driven exclusively by the economic benefits of a legal education.")

46. Ibid.

47. A. Astin, "Pre-law Students," at 73.

48. Quoted in Gee, "Current Studies of Legal Education," 32 *J. Legal Ed.* 471, 502 (1982). See also Edward O. Laumann and John P. Heinz, "Specializing and Prestige in the Legal Profession: The Structure of Deference," 1977 *Am. B. Found. J.* 155.

49. Benjamin Civiletti, "Projected Law Practice in the 1990s," *National Law Journal*, August 10, 1987, p. 22.

50. David Margolick, "Lawyers from the Old School Losing Ground to New Breed," *New York Times*, July 17, 1982, at 21, col. 1, at 22, col. 6 (quoting Gerald Edelman) ("[A]dvocacy is going down the drain. . . . [T]he law has become a business, a trade. It's not a profession anymore."); accord P. Brown, "Misguided Lawyers," *New York Times*, Dec. 6, 1983, p. A31, col. 1. See H. F. Stone, "The Public Influence of the Bar," 48 *Harv. L. Rev.* 1, 3 (1934) (evoking "pages of a glorious past" in which the bar was more committed to the public interest and less to profits); see also E. Smigel, *The Wall Street Lawyer* 304 (1964) (discussing perceptions of Wall Street attorneys in the 1950s). For the "obnoxious lawyer" quote, see *Atlantic Monthly*, April 1988, p. 66.

51. Edward O. Laumann and John P. Heinz, "Specializing and Prestige in the Legal Profession," report that the prestige of legal specialties is associated with intellectual difficulty. But with lawyers who represent opposite sides (e.g., antitrust plaintiffs and defendants, consumers and merchants) and presumably encounter comparable intellectual challenges, they found that "the side that represents the more 'established' interest is consistently rated higher in prestige."

52. Abraham Lincoln, Notes for Law Lecture, *Complete Works of Abraham Lincoln*, Vol. 2, J. Nicolay and J. Hay, ed., (Lincoln Memorial University, 1894), 142.

53. Phillip M. Stern, *Lawyers on Trial*, (New York: Times Books, 1980).

54. Sylvia Law, "Afterward: The Purpose of Professional Education," in S. Gillers, ed., *Looking at Law School: A Student Guide from the Society of American Law Teachers*, (New York: Taplinger Publishing Co., 1977) pp. 205, 212–213.

55. Quoted in the *Arizona Business Gazette*, June 24, 1985, at 1.

56. 68 *ABA J.*, 525, 526 (May 1982).

57. Ibid.

58. John H. Cardinal Newman, *Historical Sketches* 74 (London, 1872).

59. ABA Committee on Professionalism, "In the Spirit of Public Service," (1986), at 3.

60. See *Model Rules of Professional Conduct*, Rule 6.1 (Discussion Draft 1980). (Rule requiring an attorney to render pro bono public service.)

61. See G. Hazard and W. Hodes, *The Law of Lawyering: A Handbook of the Modern Rules of Professional Conduct* (New York: Law and Business, 1985) 491–92.

62. See ABA Special Committee on Public Interest Practice, *Implementing the Lawyer's Public Interest Obligation* (1977).

63. See *Model Rules of Professional Conduct*, Rule 6.1 (1983).

64. Editorial, G. Lundberg and L. Bodine, "50 Hours for the Poor," 73 *ABA J.* 55 (Dec. 1, 1987). See also *Los Angeles Daily Journal*, April 18, 1988, p. 1.

65. Ibid.

66. J. Handler, Hollingsworth, Erlanger, and Ladinsky, "The Public Interest Activities of Private Practice Lawyers," 61 *ABA J.* 1388, 1389 (1975); cf. J. Handler, E. Hollingsworth, and H. Erlanger, *Lawyers and the Pursuit of Legal Rights* 19 (New York: Academic Press, 1978). See also Barlow F. Christensen, "The Lawyer's Pro Bono Publico Responsibility," 1981 *Am. B. Found. Research J.* 1 (suggesting that the Handler, Hollingsworth, Erlanger, and Ladinsky data may underrepresent private bar contributions). See also G. Hazard and D. Rhode, *The Legal Profession: Responsibility and Regulation*, (Mineola, N.Y.: Foundation Press 1985) for an excellent discussion of issues influential in this section.

67. Self-dramatization is often apparent in attorneys' commitment to pro bono. See S. Tisher, L. Bernabei, and M. Green, *Bringing the Bar to Justice* 133 (1977): "large firm attorneys who undertook significant obligations selected only cases that promised 'prestige and public attention.' " Individuals qua performers are generally concerned "not with the moral issue of realizing [the] standards [by which they are judged] but with the amoral issue of engineering a convincing impression that these standards are being realized. . . . As performers we are merchants of morality." E. Goffman, *The Presentation of Self in Everyday Life* 251 (Garden City, N.Y.: Doubleday, 1959).

68. Editorial, 73 *ABAJ*, Dec. 1, 1987.

2

LEGAL EDUCATION: ALTERNATIVES TO COMBAT PREPAREDNESS

> One news commentator, now turned law student, placed the origins of the Watergate affair on the demeaning, aggrandizing, relativizing, inflating, mind-sharpening, boring, stimulating, feared and corrupting experience known as law school.
> —Hearings before the Subcommittee on Representation of Citizen Interests, Senate Committee on the Judiciary, 93rd Congress, 1st session, vol. 1, part 1, at 2 (1974)

Watching laws or sausage being made is not a pleasant sight. The same can be said for the making of a lawyer.

The character of lawyers reflects not only their family heritage and financial goals but also the character of their education. As Harlan Fiske Stone observed some fifty years ago, law schools are the profession's gatekeeper: they shape the character of those passing through.[1] The traditional claim is that law school teaches a unique skill of thinking ("thinking like a lawyer") and produces graduates approaching statesmen. The typical law school, however, falls short of that view.

Law study has not exactly generated the thrill of a romance novel. President John Adams found the study of law in the eighteenth century "a dreary ramble." Supreme Court Justice William Paterson found the law a "disagreeable study." Justice Joseph Story cried over the gnarled prose of Lord Coke. After the first lectures at Harvard, novelist Henry James quit because he could not understand the lecturers or the books. Poet-author-physician Oliver Wendell Holmes likened law to "sawdust without butter." "If you can eat sawdust without butter," he counseled his son, "you will be a success in the law." Oliver Wendell Holmes, Jr., reported after his first classes that he "could not make sense of one word." Felix Frankfurter was so frightened that he could not recall speaking up at all during the first year. F. Lee Bailey, on thinking back to his student days, remembered "the many nights without sleep, and the cramming to get through an exam." Scott Turow's nightmarish recollections in *One L* fit into this same tortured genre.[2]

Stone's dry observation about the impact of legal education is most perceptive, ironically, in the varied ways today's law school stamps some questionable characteristics onto future lawyers. Legal education often aggravates a combat mentality, teaches contradictory lessons about legal values, and ignores issues of grass-roots justice institutions, all in the name of "thinking like a lawyer."

CHRISTOPHER LANGDELL'S CASE METHOD

One of the most notable features of law school is that it is very bookish— and yet, at the same time, combative and narrow.

In the 1870s, Christopher Columbus Langdell, Harvard's first law dean, initiated the case method of teaching law. Legal training became a "science" of principles discoverable in appellate opinions. In Langdell's arresting analogy, the law library became for the law student what the laboratory is to the chemist, the museum of natural history to the zoologist, the botanical garden to the botanist. The case method sought to pare appellate opinions to an immutable core of universal precepts undergirding all law, these opinions being to the law student what minerals were to the mineralogist.

Langdell's premises for the case method were:

1. Law involves a scientific analysis able to reveal the life-giving principles of the common law.
2. This science of law can be advanced only by specially trained researchers—not practitioners—committed to disciplined analysis.
3. The subject most appropriate for such scientific analysis is the body of written appellate opinions.
4. Legal education means instilling techniques for scientific probing into these opinions.
5. Like other sciences law should be pursued under circumstances conducive to scientific thought, viz., in a university rather than in the hurly-burly world of law offices and courts where principles are learned, at best, unscientifically.

Langdell's case method emulated the then-fashionable scientism and Darwinism. "Self-contained" and "value free," the case method would remedy "judicial deviations" of the past and become the ideal vehicle for teaching students to "think like a lawyer." The study of appellate cases would be more enlightening than memorizing rules divorced from their evolution. Studying cases in an office could never be more than "a species of handicraft." Carried on in a university, this same study could provide mastery of ultimate legal axioms, "one of the greatest and most difficult of sciences," a metaphysics in its own right.

Langdell's hope that the case method could reveal the few basic principles of law faded, however, as law's complexity became apparent. Though Langdell confused science as an empirical and rational activity, he never wavered in his belief that law was a science and that its laboratory was not the courtroom but the library. Thus his contemporary, Thomas Reed Powell, one of the twentieth-century's eminent public law scholars, graduated from Harvard in 1904 with the firm impression that "the eternal principles of the common law" were "encased in the Year Books."[3] By 1907, Langdell's successor, Ames, put his imprimatur on the established case method:

The object arrived at by us at Cambridge is the power of legal reasoning, and we think we can best get that by putting before the students the best models to be found in the history of English and American law, because we believe that men who are trained by examining the opinions of the greatest judges the English Common Law System has produced, are in a better position to know what legal reasoning is and are more likely to possess the power of solving legal problems than they would be by taking up the study of the law of any particular state.[4]

Although Langdell and Ames emphasized the case method as a theoretical means of studying rules scientifically, they produced results tending in an opposite direction. One lasting influence was the transfer of legal education from substance to procedure, from doctrine to process, from desk law to courtroom law. Despite his dislike for the courtroom, Langdell himself set the style when his examination questions abandoned systematic exposition of rules in preference for a primitive problem method. His relentless probing helped American law assume an atomistic rather than unitary approach, with its focus on common rather than statutory law, and its emphasis on analytical rather than personal skills.

His enduring case method implies more than a subtle hint of combat. Competition inheres in the very survival of the legal principles. These rules are not obvious; they must be excavated by analytical juxtaposition of conflicting appellate opinions. The case method thus sounds dual echoes of Darwin's survival of the fittest; legal principles, although immutable, survive only in conflict with each other in differing factual settings, and they are discoverable only by "virile" law students working in competition with each other.

This combative analytical method eventually generated a role model. For Langdell, lawyering was not primarily litigating. Lawyering meant intellectual mastery of immutable legal principles. His ideal lawyer was not a combatant anxious to litigate, not the Roman "advocat" (court lawyer) nor the Roman "praetor" (magistrate) but the Roman "jurisconsult." Unlike the advocat and the praetor, the jurisconsult was a desk lawyer whose major business was giving wise advice short of litigation. Courtroom litigation to Langdell was too grossly pedestrian, too smacking of the lowly sparring techniques of an apprenticeship.

For reasons foreign to Langdell, however, his case method fostered the opposing role of the litigator by teaching that appellate opinions contained the legal rules, i.e., that litigation forged the rules. Langdell's choice of the case book pedagogy was also a crucial choice of what to exclude. The study of law shrank to but one of its sources: appellate courts reviewing adjudication. He consciously excluded the study of legislation and considered administrative law an unworthy study. With the case method modeled exclusively on common law litigation, the career role model soon became by default not the "jurisconsult" but the formerly despised litigator.

Langdell's legacy continues today in mixed form. In most law schools, the study of appellate cases remains at least the chief, if not the only, pedagogical tool. Law is thereby equated narrowly with the common law and the products of appellate courts. Litigation is seen not so much as a tool of justice but as the source of appellate opinions.

The real world shortcomings of this pedagogy escaped Langdell. The appellate review of a case hardly represents the history of a dispute. Appellate reports leach out the human context; they provide no exposure to trial, the crafting of facts that often determines success, or pretrial strategy and negotiation. An appellate report presents only a sterile opinion of those facts that percolate up from trials. Appellate judges are generals remote from the line of battle who after the fight count the wounded and lecture the survivors on what should have been done.

Despite its definitional shortcomings, Langdell's case method contains at least one valuable insight: the law student should learn not to be a litigator but to be a wise counsel, a trustworthy life advisor. Unlike the case book method, this insight has fallen into oblivion; Langdell's wise counsel has degenerated into the dogged litigator.

LAW SCHOOL CURRICULUM AFTER LANGDELL

Langdell's case method produced a model that other schools emulated. Virtually all law schools developing after 1870 were affiliated with a university. Those universities with existing chairs of law, such as Yale, Columbia, and Pennsylvania, explicitly adopted the Harvard blueprint. The innovation was not only the case method, but also the professionalization of law teaching, higher admission requirements, the sequential three-year program, and a curriculum of "pure law," excluding such contexts as administrative and international law, jurisprudence, and legal history. Contrary to the common view, many schools, elite and nonelite, resisted the case method until well into the twentieth century. Its eventual triumph rested on the financial attractiveness of large classes and high faculty-student ratios. By the 1950s, the curricular patterns established at Harvard came to dominate nearly every law school in America.

The distinguished Austrian jurist, Dr. Josef Redlich, professor of law in the University of Vienna, came to this country in 1913 to investigate legal education. Like most other scholars, Redlich considered the case method one of the great American innovations. He attributed its success strictly to "the peculiar condition in which Anglo-American law finds itself, as unwritten law.'' He found it to be demanded by the nature of the law it sought to teach:

Unchecked by the voluminous output of statutory law in all conceivable fields of law and in all the states of the Union, the law of America has still remained, above all things, common law. It may even be maintained that the numerous legislative performances that prove the incapacity of democratic bodies to give anything like correct legal expression to their products of law, and the great number of such statutes, which usually amount to nothing more than clumsy bills of particulars, with no attempt to develop legal concepts,— that all this has actually helped to preserve the ascendency of the common law in spite of its often fossilized or insufficiently developed principles. And this is so, even where, as in the field of Civil Procedure, an attempt has been made to ''codify,'' or to formulate anew, separate branches of the law. But common law is case law and nothing else than case law. . . . The whole law lies in the reports of single cases which have been accumulating for centuries. Common law is case law, and the handling of such law is the practical calling for which the American student demands preparation.

Redlich's approval of the case method was not based on the usual attributes cited in its favor—such as the suggestion that it is a scientific method, or that it trains law students to ''think like lawyers,'' or that it is relatively inexpensive in operation, allowing large teacher-student ratios. Redlich approved the case method because it was superbly suited to the law it sought to teach, the common, not statutory, law.

The case model not only trained lawyers in the not-so-gentle science of analyzing common law cases; it also produced a prolific cadre of legal scientists devoted to the scientific pursuit of uniform rules. Early law professors saw it as a weapon to downgrade apprenticeship programs and law practice so as to upgrade the academic search for immutable doctrine. Thus, in passing, was born the chasm that continues to this day to the detriment of both sides: contemplative professors in libraries, harried practitioners in offices, each rarely speaking to the other, with the professors showing particular detachment from the day-to-day operations of the very courts whose opinions they study. This continuing chasm raises the query whether law schools have had anything central to say about the legal profession as an institution and vice versa.

Though Langdell's case method continues in modified form to this day, his valuable insight about the ideal lawyer as a wise counsel has not fared as well. In Hegelian fashion, the case book method eventually generated the legal philosophy known as ''realism,'' which shifted legal education away from bookish synthesis to an activist concern for the social consequences of court rulings. The litigator, not the jurisconsult, became the realist role model, and Langdell's ''eternal principles'' became temporal tools for social change, sowing the seeds for ''value-free'' law—a law whose value lies only in effecting social change.

The kernels of this contradiction between legal principles and social change go back to early realist days when legal education shifted from a contemplative to an activist mode. When former Justice William O. Douglas first came to

Columbia University in 1922 as a student, he discovered to his surprise that learning law required not Langdell's contemplative talents but what Douglas called "predatory qualities." Even so soon after Langdell, the realist law school of that day prepared its students not to be "jurisconsults" but to be warriors trying to influence a judge-sociologist to solve social problems through legal rulings. The academic emphasis fell on creativity and combat, not on counsel or pacification.

The effect of the realists on the law was much like the role Carlyle attributed to Matthew Arnold: He led them into the wilderness and left them there. Realists killed the idea of Langdell's system. Legal logic came under suspicion. Law became socially purposive, secularized, and atomized, less a cohesive force binding together different elements in the community's city wall. It was one thing to agree that legal objectivity and neutrality were myths; it was another to destroy such myths without offering any alternatives. Such an undermining of legal foundations proved to be realism's lasting monument. Despite Langdell's efforts to the contrary, the realist law school adopted the activist private litigator as *the* career model. Armed with the wealth of the common law, the law graduate would aspire not to be legislator or administrator or counselor but to be a social reformer via courtroom litigation.

TODAY'S LAW SCHOOL EMPHASIS

Langdell's ghost remains a real presence in legal education. To be sure, law teaching has evolved to the point where the original proponents of Socratic-Langdellian teaching might hardly recognize it. Appellate cases are no longer the exclusive academic fodder. Some elective courses do emphasize practical skills. Nevertheless, law study today still more closely resembles Langdell's "science of law" than Jerome Frank's ideal of a "lawyer-school."

After the past one hundred years of its reign, advocates still contend that case instruction best teaches the inductive method to discern the law and so best directly teaches the most critical lawyering skill—the ability to "think like a lawyer." The method demonstrates that the law is a changing body of doctrine. The method forces the student into an "active" learning mode. The case method is also thought more pedagogically stimulating than more conventional methods such as lectures or the "nuts and bolts" of practice. With Langdell, proponents of the case method thus continue to see it as the best system for teaching law.[5]

Common law decisions—the kernel of the case method—thus exert a continuing influence even if, like many other legal traditions, they rule from fresh graves. Teaching students to "think like lawyers" remains the fundamental if indefinable goal. Few goals exist beyond that numbing talismanic incantation. Professors acknowledge that among their objectives are such goals as developing a skepticism about rules and generalizations, honing techniques of conceptual manipulation, and approaching cases in a "tough-minded," analytic fashion.[6] These and similar goals fall under the heading of "thinking like a lawyer," the indefinable chant whose repetition suggests sacred meaning. Arval Morris ambiguously articulates the uncertainty of this pedagogy: "the business of a university law school is thought."[7] The important question, however, is whether education focused on Langdell's common law rule-collation constitutes sufficient thought—or thought at all. Erwin Griswold put it this way:

It has often been said, for a smile, that legal education sharpens the mind by narrowing it. To my mind, there is more truth to this than we have been willing to admit. . . . [A] consequence of unthoughtful use of traditional approaches to legal instruction is the exaltation of rationality over other values which are of great importance in our society.[8]

The rules once collected need to be used. Thus ultimately, what is emphasized, sometimes subtly, in Langdell's realist-shaped law school is mercenary combat as a private means for using legal rules to address social change. Litigation receives much more attention in law schools than the legislator, the negotiator, the judge, the administrator, or the civil servant roles of lawyering. Litigation becomes for the lawyer what the operating room is for the surgeon and what the library was for Langdell: habitat, stage, and laboratory. The message is subtle but omnipresent: to be a lawyer is to wage war, with success proportionate to favorable verdicts.

Several academic trends encourage this combat mentality: (a) adjudication is presented in an abstract atmosphere devoid of its human and social context; (b) teachers emphasize the plasticity of the law to the detriment of its permanence; (c) students learn a confrontive rather than conciliatory approach to problem solving.

ABSTRACT DISPUTE RESOLUTION

The goals of compromise, negotiation, and arbitration receive comparatively little emphasis in today's law school. True, they exist as occasional electives. Courtroom litigation, however, remains among the highest legal skills, the concretization of the ineffable "thinking like a lawyer."[9] Tactical skills become highly prized. A 1977 study elicited the following comment from a student:

The primary thrust of legal education as I have experienced it has been directed at learning the naked law. No human issues have been involved. Rather, we have been trained to apply X law when a Y problem has been presented. There has been very little attention given to avoiding a courtroom conflict. We have been trained only in terms of the ultimate result, adjudication in a court of law.[10]

In the typical classroom, plaintiffs, defendants, clients, and witnesses are garbed in their legal strengths rather than in human settings.[11] Parties to litigation appear as role players useful for presenting problems from varying perspectives, movable as chess players on a board. The human context recedes. One mock court student reaction typifies this mind-set: "Wow, what a cross-examination—

he made the rape victim look like a dope-crazed whore!'' Such, one assumes, is "thinking like a lawyer."

Most schools emphasize analytical skills to dissect a problem into its parts, to parse statutes and cases, to smoke out potential opposition. Students learn solutions to problems, not how to solve them. Such discursive reasoning abstracts from the emotional milieu where legal problems arise. Rhetoric, bluffing, strategy, and power plays take center stage. Little attention falls on the human arts of negotiation, compromise, counseling, mediation, empathy, or administration, legislation, or government relations—areas that, ironically, consume a great part of practitioners' time.

The emphasis is on the single activity from which law teachers claim their professional position: doctrinal analysis of cases and statutes. The unarticulated "thinking like a lawyer" rather than the development of personal abilities is the major aim. Socratic dialogue is interspersed with lecture and discussion, but these are minor variations considering the full range of pedagogical possibilities. Huge classes, authoritarian teaching, and problem-oriented examinations—the exclusive evaluation device—predominate.

The social image inherent in this pedagogy reflects an autonomous but certain law, elite but wily lawyers, and narrow, power-oriented thinking. The atmosphere also resembles scholastic debates over angels dancing on the head of a pin—witness the medieval vagaries of real property divisions into fee simples, determinables, conditionals, executories, and extinguishables. Professors may be problem-oriented but their doctrinal problems often seem paper problems, not matters of flesh and blood. Anatole France's comment from the *Red Lily* evokes the continuing mood of Langdell's legacy:

There are bookish souls for whom the universe is but paper and ink. The man whose body is animated by such a soul spends his life before his desk, without any care for the realities whose graphic representation he studies so obstinately. He knows of the labors, sufferings and hopes of men only what can be (found in books) sewn onto tapes and bound in morocco. . . . He has never looked out of the window. Such was the worthy Peignot, who collected other people's opinions to make books out of them. . . . He conceived of passions as subjects for monographs, and knew that nations perish in a certain number of octavo pages.[12]

Whether this combination of abstraction and casuistry satisfies student, professor, or public is open to question. Whether it satisfies justice institutions is much less so. As one student put it:

Law to me at the present time tends to deal with problems only after they have occurred. Why must all disagreements be settled in court? This only brings out the worst in people. . . . Different situations in law school really frighten me. It seems that many people are losing their sense of humanity and becoming more—shall I say—''professional'' in their attitudes toward life and what part love will play in their lives. The logical, rational lawyer appears to be gaining among my classmates.[13]

MALLEABLE PRINCIPLES

According to one of Langdell's early observations, the case method would show how the law consists of fixed and "absolute" principles, the number of which is "much less than is commonly supposed."[14] By reading cases, students would learn these enduring principles and reveal the bedrock of the law. These lasting principles now appear as mere transitory solutions. Realism undermined belief in an absolute eternal body of legal metaphysics. Litigation became not so much an appeal to these principles as a means by which major social issues that could not get a fair hearing elsewhere could be resolved by institutional pressure. Lawsuits thus serve the ends not so much of justice as publicity and pressure: the eternal principles have become malleable chess players, what some economists call "weaponry."

In the first semester of law school, teachers demonstrate that certainty is illusory. The law appears an indeterminate process, not a determinate body of enduring doctrine. Any moral or logical position can be immediately met with an equally compelling argument. At a point a role reversal takes place. Having learned the techniques of legal criticism, students become skeptical at best, cynical at worst. This "dark night of the soul" causes many students to abandon their beliefs as naive and to substitute a perception of law as hopelessly indeterminate, with a counterrule for every rule, where the only uniform answer is, "It depends"—with the critical factor simply the caprice of the judge. This plastic concept of law embodies not a common sense morality but an infinite set of conflicting policy arguments that reduce legal discourse to a game in which power and guile, not justice, determine the outcome.

Many students never recover from this dark night of the soul to construct a more affirmative theory. Many succumb to techniques of cynical discourse. Some learn to counter all statements with opposing arguments as an exercise in supposed lawyerly reasoning. Such cynicism rejects any attempt to construct general theories of jurisprudence as hopeless attempts to seek permanence.

Former Assistant Attorney General Roger Cramton, former dean of the Cornell Law School, sees "the intellectual woodwork of the law school classroom,"[15] and the "prevalent orthodoxy of legal education" as a blend of legal positivism, sociological jurisprudence, legal realism, and "the functional approach."[16] These factors imply values of moral relativism. The Constitution and law become instrumental, a means to the end of victory. What counts is not the justice of one's position but whether it is victorious.

Students learn how judges supposedly achieve predetermined results and later find reasons to justify them, how judges erode precedent and change doctrine supposedly at whim. The unlimited discretion supposedly enjoyed by judges is used to fashion social solutions. No such thing as an absolute rule exists, waiting to be invoked as a guide. Rules change; what is settled today may be altered tomorrow. Today's frivolity is tomorrow's law. Laws constitute only a toolbag for manipulating adversaries.

No less important, however, the critical cast of mind of law teachers-scholars sets the tone of most law schools: students learn to be suspicious of the black letter and to look critically at all exercises of legal power rather than to accept, as Gospel, various pronouncements of "the law." They become, in short, "rule skeptics." This irreverent attitude toward law is a peculiarity and strength of the American law school.[17]

AGGRESSION AND COMBAT

Legal education in most law schools today focuses more upon private rather than public conflict. Its emphasis is on private practice of law in a firm. Law school downplays legislation, public service, judicial or administrative law. Private law, of course, is more competitive and revenue oriented than public. For better or worse, most law graduates thus take from their education a keen sense of one-on-one competition: their client against the enemy, their creativity against their fellow lawyers or the courts.

For their part, students tend to be unusually competitive even before law school. First days in class undoubtedly intensify these feelings. Students who excelled as undergraduate stars discover other students just as bright: valedictorians, class presidents, summa cum laudes, debate captains. They meet peer challenges by employing the same competitive devices that worked in the past, often relating to their peers by redoubling competitive efforts. Competition for admission, high grades, high class rank, law review editor, for victory in moot court and essay competitions and eventually for prestigious jobs shapes litigious attitudes as much as formal courses. Relentless competition inside and outside the classroom produces a highly stylized *modus operandi* that favors inductive reasoning, analytical precision, verbal onslaught, and dogged persistence.

These competitive instincts are at least partly frustrated. The ways to win in law school are fewer than the ways to lose. Only one leads the class. Only one is editor of the law review. Few receive Wall Street job offers. Meager are the rewards for client counseling or for work in poverty clinics. Competition also alienates. Scott Turow describes his Harvard experience as: "to work compulsively up to 100 hours each week; to eclipse all else, including social life; to be terrorized by the Socratic method; and to compete savagely with fellow students."[18] Turow recalls how one classmate hoarded an important library book so others could not use it. In this "growing madness in the air," students trade course summaries with friends to deny them to others. Duncan Kennedy's description of his anxiety-ridden classes at Yale in the 1970s fits this same mold.[19] The workload is often such that it is physically impossible to complete assignments on time. For some students this pressure can lead to a constant state of anxiety. The underlying dynamic parallels a highly structured initiation used by the church or the military to indoctrinate neophytes.

Though some pedagogical browbeating has lately receded, classroom aggression has hardly disappeared. Many a student is still told in first year orientation that one of three will not survive to graduate. This competition for excellence generates what Alan Stone calls a "free floating hostility."[20] Students are pressured and goaded to succeed, "to go to the top."[21] Students retain painful memories of paper-chase professors. A recent Yale class compared its instructors to a "fearful trial court judge," "an inquisitor," a "pounding . . . adversary." Some professors are unilaterally accustomed to combative, competitive, and argumentative teaching.[22] Combat colors the anticipation of practice, and in the process, represses helpful interpersonal skills. Where collaboration would be appropriate for getting along in school or in practice, students learn instead to compete when competition is counterproductive.[23]

The pursuit of grades and class rank easily promotes dishonest behavior. Carried to an extreme it may lead to plagiarizing others' work, to failing to cite sources used in papers and briefs, to cheating, to stealing books from the library, or to tearing out pages—hardly an inspiring preparation for a career in public trust. Exams and grades matter because they are important to law firms and judicial clerkships in order to sort students into a hierarchy. Grades define a pecking order as a meritocratic alternative to race, sex, religion, or family. Law school, which purports to be a value-neutral meritocracy, generates hierarchy by pushing students in directions to be judged as suitable or not for firms. Individual worth is defined by successful competition. Doing well in the subtle hierarchy of law school prepares students to accept a predictable notch after graduation.

While this psychology holds sway, another dose of competition comes from the lectern. Most teachers see private practice as the natural goal of law school and thus focus on the specialized corporate litigation of Wall Street. To this end, they regularly demolish judicial opinions to show how the results could have been manipulated to be otherwise. Sarcasm, cynicism, and abuse are frequent spices in the digestion of opinions.[24] Legal principles appear in the end as malleable by combat and rhetoric. Langdell thus stands on his head.

Yet, even as Langdell is dethroned, his case method still dominates the classroom. Ames, Langdell's successor, believing that the case method was the preeminent pedagogy, initiated a combative classroom routine that continues almost as an insult to its supposed author, Socrates:

This art or technique in general involves a discussion of the cases with different members of the class. It usually begins by one member of the class being asked to state the case. . . . The teacher . . . secures from the student a decided opinion upon the problem. Whatever it is, the instructor should be prepared to break him down. . . . If the instructor can break the student expert down and force a reversal of his opinion and then start in on him again and break him down a second time, so that he is forced to admit that his first opinion was right, the instructor will score a considerable success.[25]

Course offerings reinforce this combative view. Law school subjects cover rules of evidence and procedure, trial practice, appellate advocacy, litigation strategy, and courtroom techniques. Economics courses emphasize tactics such as "bluffing" and "chicken" and game theory. Contrary to Langdell, many teachers now spend time asserting that there is no such thing as "law of contracts" or "law of torts." Required course offerings convey that the stereotypical lawyer (the paragon of "thinking like a real lawyer") is not a municipal bondsman nor legislator nor judge nor public servant nor court administrator but litigator.

Skills learned are consistent with this emphasis. A 1978 Law School Admission Council study of 1600 practicing lawyers who graduated from law school in 1955, 1965, and 1975 indicated that law schools developed few practical skills considered essential in office practice apart from the courtroom.[26] For example, 77.3 percent said that law school provided either no training at all or no helpful training in negotiation skills.[27] Further, 68.6 percent said that their legal education provided no training at all or unhelpful training in counseling clients.[28] Forty-four percent said that law school provided either no training or unhelpful training in the ability to draft legal documents.[29]

As they internalize the combative model, students may emphasize posturing and overestimate the merits of intractability. Course offerings imply values in stonewalling. They lean more toward conflict than toward the gentler arts of legislation, reconciliation, and accommodation. This tilt is all the more misplaced because in practice litigation is dwarfed by the many varieties of "desk" law.[30] Even in litigious areas of the law, such as personal injury and contracts, more than 90 percent of cases filed are resolved without litigation via settlement skills.

A large segment of the practicing bar has found that not a single one of the interpersonal skills comes through formal legal education. These skills have to be developed through experience in practice.[31]

There then begins a process of developing skills in the dialectical method of law. Ultimately, students learn to depend on these skills to provide solutions to many real and different problems in life about which they must make decisions. An orderly process of weighing and interpreting many life events results. The analytic experience is made easier by the fact that the entire process and result is impersonalized and viewed largely from an intellectual context. So far as the experiencing of problems, particularly other persons' problems, is made completely impersonal, the development of legal skills is reassuring. At the same time, these may not reach and probably do not touch upon the psychological sore-points that create anxiety for the individual student-lawyer.[32]

As a result of this combative, common law pedagogy, American law schools have turned loose on society a thundering herd of combative litigators at the expense of compassionate peacemakers or justice devotees. Professor Roger S. Haydock recently observed:

We do a fairly good job of teaching students to be top gun litigators and be a jerk if they have to be, but (we're) woefully inadequate in showing students how to be compassionate and yet still be effective to the client. . . . We've given them lots of ways to be jerks.[33]

THE AGENDA

The old house of legal education has stood now for over a century. It is built on a foundation set deep in the conflicts of the industrial and social revolutions following the civil war. The house is guarded by the ghosts of Langdell, as well as ghosts of scientism and rationalism. It is a house decorated with perversions of Socrates' teaching with little announcement of its purpose other than inane inscriptions of "thinking like a lawyer."

Langdell would be flattered as law schools copied his Harvard model. Today, more than a century after his innovations, he would be comfortably at home in most law schools. Education has progressed from the day when lawyers were a caste apart, semipriestly in nature, and when the law was little more than a set of rules. The case method has allowed students to examine "primary" materials in the form of appellate cases.

However, real life cases are rife with confusion and complexity, which appellate reports reduce to legal skeletons. With or without the case method skeletons, legal education of the 1980s still shows ample contradictions. At bottom is the absence of any in-depth self-examination by law schools of their goals regarding justice institutions. At most schools, the purposes of legal education and the pursuit of justice itself are seen as unfruitful, if not unfit, topics for conversation. Of almost two hundred journals of legal scholarship, only one regularly addresses education. Questioning any part of the belief structure underlying education brings into question the entire structure, as if pulling on a single thread would unravel the entire garment.

The garment of legal scholasticism needs unraveling and refashioning. Much legal education appears related to legal practice and its institutions as oil to water. The conflict, at bottom, is not that of theory/practice, contemplation/action, or clinic/doctrine but a loss of moral vision, of "soul." Instead of being laboratories of justice, inspiring future attorneys with a honed pursuit of justice, law schools remain to a large extent grading mills ordered internally to doctrinal scholarship and outwardly to employment of attorneys graduating with the nineteenth-century mind-set of common law combat litigators. The narrowing spiral of legal scholarship reflects the continuing effort to unmask common law doctrine but not to unmask its twentieth-century failures via social science studies of delivery of legal services by law firms, courts, and bars. Legal scholarship has much to do with tenure and pocketbook and little to do with practical aspects of healing fractured social relationships within the city wall. No one seems to care to shepherd justice. Legal education seems unable to inspire students with a mission to mend, much less to cultivate ideals worth working, fighting, or even dying for. Rather than producing lawyers as grass-roots, justice-minded magistrates or walking peacemakers, law schools have degenerated into grading mills anesthetized from any indignation at the moral relativism of its education and the Machiavellian character of its graduates. Each of these factors deserves a place on an agenda for reform.

THE CURRICULUM

When the garment of legal scholasticism is rent, disturbing patterns appear. First, the required curriculum of the first year has been virtually identical in every law school for most of this century. Subjects emphasize the private and the individualistic with a strong common law orientation mainly located in the opinions of appellate court judges. Courses rarely deal with any form of organization—corporations, families, labor unions, lobbies—or with the way the legislative and executive branches function. Little to nothing exists on state and local government, or public taxation or expenditures, and nothing at all on judicial institutions, or on law-related, nonlawyer careers as politicians, legislators, social activists, or public administrators.

The conventional explanation for this uniformity is the weight of history. Traditional first-year subjects reflect the legal world of a century ago: private transactions, common law litigation, and relations among individuals in the era of Langdell's industrial revolution. The "real" law thus appears as the common law facilitating private commercial transactions. The second-year statutory curriculum exists only to fill in the details of this real law. In this dichotomy, regulations and statutes become abnormal and suspect. In the common law, rules seek individual justice via litigation with its elaborate and expensive procedural mechanisms. By contrast, the statutory goal is rough justice over a large number of cases via rules that more or less, most of the time, deal fairly with masses of people without individualized adjudication.

Theoretical assumptions underlie this dichotomy. First, the traditional common law incorporates the assumption that the core value of law is individual self-assertion within the context of free enterprise. Old cases thus invoke notions of "progress" in holding that entrepreneurs are responsible for injuries only if the injured person proves fault. Holmes, for example, thought it self-evident that

the public generally profits by individual activity. As action cannot be avoided, and tends to the public good, there is obviously no policy in throwing the hazard of what is at once desirable and inevitable upon the actor.[34]

This laissez-faire model of an informed consumer casting a voluntary vote in a free market bears little relationship to today's economic model. The older model assumes a competitive market when in fact today many barriers impede free competition. Many of the things we most want cannot now be purchased individually: clean air and water, safety, security, and decent health care can only be purchased collectively through government help.

This traditional curriculum also assumes that consumers make informed choices when, in fact, such choices are often impossible. The curriculum sidesteps questions about persisting inequalities in the distribution of wealth. The common law focus also encourages the belief that personal relationships are reducible to a series of quid pro quo commodity exchanges: health care involves not a healing relationship between two people but a transaction in which a medical provider sells a service to an insured as a grocer sells an apple to a shopper. Human relationships, at bottom, are binary and adversarial; we are in Sartre's world, where hell is the other person, a potential adverse party in an either/or world of vendor/vendee, where the rule of thumb is "beware."

The traditional case method, in sum, has a historically narrow focus, is the wrong end of the judicial process to show students first, encourages passive learning, imposes binary adversity on parties and lawyers, and omits social science inquiry by continuing to voice Langdell's science of law dogma.[35] The legal temper has changed. Over the past one hundred years the law has seen the birth of tort in the Industrial Revolution, and, in Grant Gilmore's phrase, the death of contract. Legislative and statutory law have achieved a prominence unthinkable at the turn of the century. The codification movement of David Dudley Field has captured legislative halls. Land use controls, zoning, the Internal Revenue Code, environment and securities regulation, worker's compensation, social legislation, and the extraordinary development of the administrative agency have replaced the industrial revolution mentality. In a word, much common law has been supplanted by statute and agency law, just as our modified welfare state has replaced laissez-faire commercialism.

THE ROLE MODEL

The business world scholasticism of this traditional curriculum contains an implicit role model. The ideal lawyer in this view becomes the expeditor of commerce, i.e., the commercial lawyer allied to dominant mercantile institutions. The role model lawyer is the corporate sidekick furthering its economic advantage. The corollary message is elevation of the litigation model of dispute resolution as the norm. In this tradition, disputes are to be resolved by courts and lawsuits.

In fact, however, large numbers of lawyers increasingly deal with administrative and statutory laws and alternate modes of dispute resolution. Common law combat litigation becomes of lesser importance in an increasingly administrative society operating more often under statute than under common law. As common law adjudication slowly becomes so elaborate as to be archaic, the subtle specter of the combative commercial litigator lurking behind legal education needs to yield to other role models: the public servant, administrative head, politician, and legislator, to name but a few necessary additions. In particular, the deservedly poor public image of politicians and legislators cries out for professional career preparation in law school in ways conducive to avoiding the dishonesty, demagoguery, and pandering popularly attributed to these careers. A balanced curriculum emphasizing alternatives to the litigation model could reduce the combative atmosphere and, in its place, encourage healing-oriented public careers for more idealistic reasons than wealth, power, and service to industrial clients.

The lawyer's many roles as mediator and facilitator could well lead educators to teach skills beyond the mere ability to critically analyze cases. The varied roles of investigator, counselor, negotiator, advocate, and peacemaker should be a major addition to the current curriculum, if for no other reason than the practical reality that 90 to 95 percent of criminal and civil cases terminate without trial. Negotiation, settlement, leadership, administrative, and "healing" talents are more immediately important than warrior tactics in solving modern legal problems.

COMBAT AND DICHOTOMY

Combative attitudes stem in part from our American heritage. Competition has been the driving force of our economy and of our judicial process. The authors of the Constitution in 1787 designed a framework for governing individuals defined as atoms of self-interest. In the struggle for power, the Constitution and the Bill of Rights define zones of autonomy and noninterference. In this view, safety from aggression lies not in connection with others but in rules reinforcing individualism, self-assertion, isolation, and noninterference.[36] Such is the Hobbesian ethos of our founding documents.

This insular mentality, so characteristic also of social Darwinism, interferes with peacemaking roles. It generates an either/or, "winner/loser," or "me vs. you" attitude in inappropriate places. The mentality of winner/loser permeates adversary adjudication. Lawyers in divorce cases, for example, often leave the parties angrier with each other than they were initially because they impose the antagonisms of the adversary system differently from the way in which the parties want to treat each other. At conventions of prosecutors, speakers appear as cheerleaders uttering cries of "kill, kill, kill" the defendant, who has become the "enemy." Anyone who gets in the way of destroying that enemy, including judges and defense lawyers, becomes another enemy. A similar polarity exists at the opposite table: defense groups struggle with how best to help clients who have conceded misconduct prevail or how to get back at vindictive prosecutors. Justice in this form of adjudication becomes equated with defeating the adversary in a win/lose dichotomy.

In fact, however, from the more global viewpoint of the city wall, much of the best legal practice is not about pushing opponents to the wall but seeking to acquire confidence, to make others believe in justice, to reduce rather than exacerbate differences. That process requires more complex interpersonal skills than the separatist binary dichotomies of the adversary system. Many lawyer tasks are better done with skills different from the macho attitude nurtured by adversary combat. Abstracting legal issues from their social context is consistent with the adjudicative model where issues and evidence are narrowed for decision making. But adjudication is often antagonistic to the real-world situations from which controversies evolve. The end of a lawsuit is only one step in what many litigants hope will be a continuing friendly relationship. Many a business person rightly fears that lawyers translate a good working relationship into a terminal fight. Promoting litigiousness neglects such broader goals. In sum, the binary language and adversarial polarity of adjudication need to be relaxed by deconstruction techniques; either/or posturing leads to exaggeration, bluffing, and intractability hostile to peacemaking.

JUSTICE INSTITUTIONS

Law alone no longer can be studied in splendid isolation from its institutions. It should relate both to other academic disciplines and to the institutions that embody legal principles. The traditional notion of the discrete study of law as an end in itself should have died in the Industrial Revolution. Law schools need Husserl's *epoché* to dispel the provincial Anglo-American parochialism that sees legal institutions as perfect just because they have roots in the Magna Carta. Within our own heritage, students should be required to study justice institutions, jurisprudence, legal history and philosophy, and especially an appropriative comparative law. Much can be improved by copying. West Germany's court system, for example, shows how a federalist system like ours need not require a side-by-side duplication of federal and state courts. England's division between barristers and solicitors suggests an avenue for improving courtroom litigation by special licensing for trial experts. Even the USSR's legal system offers alternative ways of addressing plea bargaining and comparative negligence.

RESEARCH MODES

Law schools need to abandon their traditional lofty detachment from justice institutions. The schools have done far too little intensive scrutiny of the adversary process with a view to its improvement. The academic exaltation of "advocacy" as the stuff of litigation courses perpetuates the law's rhetorical posturing. Instead, the schools need to become laboratories for justice improvement. In addition to generating obscure law review articles and nourishing their private practices, professors could help more by devising improvements in existing justice institutions and expediting delivery of legal services.

Sharing Langdell's disdain for the crankings of the courts, professors have ignored the brutal fact that these mechanisms with all their flaws generate our only public justice. They rarely address such prosaic but real social science issues as lower court chaos; delays in getting to trial; plea bargaining; jail overcrowding; the bar's ethical violations; prohibitive costs of litigation; contingent fees and their effects on the distribution of legal services; the filing of spurious law suits, as in medical malpractice and automobile accident cases; excessive procrastination that wears down the other side and uses up scarce court resources; litigiousness that keeps disputes alive to the detriment of both the client and the larger society; the reduction of courts to theaters; and the drift of lawyers away from their historical role as officers of the court to being Machiavellian hired guns. Law faculties could undertake fruitful social science research about these basic problems of the real-world justice system, train students in voluntary mechanisms to resolve disputes without going to court in the first place, and create new institutions like court-annexed dispute resolution centers more efficient than traditional law firms or courts for delivering legal services to the poor and middle class.

Law schools have effectively resisted such practical inquiries. Much of the resistance stems from the common elitist backgrounds of teachers[37] and the difficulties of instituting change among tenured faculty with a stake in publishable research interests. The independence of the judiciary pales by comparison with that of a law faculty. As Woodrow Wilson observed, changing a curriculum is like moving a graveyard.[38] Professors enjoy their "Lone Ranger" status, doing their own thing in their own way at their own pace, resisting efforts to think about justice and easy access to its institutions. Although some professors do inject history, sociology, and economics into discussions, many faculties still contain doctrinal scholastics not inclined to risk a pleasant routine for something as ineffable as the improvement of justice. Unless they move into more justice-oriented roles, law schools risk remaining grading mills anesthetized from the cumbersome system they feed.

Law professors, not to mention judges,[39] need to reflect on the fact that if the justice system is ever to be made more responsive, it is only likely to occur through their efforts:

If we are to achieve that more perfect system of justice, it is we lawyers, judges, and professors of law . . . who must educate the public on the needs of the justice system and on how to get them. If we of the justice system do not do this leadership job, it will not be done at all.[40]

Understanding institutional characteristics requires broader knowledge than is required for analyzing legal dogma in constitutions, statutes, judicial opinions, and rules. Institutional analysis must draw on philosophy and the social sciences. Even national law schools do not appear able to advance such analysis. The overwhelming concern of law teachers and students is the study of doctrine, not institutions. A course in civil procedure is a course about procedural law; a course in federal courts is about doctrines of federal jurisdiction. Neither course traditionally talks in detail about delivery of doctrine. Courses that explicate statutes are taught but courses in legislation are rare. Questions of court congestion and delay, judicial selection, promotion, ethics, and quality of judges would fetch a big yawn among the mercantile masses.

Langdell felt that all the principles that a judge needed to decide a novel case could be found in appellate opinions; therefore, he concluded, the way to learn law was to read cases and deduce these principles. Such doctrinal analysis can no longer be isolated from institutional problems, judicial selection or compensation, the causes of caseload growth, or the relative merits of general and specialized courts, all of which are informational issues as well as methodological. Appellate opinions address rules but they do not convey the quantitative data and facts necessary for the analysis of legal institutions. The appellate process bleaches out the true colors of a dispute by winnowing out human and institutional data.

Law schools encourage little social science inquiry. For the most part, faculty are not trained to do research in the social sciences, and law students have little interest in the scientific study of justice delivery. The vast majority sign up only for studies that contribute directly to financial success. There is little interest in applying economics to judicial administration, and there is virtually no market for the research skills necessary for social scientific studies of justice delivery. If all research corrupts, empirical research corrupts absolutely.

Yet, the need for hands-on social studies is great. Ideally, courses in judicial administration and administrative law would deal with issues such as the demand for and supply of litigation; the recruitment, compensation, and evaluation of judges; the organization of agency and court systems, state and federal, United States and foreign; the causes of litigation; court and agency delay; the history and contemporary role of the jury; arbitration and judicial supplements; the pricing of judicial services; the role of specialized courts; the delegation of judicial adjuncts; access to courts by poor and middle-class persons. Such courses could not, of course, be taught from the conventional law school course materials, nor by a lawyer unversed in social science. The end result ought to be more sensitivity about the gap between justice and its institutions—and how to narrow it.

Ultimately, legal education needs a double infusion of idealism and practicality to resuscitate its soul and that of its graduates. One way to achieve this goal is by expanding its orientation from its present narrow goal of training lawyers to the broader goal of educating "public trustees." In this format, a school would train not only traditional lawyers with the traits described in the preceding chapter but also educate (literally, "draw forth") advocates inspired with the pursuit of public social justice. To reflect this broader philosophy a law school might change its name to the "school of law and public trust." It would attract not only conventional lawyers-to-be but also an attitude now at a premium: persons broadly committed to careers in public trust, such as politics, legislation, judging, court administration, agency administration, diplomacy, and other forms of broadly defined social service, including community legal services and Peace Corps-minded social activists.

The education of these public trustees should include law, of course, but go beyond it to embrace social theory, social relations, the integrity and functions of social and political organs, the distribution of wealth, access to justice, and responsiveness of public institutions. These secular apostles would resemble Langdell's jurisconsult rather than the realists' litigator; they would carry Band-Aids in their briefcases rather than lawsuits. They would seek social justice for the broader clientele of society at large, and their tools would include not only traditional legal skills but also mediation, community organization, motivation skills, and peacemaking and sociological skills useful for cohesive social ties within the city's wall.

Such a school would uniquely achieve the boast that most now make of being "national," for their students and faculty would care about the welfare and cohesion not simply of individual clients but of larger social and political units. Its graduates would not be Nietzsche's "walking legislators" but would be blessed with an analogous spirit able to move beyond, at appropriate times, the common law's binary dichotomies of win/lose, grant/deny, right/wrong to work in the vast open plain of shadows of gray where these binary divisions do not alienate.

For those so choosing, such advocacy as a public trustee could well be a lifelong career. For all students, there could be a required year-long internship or "trusteeship" before bar admission, coupled with a recurring sabbatical "advocate" year to be spent at least part-time in pro bono work. The ultimate message of such a public trusteeship is that, despite our individualism and self-assertion, we constitute a society able to achieve more benefits through cooperation than alienation.

VALUES AND THEORY

Finally, law school temerity in dealing with theory and values needs to be reduced. Serious study into theoretical bases of law is needed for context and value. Even in the heyday of realism, legal analysis involved the application of sociology, political science, psychology, and economics to law by legally trained teachers who acquired limited skills in these other disciplines. Rarely have professional philosophers raised in law school basic questions about the source of law, the meaning of obligation, and the "naturalness" of basic human rights. Yet, as opposed to the "hard sciences," the law concerns primarily matters of value—values relating to the conduct of individuals and groups, how those individuals and groups should act in relation to each other and to the state. Such conclusions cannot be empirically derived. David Hume's success at a particular moment in history rested not so much on his method as on the fact that his method was tied to the law then perceived as an autonomous inductive mechanism free of values, unconnected to and independent of the men and women who make it—a view now deservedly outmoded.

Today, contrary to Langdell, we know that law cannot be reduced to an empirical basis. Morality is not an empirical science. A knowledge of empirical or nonmoral facts does not provide a sufficient basis upon which to make a right decision. Lawyering is a moral function in a sense that other professions, such as medicine, are not. Lawyers do not merely render to the community a social service; their functions are in a broad sense political because private individuals cannot secure justice without their aid.

To acknowledge the value choices inherent in the work of the lawyer is not to actually make value choices for the student. A conscientious teacher may refrain from making a student's ultimate choice; it is another thing to refuse to come to grips with these fundamental issues. A strong message regarding the place of values now pervades the academy's approach to lawyers; it is a message, at best, of the low priority of values or of their total irrelevance, or, at worst, of the relativity of legal and moral rules in the practice of law.

Were such a value-free science of the law possible, it would be a science of technical expertise. But there is no such thing as a value-free human enterprise, most certainly not in the law, the very embodiment of authoritative values. At the most practical level, without some philosophical basis for legal values, rules become as arbitrary as positions and outcomes on a chessboard. If an education implies that legal victory and defeat are merely arbitrary results manipulable by skill and power, it ultimately conveys a devastating message to disputants: they could win if only they had more skill, money, or power to play the "game" endlessly.

Conversely, in a value-laden theory such as natural law, there is a metaphysical difference between right and wrong, and at least some legal results follow moral desert. Basic legalities, including litigation, reward "right" behavior and punish "wrong" behavior at some objective, rockbound level that constitutes the stopping place for litigation not because of exhaustion but because of the moral desert that separates winner from loser. It is a lesson that needs to be heeded if justice is ever to return from the divinity school to the law school.

The search for moral truth remains a central commitment of the legal scholar, lawyer and public trustee. A renewed understanding of what it means to be a professional should include a commitment to something other than wealth acquisition. As Montaigne once observed: "To compose our character is our duty, not to compose books, and to win, not battles and provinces, but order and tranquility in our own conduct. Our great and glorious masterpiece is to live appropriately."

NOTES

1. H. F. Stone, "Public Influence of the Bar," 48 *Harv. L. Rev.* 1, 14 (1934). For an excellent overview of legal education, see C. Woodard, "Justice Through Law—Historical Dimensions of the American Law School," 34 *J. Legal Ed.* 345 (1984), to which this chapter is partly indebted.

2. S. Turow, *One L* (New York: Putnam, 1977).

3. C. Woodard, "Justice Through Law—Historical Dimensions of the American Law School," 34 *J. Legal Ed.* 345 and ff. (1984).

4. Quoted in P. Carrington and J. Conley, "The Alienation of Law Students," 75 *Mich. L. Rev.* 887 (1977).

5. Albert J. Harno, *Legal Education in the U.S.; A Report Prepared for the Survey of the Legal Profession*, 51 (San Francisco: Bancroft-Whitney Co., 1953).

6. These are the tenets of the "ordinary religion" of the law school classroom as

described in Roger C. Cramton, "The Ordinary Religion of the Law School Classroom," 29 *J. Legal Ed.* 247, 248 (1978).

7. Arval A. Morris, "Legal Education: Cognitive Development or Psychological Adjustment," 53 *N.Y.U. L. Rev.* 635, 641 (1978).

8. E. Griswold, "Intellect and Spirit," 81 *Harv. L. Rev.* 292, 301 (1967).

9. Howard S. Erlanger and Douglas A. Klegan, "Socialization Effects of Professional School: The Law School Experience and Student Orientations to Public Interest Concerns," 13 *Law and Society* 11, 30 (1978). Lon Fuller reminded law teachers that "the slogan, 'We teach men to think,' has been the last refuge of every dying discipline from Latin and Greek to Mechanical Drawing and Common-Law Pleading." L. Fuller, "What the Law Schools Can Contribute to the Making of Lawyers," 1 *J. Legal Ed.* 189, 190 (1948). For useful previous discussions of "thinking like a lawyer," see Gordon A. Christenson, "Studying Law as the Possibility of Principled Action," 50 *Den. L. J.* 413, 430–33 (1974); John O. Mudd, "Thinking Critically About 'Thinking Like a Lawyer'," 33 *J. Legal Ed.* 704 (1983).

10. Morris L. Cohen, *Legal Research in a Nutshell*, 11 (St. Paul: West Pub. Co., 1978). See also E. Walter Van Valkenburg, "Law Teachers, Law Students, and Litigation," 34 *J. Legal Ed.* 584 (1984).

11. Jack Himmelstein, et al. "Reassessing Law Schooling: An Inquiry into the Application of Humanistic Educational Psychology to the Teaching of Law," 53 *N.Y.U. L. Rev.* 561 (1978).

12. Quoted in A. Gerson, *Lawyers' Ethics*, 53 (New Brunswick, N.J.: Transaction Inc., 1980).

13. T. Shaffer and R. Redmount, *Lawyers, Law Students and People*, 197 (Colorado Springs: Shepard's, 1977).

14. C. Langdell, *A Selection of Cases on the Law of Contracts*, vii (1871). Of Langdell's contracts casebook, Holmes wrote in an anonymous review, "There cannot be found in the legal literature of this country, such a tour de force of patient and profound intellect working out original theory through a mass of detail, and evolving consistency out of what seemed a chaos of conflicting atoms. But in this word 'consistency' we touch what some of us at least must deem the weak point in Mr. Langdell's habit of mind. Mr. Langdell's ideal in the law, the end of all his striving, is the *elegantia juris*, or logical integrity of the system as a system. He is, perhaps, the greatest living legal theologian." 14 *Am. L. Rev.* 233 (1880).

15. R. Cramton, "The Ordinary Religion of the Law School Classroom," 252.

16. Ibid.

17. C. Woodard, "Justice Through Law—Historical Dimensions of the American Law School."

18. S. Turow, *One L* (New York: G. P. Putnam, 1977). See also P. Stern, *Lawyers on Trial*, 173 (New York: Times Books, 1980).

19. D. Kennedy, "How the Law School Fails: A Polemic," 1 *Yale Rev. L. & Soc. Action* 71, 73 (1970). Mr. Kennedy is now a professor at Harvard Law School. For his later articles see "First Year Law Teaching as Political Action," 1 *Law & Soc. Prob.* 47 (1980) (speech at 1978 Conference on Critical Legal Studies); and "Legal Education and the Reproduction of Hierarchy," 32 *J. Legal Ed.* 591 (1982). For a similar condemnation of legal education, see Paul N. Savoy, "Toward a New Politics of Legal Education," 79 *Yale L. J.* 444 (1970).

20. A. Stone, "Legal Education on the Couch," 86 *Harvard L. Rev.* 392, 442 (1971).

21. T. Shaffer and R. Redmount, *Lawyers, Law Students and People*, (1977) at 161.

22. Robert Stevens, "Law Schools and Law Students," 59 *Va. L. Rev.* 551, 646, 647 (1973).

23. T. Shaffer and R. Redmount, *Lawyers, Law Students and People*, at 212.

24. Ibid. at 158.

25. Carrington, "The Alienation of Law Students."

26. Leonard L. Baird, "A Survey of the Relevance of Legal Training to Law School Graduates," 29 *J. Legal Ed.* 264 (1978).

27. Ibid. at 273.

28. Ibid.

29. Ibid. See also W. Thielens, *The Socialization of Law Students: A Case Study in Three Parts*, at 163 (New York: Arno Press, 1980).

30. Jeremy Bentham, in his *Comment on the Commentaries and A Fragment on Government* (Atlantic Highlands, N.J.: Humanities Press), observed: "If there be a case in which students stand in need of instruction most it is where the generality of books that come into their hands represent things in a different light from true ones. True it is, that after many errors and disappointments, observation and practice may let a beginner into the bottom of these mysteries; but what sort of an excuse is it to give feeding him with falsehood, that some time or other he may chance to find it out?"

31. F. Zemans and V. Rosenblum, *The Making of a Public Profession* (Chicago: American Bar Foundation, 1981) at 137.

32. R. Redmount, "A Conceptual View of the Legal Education Process," 24 *J. Legal Ed.* 129 (1972).

33. Roger S. Haydock, quoted in the *Los Angeles Daily Journal*, August 10, 1987, p. 16, "Law School News," col. 5.

34. O. W. Holmes, *The Common Law* (Mark Howe ed., Boston: Little, Brown and Co., 1963) at 77.

35. *Montana Law School Report*, 6–7 (1987). See also J. Mudd, "Beyond Rationalism: Performance-Referenced Legal Education," 36 *J. Legal Ed.* 189 (1986). Several law schools have adopted some of these humanist principles in implementing new approaches to legal education. The C.U.N.Y. Law School was conceived and staffed by several of the leading humanist scholars. The University of Montana School of Law, established in 1911, revised its first year curriculum in 1984 after an extensive reevaluation. The predecessor to these schools was Antioch Law School, which integrated clinical and substantive law training in an effort to train lawyers in large part for public interest and poverty law careers. The "humanists" are perhaps best represented by E. Dvorkin, J. Himmelsmith, and H. Lesnick, *Becoming a Lawyer: A Humanistic Perspective on Legal Education and Professionalism* (St. Paul, Minn.: West Publishing, 1981) and the program adopted at C.U.N.Y. Law School at Queens College. The "humanities" have been defined as "the system of values, traditions and customs with which we live and which we may wish to change." S. Byman, "Humanities and the Law School Experience," 35 *J. Legal Ed.* 76 (1985). The humanists' stated purpose is to broaden "the scope of traditional education to include a focus upon the persons of teachers and students, the human dimensions underlying the subject matter, and the experience of learning" (ibid). The goal of this approach, however, "is not to replace the traditional strengths of the profession, but to include them in a larger context" (ibid). See also the extended discussion on humanism in 10 *Nova L. J.* 504 (1987).

36. See generally A. Bloom, *The Closing of the American Mind*, 187 and passim (New York: Simon and Schuster, 1987).

37. Thomas Shaffer and Robert Redmount comment, ''Innovation in legal education comes hard, is limited in scope and permission, and generally dies young.'' Shaffer and Redmount, *Lawyers, Law Students, and People*.

38. Quoted in L. Baird, ''A Survey of the Relevance of Legal Training to Law School Graduates,'' 29 *J. Legal Ed.* 264 (1978).

39. Richard A. Posner, *The Federal Courts: Crisis and Reform* 326 (Cambridge: Harvard Univ. Press, 1985), to whom part of this critique is indebted.

40. *National Observer*, October 2, 1976, quoting Charles Rhyne, President, World Peace Through Law Center.

3

BAR EXAMS AND MORAL CHARACTER: INQUIRIES WITHOUT CHARACTER

> There is, perhaps, no profession, after that of the sacred ministry, in which a high-toned morality is more imperatively necessary than that of law. There is certainly, without any exception, no profession in which so many temptations beset the path to swerve from the line of strict integrity; in which so many delicate and difficult questions of duty are continually arising.
> —G. Sharswood, *An Essay on Professional Ethics* (1860)

> Give me a room full of educated adults five nights a week for four weeks and I could probably get them through the bar exam. The bar exam is nothing but regurgitation of some very specific information.
> —David Epstein, Emory Law School Dean (1986)

After graduation, the aspiring lawyer confronts bar admission and learns that the legal profession that helps set rules by which the rest of the public must act often falls short of principled rulemaking for itself.

In *The Lawyer from Antiquity to Modern Times*, Roscoe Pound argued that an organized profession like the bar is not the same "as a retail grocer's association."[1] The divergence may be disputed. The bar sometimes differs from trade unions only in sanctimoniousness,[2] particularly in its control of its own admission standards. Some segments of the bar believe that lawyers are somehow special, not subject to the internal standards of other professionals. The legal field is so specialized, some say, so beyond ordinary understanding in its sacred pursuit of justice that entry to it cannot be reduced to ordinary judgment. Similarly, the fact that lawyers are not universally loved perhaps can be attributed to some innate human perversity related to original sin.[3]

Such at times is the scenario of sanctimoniousness surrounding the bar's entry to its own ranks.

Typically, there are two gateways to the bar for law graduates: examinations and moral character review.[4] These dual gateways seek to assure professionalism; for differing reasons both fall short of that goal.

THE BAR EXAMINATION

The bar examination usually includes three state-administered exams: (1) a multiple-choice, multistate exam of some two hundred questions (MBE), (2) several essay questions, and (3) an ethics exam.

MBE exams test basic verbal logic, knowledge of legal vocabulary, and ability to function under pressure. In law practice, more important skills predominate: the ability to negotiate, to ask productive questions, to find and apply differing laws, and to get along with individuals in distress. No exam directly addresses these skills. The MBE yields scores that reflect the relative success of candidates. There is no passing score nationwide; each state chooses its own. Since each score reflects only relative performance, each state opts for a probable pass rate when it chooses a passing score. The arbitrary passing score makes it virtually impossible for all to pass. Differing state passing standards balkanize the admission process.

Some candidates whose abilities are virtually indistinguishable pass or fail due to an error of measurement that results in almost one-third of the candidates clustering around the average correct score of 140 of 200 questions. The MBE thus shares the infirmities that infect the LSAT, but law school admissions offices readily treat chance differences as no difference at all. Where the candidate's LSAT score is inconsistent with others, the score can be disregarded. These safeguards are unavailable for the multistate examination. Since a single passing score is chosen for all candidates within a state, scores just below passing due to an error of measurement become failing.

The bar examination also typically includes an essay portion that asks examinees to discuss legal points of a factual problem. While it forces candidates to write and analyze, the essay requires a sufficiently strong memory of legal rules to permit issue recognition, which, rather than correctness, is the bellwether of a good answer.

The ethics portion (MPRE) of the bar exam tests knowledge of lawyers' ethical rules. To the uninitiated, successful completion suggests virtue. In fact, the MPRE does not test honor, integrity, character, or even general morality but only knowledge of lawyers' professional rules. A totally immoral person could easily pass the MPRE; the exam tests good memory, not good character. Lawyers do not become ethical simply by passing the MPRE. The real issue in lawyer ethics is not memorization of rules; it is policing practicing lawyers who lack integrity regardless of their ethics scores. A personality test measuring greed or alcoholism might offer a more realistic prediction of ethical compliance.

The ethics exam also enforces an ethics of a specified minimum. The MPRE requires students to think as people subject to a code like the Internal Revenue

Code. One can know the law of professional ethics but not have any realization of either ethics or professionalism, just as one may know the letter of the rule and disregard its spirit.[5]

For decades, lawyers have talked about the desirability of a national bar examination, but progress in that direction has been painfully slow. The practice of law is interstate these days, but the bar exam is a hanging-on from days gone by, an old states' rights issue. Since 1972, each state has had the option of replacing its multiple-choice test with two hundred computer-graded questions. All but Louisiana, Washington, Indiana, and Iowa use the multistate test. Even though bar applicants in several states now answer all the same questions, each state still sets its own passing score. Most years, Idaho passes nine out of ten candidates who take the bar examination. Vermont and California pass only about half their applicants. The profession that extols equal treatment contradicts its ideals even for its own.

In at least ten states within recent years, lawsuits have challenged bar examination results. Their thrust is similar: the examination discriminates against minority candidates and is administered arbitrarily. The suits have all been unsuccessful. They have also missed the central point regarding bar exams: with very narrow exceptions, the present examinations test memory and few if any of the skills needed for competency. The rigorous standards courts require for other employment tests are irrelevant to bar admission; only a loose "rational" relationship between the examination and the practice of law is required. In bar exam litigation, this standard is typically met by bar examiners' testimony that they themselves once took a similar examination. Statistical proof is also offered to demonstrate that exam results closely reflect law school grades. Evidence that the examination reflects the practice of law in any way is rarely presented; it is thought superfluous.

The exam format is regularly justified by pointing to the correlation between exam results and law school grades. Not surprisingly, there is a similarity between MBE and essay scores. There are also high correlations among MBE scores, law school grades, and LSAT scores. Applicants who do well on the MBE are almost always the same who do well in law school and on the essay exam. This correlation hardly refutes the possibility that an applicant's score on the MBE is a function of knowing how to take multiple-choice tests rather than legal skills.[6]

Defenses of the examination's format constitute a vicious circle of justifications. The LSAT is justified by its correlation with law school grades and with the results of the bar examination. The bar examination is justified by comparison with GPA and LSAT results. The LSAT, law school GPA, and bar exams self-validate because they mutually validate. They mean only that people who test well do so consistently. Their only meaningful distinction is between those who test well and those who do not, i.e., those who analyze and remember well and those who do not. In sum, the bar exam says much about good test memory and nothing about lawyer competency or integrity.

Despite the correlation among LSAT, grade average, and bar examinations, there is no evidence that any of the three relate to competence in practice.[7] Some empirical data suggest that legal education provides poor training in essential practice skills such as negotiation, interviewing, and drafting legal documents.[8] None of these skills appears on traditional bar examinations. In sum, the exams test little beyond short-term rote memory—the same memory that rises and quickly falls to meet the similar challenges of LSAT and law school exams.

Not surprisingly, though nine lawyers in ten (88 percent) think that bar exams should continue in some form, by a nearly three-to-one margin (70 to 26 percent) they agree that current bar exams do not measure the ability to practice law, do not measure competence in a meaningful way, do little to protect clients ethically, and do even less to protect law firms.[9] When passed, bar examinations create the illusion of success both for examinee and alma mater, which often treasures this batting average as the badge of its success. The exams create only an illusion of competency; the public is led to believe that the successful examinee can practice law generally. In fact, however, the examination tests a memorized legal catechism so broadly oriented toward common law doctrine as to be largely irrelevant to competency even in the simplest specialty. Specialization is rarely raised in law school and more rarely tested or questioned; the issue disappears under reassuring rhetoric about how hard the exam is (meaning, how taxing to memory and logic) and how it nicely correlates with LSAT and law school grades. The current bar exams thus remain a ceremonial entrance rite with little relevance to practice or character.

CHARACTER AND FITNESS REVIEW

History

Moral character as a professional credential for lawyers has an extended lineage dating to Rome's Theodesian Code. Its Anglo-American roots reach to thirteenth-century England. By the 1400s, attorneys' conduct was questionable enough to inspire oath-taking:

> Item, for sundry damages and mischiefs that have ensued before this time to divers persons of the realm by a great number of attornies, ignorant and not learned in the law, as they were wont to be before this time: it is ordained and established that all the attornies shall be examined by the justices, and by their discretions their names put in the roll, and they that be good and virtuous, and of good fame, shall be received and sworn well, and truly to serve in their offices . . . ; and the other attornies shall be put out by the discretion of the said justices.[10]

Taken by lawyers of that era, this oath was thought sufficient to encourage virtue. By 1701, the lawyers of Massachusetts were required to take yet another oath demanding that a lawyer do no falsehood, nor consent to any to be done in the court; advise the court of any falsehoods of which the lawyer had knowledge; avoid the procurement or promotion of false or unlawful suits, nor consent nor aid the same; delay no man for lucre or malice; perform the duties of his office to the best of his learning and discretion with all good fidelity as well to the courts as to your clients.[11]

These historical examples suggest a belief that virtue derives from repeated oath-taking. Perhaps repeated oaths serve as a reminder of easily forgotten ethical duties or of the somber thought of Lord Bolingbroke: "the profession of the law, in its nature the noblest and most beneficial to mankind, is in its abuse an abasement the most sordid and pernicious."[12]

History can be read not only as a pursuit of ethics but also as a recurring demand for lawyer control. As early as 1817, a Maryland law professor, David Hoffman, proposed "Fifty Resolutions in Regard to Professional Deportment"[13] as guidelines for conduct by new attorneys. As much concerned with etiquette as ethics, Hoffman prescribed standards uncompromising in both respects. Lawyers should renounce all activity that might compromise professional dignity or personal honor: no self-promotion, unjust causes, or disingenuous tactics.

In 1854, as a Pennsylvania trial judge, Justice George Sharswood wrote "A Compend of Lectures on the Aims and Duties of the Profession of the Law," as a body of rules accepted by the profession as standards for other lawyers' conduct.[14] Although echoing Hoffman's distaste for commercial rivalry, Sharswood's essay articulated a complex notion of the clubbish obligation of the lawyer to his fraternity. A magnificently clubable man, Sharswood told his students that they would not go wrong to imitate their professional elders—a point of view also prominent in the stories of Louis Auchincloss and James Gould Cozzens. Today's law students, of course, are familiar with their elders' involvement in, among other notorious matters, Watergate and stock market frauds.

Many formal codes have been adopted by bar associations and courts, led by Alabama in 1887 and followed by the American Bar Association in 1908.[15] These codes suggest that virtue flows from ceaseless enactment of rules and repeated oath-taking.

The necessity of good moral character originates in the trustee nature of the practice of law. As Justice Frankfurter once explained, lawyers hold others' rights in trust:

All the interests of man that are comprised under the constitutional guarantees given to "life, liberty and property" are in the professional keeping of lawyers. . . . From a profession charged with such responsibilities there must be exacted those qualities of truth-speaking, of a high sense of honor, of granite discretion, of the strictest observance of fiduciary responsibility, that have, throughout the centuries, been compendiously described as "moral character."[16]

Historically, the bar's character and fitness requirements have been used to preclude the socially unpopular and to keep down the underdogs, under a belief that diseased dogs should be refused entry before their first bite. Entry restrictions intended to maximize public protection still remain largely ineffective in identifying those likely to engage in misconduct.

With the exception of the early 1950s when they were used to exclude suspected left-wingers, the bar's character requirements have been largely honored in the breach. In the abstract, of course, to be a good lawyer one must be a morally good person. This assumption underlies all the current moral character and fitness tests:[17] if one is not a morally good person, one will not be a good lawyer.[18] Consequently, bar examiners disqualify individuals who seem not to be morally good.[19]

What makes for a morally good person, however, is defined nowhere.[20] Bar committees and courts have had to decide, among other such issues, whether homosexual orientation, membership in a communist organization, declaration of bankruptcy, or brewing home beer are moral reasons to exclude a candidate. Whether this arbitrary moral investigation protects society or the bar is doubtful.[21] The present character inquiry disserves both the bar and the public; it discriminates among lawyers and fails to protect the public.[22]

Caprice of Bar Admission Standards

A recent *Bar Examiners' Handbook* candidly concedes: "No definition of what constitutes grounds for denial of admission on the basis of faulty character exists."[23] Indeed, moral fitness is heavily subjective. Definitions of fitness reflect the prejudices of the definer.[24] To Justice Holmes the standard expresses "an intuition of experience which outruns analysis."[25] Courts require that moral criteria have a "rational connection with the applicant's fitness or capacity to practice law."[26] Unfortunately, this description offers little assistance. No objective guidelines exist as to what is a "rational connection" between practice and the determination of good moral character.[27] "Rational connection" remains as subjective as "moral fitness."

Here are some examples of the varying tests used, with differing results, that poorly elucidate that connection.

Prior Illegal and Immoral Conduct. The Code of Professional Responsibility prohibits lawyers from engaging in illegal conduct and moral turpitude. What constitutes moral turpitude, however, is circular:

Fundamentally, the question involved in both situations is the same—is the applicant for admission or the attorney sought to be disciplined a fit and proper person to be permitted to practice law, and that usually turns upon whether he has committed or is likely to continue to commit acts of moral turpitude.[28]

The bar's Code of Professional Responsibility defines good moral character as "qualities of truth, of a high sense of honor, of granite discretion, of the strictest observance of fiduciary responsibility.''[29] For its part, ''moral turpitude'' means ''baseness, vileness or depravity in the duties which one person owes to another or to society in general.''[30] In short, ''good moral character'' is goodness; ''moral turpitude'' is badness. The good and bad are defined by synonyms, not by definitions. ''Moral turpitude'' is a virtually useless standard to measure lack of moral character. Good moral character remains unknown.

''Rational connection'' is also circular. Though at common law attorneys were disbarred for fraud or dishonesty, most courts scrutinize the nature and proximity of criminal conduct for any connection with law practice.[31] Prohibiting ''illegal'' conduct reflects a concern for limits in furthering a client's interests. Prohibiting moral turpitude smacks of a morality of professional appearance as distinct from legality. The present character rules do not provide a workable standard for identifying or separating either, nor do they reveal any connection, rational or otherwise, to law practice.

Personal Data. Character of candidates is assessed through information from questionnaires, letters of recommendation, follow-up investigations, interviews, and hearings. To Justice Frankfurter, this decision-making process requires ''delicate'' judgment:

No doubt satisfaction of the requirement of moral character involves an exercise of delicate judgment on the part of those who reach a conclusion, having heard and seen the applicant for admission, a judgment . . . that . . . expresses ''an intuition of experience which outruns analysis and sums up many unnamed and tangled impressions which may lie beneath consciousness without losing their worth.''[32]

These ''tangled impressions'' rest on a devastating and sterile paperload. Here is the way one bar official explains the bar's crushing paper chase for moral turpitude:

We contact every high school, university and law school attended by the applicant. Every employer since age 18 regardless of whether it was part-time, casual, contract, etc. Then, for every locality in which the applicant has resided, three references for each. For those admitted elsewhere, we contact partners, co-workers, associates in law firms, plus legal references (other attorneys, judges, etc.) for every locality in which they have practiced, and three clients for every locality of practice.

When responses are received from the above, they are read carefully for negative responses. If found, ''red-flagged'' in order that a committee member will immediately see. Examples of red-flagged comments would be poor attitude, bad work habits, fired, drinking problems, personality conflicts, and innuendos! The application itself would have already been red-flagged for negative responses that the applicant provided, such as proliferation of violations, law suits, academic problems.[33]

A more crushing pursuit of diminishing returns would be hard to imagine.

Bar applications typically begin with an extended series of pedigree questions: half (57 percent) ask who the candidate's parents are; over a quarter (29 percent) seek parental occupations.[34] Some question parental birthplace (4 percent), mother's maiden name (10 percent), siblings' names or occupations (6 percent), grade school (10 percent), junior high school (24 percent) or extracurricular activities (4 percent). Disciplinary sanctions in high school (63 percent) and college (86 percent) are common inquiries. Several states, including New York, inquire whether applicants have ever been denied academic admission for character defects. How candidates would have this information is unclear.

Employment inquiries are equally inept. About a third of the states demand employment histories from age sixteen or earlier. Half ask about dismissals or resignations for unsatisfactory work (22 percent) or any other causes (24 percent), or accusations of dishonesty (10 percent). Several states (8 percent) seek an accounting for all time periods since age eighteen by requiring "where you were and what you did" during times not covered by other questions. Sometimes the clairvoyant candidate must identify future employers (6 percent).

All states inquire about criminal proceedings. Over half (59 percent) demand disclosure of all convictions, including misdemeanors, and all arrests (51 percent). Many jurisdictions include expunged (24 percent) or juvenile (20 percent) offenses, and parking violations (14 percent). Some inquire about accusations (8 percent), warnings (4 percent), testimony (6 percent), refusals to testify (6 percent), and requests to appear before an investigative agency (6 percent). New York even asks the number of unpaid traffic tickets. About two-thirds of the bars ask if the applicant has been involved in any civil proceedings (63 percent) or has any unsatisfied judgments (67 percent). Some jurisdictions inquire about bankruptcy (63 percent), divorce (43 percent), debts past due (27 percent), and dishonored checks (4 percent).

Personal History Questions. Every jurisdiction requests extensive information about prior residences. A quarter demand a ten-year itinerary, which for many graduates begins at age fourteen. A minority of states require photographs (25 percent), birth certificates (6 percent), physicians' certificates (4 percent), law school applications (2 percent), and high school grade transcripts (2 percent). Usually nothing is done with this burdensome information apart from a check of local law enforcement records.[35]

Almost all states require personal references of varying form and number, often three or more from each place the applicant lived. Some states even allow applicants to submit completed reference forms themselves. A minority of states seek self-serving assurances. About a quarter ask if the applicant intends to comply with the Code of Professional Responsibility.[36] Eleven states inquire if the applicant has read the Code of Ethics. Three states ask about compliance with it. To obtain a handwriting sample, North Carolina makes applicants explain why they want to practice there. Maryland demands an essay on one Canon of Ethics that the candidate personally thinks is important.[37]

Inquiry on a candidate's application may extend to matters that rarely involve discipline for a practicing attorney: bounced checks (76 percent), involvement in litigation (52 percent), and high levels of debt (56 percent). Many jurisdictions investigate psychiatric treatment (98 percent), misdemeanor convictions arising from sit-ins (80 percent), and sexual conduct or life-style (49 percent). All these issues would be ignored in a practicing attorney's life-style.

Arbitrary Decisions Regarding Respect for Law. No consensus exists as to what general types of conduct disqualify an applicant. The only factor commanding majority agreement is a criminal record (47 percent). Yet bar investigations frequently probe into juvenile offenses and parking violations. Candidates have been excluded for traffic convictions and cohabitation.[38]

While courts stress some rational relationship between conduct and fitness to practice, decisions on whom to exclude show few standards. "Disrespect for law" as a criterion for exclusion yields inconsistent results. Violation of a fishing license statute ten years earlier caused one local Michigan committee to decline certification; in the same state, at about the same time, other examiners admitted individuals convicted of child molesting and conspiring to bomb a public building.[39]

Convictions for marijuana are taken seriously in some jurisdictions and overlooked in others. By their own admissions, many Boards of Examiners function under a double standard: Board members say nothing about the guy who gets in brawls and fistfights in bars because they figure he's "just a good ol' boy," but many boards get upset about drugs, even in small amounts. Courts, too, frequently divide over drug and alcohol addiction; for some, it is an adequate mitigating circumstance; for others it is reason for denial.[40]

Cohabitation and homosexuality generate similar diversity. Some examiners consider such activity only when it becomes a public nuisance or a crime. Thus, the Arizona admissions committee does not set itself up as a "moral judge," because "in this day and age living together is accepted." In other jurisdictions, however, cohabitation and homosexuality trigger extensive inquiry with some possibility of denial. "Disrespect for law" may be either honor or shame.

Political Expression. Responses to political activity are highly unpatterned. The Secretary of Arkansas' Board of Law Examiners looks at political dissent "with a blink." In other jurisdictions such as Nevada, misdemeanor arrests arising from free speech "raise eyebrows," and cause some applicants to be "harried." Any disruptive activity triggers review in one Missouri district. In Idaho, only membership in the "Red Brigade" would arouse interest. In Virginia such associations would not be "any of [the committee's] business." Yet to the California Supreme Court, acts of civil disobedience reflect the "highest moral courage."[41]

Political belief provides some of the bleakest chapters in bar admission, with outrageous cases abounding. A conscientious objector to military sevice, an applicant named Summers,[42] was denied admission because he could not swear to uphold the state constitution provision requiring men of Summer's age to serve in the state militia in time of war. Another conscientious objector, Brooks,[43] violated a criminal law by refusing to report for alternative service in a civilian labor camp. Ten years later, he was denied bar admission because "age alone has not reduced his potential for war resistance to zero. . . . An old lawyer can impede his country's war effort in many ways as well as a young one.''[44]

Asked on a bar application to identify the principles underlying the Constitution, applicant Anastaplo[45] referred to the same right of revolution against an oppressive government asserted in the Declaration of Independence. This response triggered lengthy hearings in which Anastaplo was asked whether he belonged to the Ku Klux Klan, the Communist Party, and any of the Attorney General's listed subversive organizations, and whether he believed in a Supreme Being. Anastaplo refused to answer some questions on First Amendment grounds. He was subsequently denied admission for failure to cooperate, notwithstanding what the dissent called ''a mountain of evidence so favorable to Anastaplo that the word 'overwhelming' seems inadequate to describe it.''[46]

This pattern continues today. Nevada inquires if the candidate is a Communist. Tennessee requires disclosure of all organizations to which the applicant belongs, a question flatly inconsistent with Supreme Court holdings. Eighty percent of all jurisdictions investigate conduct such as sit-ins resulting in misdemeanor convictions or membership in radical organizations. Court decisions suggest that such activities could not legitimately warrant exclusion from the bar.

Candor, Remorse, and Inconsistency. The ultimate vulnerability in most jurisdictions remains nondisclosure of even trivial matters. Committees place a high premium on candor and remorse. Appealing to a higher personal ethic or protestations of innocence are generally useless. Perplexing inconsistencies result. A repentent bomber in Michigan was thus admitted to the bar despite several years in a maximum security prison; North Carolina's unconfessed ''peeping Tom'' was thought too great a threat to be certified as a lawyer.[47] In the late 1970s the usual disciplinary sanction in Florida for failure to file income tax returns was a public reprimand.[48] At the same time, a Florida bar applicant was denied admission for the identical offense.[49] In December 1987, former federal Judge Harry Claibourne was readmitted to practice in Nevada, without discipline, after serving seventeen months in prison following impeachment and convictions for failing to report taxes in 1979 and 1980. A less illustrious applicant might well have been refused admission. In Maryland, in 1981, admission was denied to an applicant convicted of stealing sleeping pills and leaving the scene of an accident, notwithstanding a psychologist's report that his problems were resolved. In 1982, the same Maryland court ordered that the convicted driver of a getaway car in a bank robbery who failed to fully disclose the conviction on his application be admitted to that bar.[50]

Ceremonial Interviews. Similar useless pomp pervades mandatory candidate interviews. Each year, over eleven thousand law graduates—more than a quarter of those admitted to practice—must submit to character interviews. The claim that this is an opportunity for seasoned guidance by elder statesmen is belied by its cursory and pontifical nature. The eight- to ten-minute conversation usually centers on what it means to be a lawyer, the candidate's background, reasons for legal study, weather, mutual acquaintances, and future job prospects. Some committee chairs see their only purpose in such a tête-à-tête as determining compliance with residency requirements or the criminal law, issues resolved well prior to the interview. Applicants can easily survive the interview by sweet talk or lying, an ominous initiation to a career in public trust.[51]

LAW SCHOOL DISINTEREST IN CHARACTER

Consistent with their detachment from the legal world's ethics, law schools show only a perfunctory interest in this paper mill, matching a correspondingly low interest in the character of their graduates. Their obligation to report character defects dates from days when the schools were intimate enough that the faculty knew students well enough to say, "Yes, that's a person who ought to be admitted to the bar." At most schools today, mass education no longer permits anyone to say, "We as a faculty know Mary Smith is a person of quality who ought to be a practicing lawyer." The school can only say at best, "Our records show that Mary Smith took the requisite number of hours and received the grades necessary to graduate."[52]

Law schools traditionally have been ambivalent over the obligation to screen morality, specifically over whether to discipline individuals who have sold drugs, engaged in disruptive political demonstrations, or shown other signs of "moral turpitude."[53] Plagiarism is equally controversial. By law school standards, conviction for a felony is viewed about as seriously as improprieties regarding the LSAT or the law school's application form. In fact, once an applicant is admitted to law school, discipline for academic offenses such as cheating (94 percent), plagiarism (86 percent), or misuse of the library (84 percent) is considered more appropriate than discipline for a felony (56 percent) or sale of hard drugs (54 percent). Law school faculties see themselves as protectors of academic values, not as screening agents.

This detached view is contrary to that of many members of the bar and judiciary, as well as of character and fitness committees. For example, in 1965, Associate Justice Lewis F. Powell, then president of the American Bar Association, said in a speech:

Obviously, it is wise to screen out the undesirables at the earliest possible date. . . . The law schools have at least two opportunities to screen out undesirables. One is at the time of application and the other is prior to awarding a degree. . . . I am sure that every dean, and indeed perhaps almost every faculty member, is conscious of the problem—and I suspect that many of you would like to have less rather than more to do with it. We all know that character screening is an unwelcome task.[54]

Academic confusion over what, if anything, to do about student character defects runs deep. In one 1970 survey, accredited law schools were evenly divided over whether to admit to the bar a qualified applicant who posed no threat of danger to the academic community but who was denied admission on grounds of moral character.[55] Of twenty-three faculty and administrators more recently interviewed, ten (43 percent) believed they should not perform a screening function for the bar; their role, they said, is not to police the profession but only to provide legal education. By contrast, thirteen faculty and administrators (57 percent) felt that law schools had an obligation to assess character and fitness of their graduates. One director of admissions indicated that law schools should "play a much stronger role than they do. . . . There are so many lousy lawyers who, I imagine, grew out of lousy little boys."[56]

Regardless of policy preferences, deans lack the resources for insightful character evaluation. Unless the dean becomes aware of a character problem, no academic investigation occurs. Faculty, too, rarely if ever become aware of character problems. Yet, laws in thirty states continue to require character certificates from law schools. In Virginia, certification by in-state law schools constitutes proof of fitness to practice law. There the dean of the University of Virginia Law School notes that bar examiners

seem to think of law schools as small homey places where everyone knows everyone. . . . The belief that I am a good judge of character of the 375 students that emerge from here every year is mind-boggling. . . . I am not a good judge of candor, let alone character.[57]

During his six-year tenure, the dean of the T. C. Williams School of Law in Richmond, Virginia, has never failed to certify a student.[58]

Some schools even deliberately avoid exposure to questionable character traits. Not uncommonly, academic officials sometimes prefer to keep themselves in the dark:

In many law schools, the rules are that the dean says to the faculty at the beginning of the year, I don't want you to tell me anything about anybody—you understand—because I want to be able to sign this certificate truthfully and if you start telling me about these people, I'm going to have trouble. Whatever you want to tell each other about the students, that's your business; don't tell the dean so I can sign the certificate saying that to the best of my knowledge, I don't know anything about this individual.[59]

EVALUATION

Taken as a whole, the current certification process for potential lawyers is an extraordinarily "hot" means of providing public protection—"hot" in Levi-Strauss's sense of devouring itself. Great amounts of paid and volunteer time are consumed in screening routine applications without serious character questions. Arbitrary but lasting decisions to admit or exclude are often made by whim. Pedigree inquiries about parental occupation, maiden name, birthplace, employment, extracurriculars, precollege school affiliations, boyfriends, girlfriends, and marriages invite class and ethnic biases. This heated inquiry is also misdirected. It is hardly an appropriate vehicle for collecting speeding tickets, child support payments, or student loans, all of which debase the enterprise. Like Levi-Strauss's modern social system, these character inquiries are overdrawn, energy-intensive, and concerned more with public image than substance.

At times the process is also illegal. Requiring revelation of all arrests, including expunged offenses, violates statutory provisions in most states shielding such information from compelled disclosure.[60] The public policy underlying such legislation—that adverse inferences should not be drawn from conduct of marginal probative value—is applicable to other licensing determinations but strangely inapplicable to bar candidates. This traditional inquiry into character provides no fair notice to candidates, nor does it assure consistent treatment among applicants, nor does it really protect the distant public. It provides no means of measuring a character decision, and permits discrimination against unusual people merely because they are unusual. The consuming public receives only haphazard protection and loses valuable dissident voices able to speak with courage for unpopular views.[61]

The present character assessment is also internally ambiguous.[62] Definitions of virtue are circular or conclusory or highly personal to the examiner. Disagreement even exists about the same conduct: bankruptcy, barroom brawls, bounced checks, sexual activity, drug or alcohol usage, civil disobedience, and psychological problems all yield different results. Character decisions are so imprecise as to be virtually unreviewable. The unprincipled assessment of character turns loose a vast cadre of untested lawyers who learn at least one thing about the relationship of character to law practice: it can be faked.

The traditional view that character decisions involve an ''intuition which outruns analysis'' as the product of ''unnamed and tangled impressions'' which ''lie beneath consciousness'' does not provide consistent ground rules. Like the pro bono requirement that is made a nonrequirement in Rule 6.1 of the Model Rules of Professional Responsibility, the character investigation suggests that hyprocrisy is the bow that vice pays to virtue.

THE AGENDA

Other tributes are available. Abolition is not among them. Several scholars do advocate the abolition of the character requirement,[63] to dispense with the hocus pocus that is now the admission price at the gate of the great temple. Abolitionists believe that graduation from law school alone is sufficient certification of moral character. Given the law schools' disinterest and perfunctory certification policy, completion of law school alone hardly gives reassurance. The profession suffers more from sharp practices than from ignorance of legal principles. Because law is the vital core of justice, it should not be an open market.[64] Good moral character still needs to be assessed to ensure that both clients and justice are served responsibly.[65]

What, then, should be done? First, the exam process needs rethinking on a national level. The state-based system of bar admission is anachronistic. Ours is an era of multistate, even multinational, law firms. The practice of law is frequently multistate, but bar admission still occurs one state at a time. Legal experience is the only central bar admission criterion for which no national standards exist, especially ironic since admission based upon proof of legal experience in another state is inherently an interstate concern. The absence of national standards leads to ad hoc local decision making, an administrative nightmare for bar examiners and a costly roulette for bar applicants. The solution is a single bar exam across the country with local tailoring for local procedures.

Second, the examination process could well become the final step within the three-year law curriculum. Bar review courses could be coordinated within the third year using nationally administered and graded examinations as part of the admission process. A one-semester comprehensive review course would not impinge on the academic freedom of the law school and might even be welcomed by typically bored third-year students.[66]

The justification for current bar examinations—that they accurately reflect LSAT and law school grades—is circular. It would be a modest advance for the bar to acknowledge the circularity. High scores on any test—LSAT, law exam, or bar exam—say much about memory and little if anything about competence and integrity. The framework for scrutinizing admission to the bar lies elsewhere than in the incestuous correlation among UGPA, LSAT, and bar exam.

Fourth, bar examiners need to define competency and tailor exams accordingly. Whatever it means, competency involves far more than the rote memory skills of common law rules tested on present bar examinations. The bar has not yet agreed on answers to two fundamental questions: what is lawyer competence, and how should we best train for it? One judge's humorous explanation is probably universal: "I cannot define it but I know it when I see it."[67] Competency is the subject of no consideration in law school. "Thinking like a lawyer" is too vacuous for any realistic assessment of competency. At a minimum, competency requires skills of analysis, interpretation, creativity, writing, counseling, mediating, and integrity, few of which are tested on the present examinations. Once competency is defined, examinations need to test the skills that make for it. If it is a skill at all, memory is a much lower priority.

Legal practice provides one clue to competency. In order to assure a minimum level of competence, an attorney must keep up to date on a specialized area of practice. As presently constituted, the exam has very little to do with specialty competence. The bar grants a general license without limitation, yet nearly all attorneys practice in one or two specific areas. The examination does nothing to ensure competence in the area of actual practice. An attorney practicing in the immigration area, for example, is hardly competent to handle an estate planning case. Since the Supreme court held that lawyers may extol their own virtues by advertising, the question arises: what representation should a lawyer be able to make relative to special competency?

A bar license now given is a license for life. The bar has no mandatory continuing education requirements, ironic in a profession where information changes so radically. Curiously, after establishing a system where thousands of students spend three years and a small fortune, the bar allows those who pass a general test to practice in any chosen specialty and remain untested again until they die. Specialized bar exams for specially prepared candidates with mandatory periodic retesting is the obvious solution.

As part of the need for specialty testing, there is the further need for practice-oriented testing. At present, the most realistic assessment of lawyer skills comes from only one part of the exam in one state—California's "Performance Exam." There the performance test measures an applicant's ability to use skills to complete a writing and thinking task that a lawyer should be able to handle in the early stages of law practice.

Whereas essay and MBE tests measure an applicant's capacity to analyze issues based on memorized legal rules, performance tests call upon the applicant (1) to sift through detailed factual material to separate relevant from irrelevant facts; (2) to analyze statutory, case, and administrative materials for rules of law; (3) to consider ethical rules of practice; and (4) to apply the law to the relevant facts in a manner likely to resolve the problem.

The performance test consists of two parts, the "File" and the "Library." Facts are contained in a package of source documents called the "File," with transcripts of interviews with clients or witnesses, transcripts of hearings or trials, pleadings, correspondence, newspaper articles, medical records, official records, police reports, and lawyer's notes. The facts necessary to solve the problem are not given in a synthesized form. Relevant as well as irrelevant facts are included. Facts in performance tests are sometimes ambiguous, incomplete, or even conflicting. Applicants are expected to recognize inconsistencies, missing facts, and the need for additional facts. This exam format needs to be widely adopted across the country to assess one phase of competency.

Given these observations, the most practical solution to these examination procedures is to divide lawyer examination into two parts: a general exam to be taken for "general admission only" to the bar, followed by a "specialty exam" to qualify for specialized work. General admission would allow legal work to be done only under supervision; to work without supervision would require passing a specialized exam, which would authorize work confined only to the specialty. The specialty license would need to be renewed after seven years; a lapsed specialty license would require legal work to be done only under supervision of another.

Such a bifurcated examination process reflects several realities: first, the fact the law school's common law orientation is, at best, only a historically dated appetizer to law practice; second, that specialization will increasingly characterize the profession, and no form of it can be well taught in law school; third, that turning a general common lawyer loose to do specialized work without supervision evokes Hegel's dark night in which all cows are black. Because specialty knowledge is rapidly changing, the specialty license needs renewal via retesting every several years, and the seventh year, being sabbatical, seems most sanctified for this purpose. Mandatory continuing legal education would obviously help toward renewal.

Character and Fitness Review

Several novel ways exist by which the public can receive protection from unqualified lawyers. One is to insist that law schools or bars provide it via a one-year, specialized, lawyer-supervised internship or trusteeship prior to admission. Law schools could well fill the gap in providing the necessary training until internships are legislatively mandated, as they deserve to be if the schools do not take the initiative. Such trusteeships in public service would correlate exactly with the advocacy internship discussed in the preceding chapter.

A current law school graduate has been trained in law school to be one of three things; an associate in a big law firm, a clerk to an appellate judge, or a law professor. These jobs, naturally enough, are few and far between. The rest of the crop of new practitioners is dumped unceremoniously on an unsuspecting public. It's not that people don't need good, reasonably priced legal services— Jacoby & Meyers has shown us that they do—but middle-class people who need lawyers cannot afford competent ones. People who can afford competent counsel have a surfeit of competitive novices to choose among.

An internship before admission could be done in teaching law offices, like teaching hospitals, with these teaching offices linked with courts and administrative agencies to allow these novices to represent and counsel real clients with real problems. The idea of a teaching law office is, of course, not a new one. The profession itself, and most particularly legal education, is unable to wrench itself away from a tradition of training that is turning out an unfit product.

The bar's current character investigation is both too early and too late; it occurs before applicants face practical ethical situations and after such a significant investment in legal training that denying admission becomes difficult. The investigation fits more logically after the graduate completes a pro bono trusteeship and several years of supervised practice. Lawyers should be required to take and pass an ethical audit examination after seven years of practice, analogous to an income tax audit, to determine compliance with ethics. This audit could include a written test based on ethical principles, an oral interview, and a peer review evaluation by employers and fellow members of the bar, especially opposing counsel.

The concept of lawyer peer review—studied in depth in a 1980 American Law Institute-American Bar Association (ALI-ABA) project—makes sense in today's competitive legal market. Evaluating peers prevents any one lawyer from becoming too autonomous and makes it easier to detect alcohol, drug, and other personal problems. It might even encourage professional courtesy. Despite those benefits, most law firms resist formalized peer review, and the bar itself has shown little organized interest, perhaps from peer fear.

The regulatory difficulties in determining character and fitness raise a fundamental question about lawyer professionalism. If we can't adequately measure it, screen for it, prepare for it, or monitor it, what is "it" that justifies the claim? The bar persistently ignores that question. In a recent survey of ABA members, over three-fourths of the respondents agreed that self-regulation had proved successful and should be continued. Yet no one had any idea what it entailed in practice.[68]

The public ultimately is best served by making the data discussed above accessible. At present the potential client has no way to assess lawyer competency except by hearsay. Bar associations need not only list lawyers by specialty license but also have available for public consumption data on competency, character, and discipline. Ideally this information should be as accessible to the consumer as business information is available through the Better Business Bureau.

Finally, a word on soul—the same "soul" found lacking in the prior chapter. Promoting desirable lawyer behavior can appear as a morality of duty or a morality of aspiration. In a morality of duty like the tax code, minimal standards are established to mark boundaries of violations. The focus in the admission process now is on the "rule," i.e., learning what not to do rather than what ought to be done. If professionalism means anything, it means living not by a series of negatives but by internalized goals that inspire conduct rather than constrict it. That code has hardly been the hallmark of legal education or the bar. To many lawyers, ethical rules are like road signs: not models of good behavior to emulate, but signposts of how much misbehavior is tolerable. The purpose of drawing a line in the sand has been to see how close one can come without stepping over it. This "stepping over the line" mentality continues to color character and ethical assessments. Prospective lawyers learn where the line is and how close to come to it. Character determinations now assess more social conformity than moral integrity. The end result is the inculcation of the widespread minimal morality of "how much can I get away with." In lieu of this morality of minimal duty, the legal profession needs more uplifting standards of character to inculcate "soul" rather than merely toeing the mark. Socrates, Atticus, and Thomas More could well be reborn as living guides for ethics and character in a profession whose lessons seem increasingly to come from Machiavelli.

NOTES

1. R. Pound, *The Lawyer from Antiquity to Modern Times*, 89 (1953).

2. E. Freidson, *Profession of Medicine: A Study of the Sociology of Applied Knowledge*, (New York: Harper and Row, 1970), p. 369.

3. D. Mellinkoff, *The Conscience of a Lawyer* (St. Paul, Minn.: West Publ. Co., 1973). See also A. Marie, "Competency and the Legal Profession," *Insurance Counsel J.*, January 1986, 72, 87.

4. L. Patterson and E. Cheatham, *The Profession of Law* 281 (Mineola, N.Y.: Foundation Press, 1971); see also B. Harnett, *Law, Lawyers and Laymen: Making Sense of the American Legal System* 46 (New York: Harcourt Brace Jovanovich, 1984). See

generally S. Duhl, ed., *The Bar Examiners' Handbook* (Chicago: National Conference of Bar Examiners, 1980), 14–23 (general overview on admission to the practice of law in the United States).

5. T. Morgan, "The Rise and Fall of Professionalism," 19 *Rich. L. Rev.* 451, 458 (1985).

6. *Syllabus*, September 1982, at 3 (1982).

7. D. White, "The Definition of Legal Competence: Will the Circle Be Unbroken?" 18 *Santa Clara Law Rev.* 641 (1978). See also *Richardson v. McFadden*, 540 F.2d 744 (4th Cir. 1976); E. Gee and D. Jackson, "Bridging the Gap: Legal Education and Lawyer Competency," 1977 *B.Y.U. L. Rev.* 695, 712 (1977).

8. See F. Zemans and V. Rosenblum, *The Making of a Public Profession*, 134–50 (1981); L. Baird, "A Survey of the Relevance of Legal Training to Law School Graduates," 29 *J. Legal Ed.* 264 (1978).

9. "Bar Exam Blues," 34 *ABA J.*, July 1, 1987.

10. 4 Hen. 4, ch. 18, quoted in *State v. Cannon*, 206 Wis. 374, 240 N.W. 441, 446 (1932).

11. O. Phillips and P. McCoy, *Conduct of Judges and Lawyers: A Study of Professional Ethics, Discipline & Disbarment*, 9–10 (Los Angeles: Parker and Co., 1952) (quoting J. Cohen, *The Law: Business or Profession* 87 (rev. ed.; New York: G. A. Jennings Co., 1924)).

12. Quoted in *People v. Salomon*, 184 Ill. 490, 501 (1900).

13. Reprinted in G. Costigan, *Cases and Other Authorities on the Legal Profession and Its Ethics*, 695–709 (2d ed. 1933).

14. Later published as *An Essay on Professional Ethics* (5th ed. 1884).

15. O. Carter, "Ethics of the Legal Profession" (pt. 1), 9 *Ill. L. Rev.* 297, 308 (1914).

16. *Schware v. Board of Bar Examiners*, 353 U.S. 232, 247 (1957) (Frankfurter, J., concurring).

17. All states make good moral character a condition for admission to the bar. Model Code DR 1–101(b) provides that "[a] lawyer shall not further the application for admission to the bar of another person known by him to be unqualified with respect to character, education, or other relevant attribute."

18. Model Code EC 1–5 provides that "[a] lawyer should maintain high standards of professional conduct and should encourage fellow lawyers to do likewise. He should be temperate and dignified, and he should refrain from all illegal and morally reprehensible conduct."

19. J. Auerbach, *Unequal Justice: Lawyers & Social Change in Modern America*, (New York: Oxford Univ. Press, 1976), 94–101. See also D. Rhode, "Moral Character as a Professional Credential," 94 *Yale L. J.* 491 (1985), to which this essay is indebted for original research. See note 34 infra.

20. For a discussion of what makes a morally good person in the legal setting, see Frederick A. Ellston, "Character and Fitness Tests: An Ethical Perspective," 51 *Bar Examiner*, August 1982, pp. 8–16.

21. The states have the power to determine who shall be admitted to the practice of law. In a majority of states, the state supreme court acts as the general overseer of the bar, delegating admission to a committee of bar examiners, whose responsibility is to govern admission of the applicant to the bar. See Comment, "Bar Examinations: Good Moral Character, and Political Inquiry," 1970 *Wis. L. Rev.* 471, 472.

22. See *Law Students Civil Rights Research Council, Inc. v. Wadmond*, 401 U.S.

154, 159 (1971); *Ex parte Minor*, 280 So. 2d 217, 220 (La. 1973) ("Good moral character is an indispensable qualification for admission to the practice of law"); C. G. Carothers, "Character and Fitness: A Need for Increased Perception," 51 *Bar Examiner* 25, 25 (Aug. 1982) (affirmative demonstration of character and fitness is a necessary ingredient for bar admission); W. Shafroth, "Character Investigation—An Essential Element of the Bar Admission Process," 18 *Bar Examiner* 194, 208 (1948) (character and fitness are "essential conditions to a better bar").

23. *Bar Examiners' Handbook*, 123 (general overview on admission to the practice of law in the United States).

24. *Konigsberg v. State Bar of California*, 353 U.S. 252, 263 (1957) (footnote omitted); see also *Application of Klahr*, 102 Ariz. 529, 531, 433 P.2d 977, 979 (1962). ("The concept of 'good moral character' escapes definition in the abstract. Instead . . . an ad hoc determination in each instance must be made by the court.")

25. *Schware v. Board of Bar Examiners*, 353 U.S. 232, 248 (1957) (Frankfurter, J., concurring) (quoting *Chicago, Burlington & Quincy Ry. Co. v. Babcock*, 204 U.S. 585, 598 (1907).

26. Ibid., 353 U.S. at 239 (majority opinion).

27. See *Law Students Civil Rights Research Council, Inc. v. Wadmond*, 401 U.S. 154 (1971); *In re Stolar*, 401 U.S. 23 (1971); *Baird v. State Bar*, 401 U.S. 1 (1971).

28. *Hallinan v. Committee of Bar Examiners*, 65 Cal. 2d 447, 453, 421 P.2d 76, 81, 55 Cal. Rptr. 228, 233 (1966); see also *In re H.H.S.*, 373 So. 2d 890, 893 (Fla. 1979) (Adkins, J., dissenting).

29. *Model Code of Professional Responsibility*, Canon 1, n.14 (1982) (quoting *Schware v. Board of Bar Examiners*, 353 U.S. 232, 247 (1957) (Frankfurter, J., concurring).

30. *Model Code of Professional Responsibility*, Canon 1, n.13 (1982) (quoting *Committee on Legal Ethics v. Scheer*, 149 W. Va. 721, 726–27, 143 S.E.2d 141, 145 (1965).

31. See, e.g., *Schware v. Board of Bar Examiners*, 353 U.S. 232 (1957).

32. *Schware v. Board of Bar Examiners*, 353 U.S. 232, 248 (1957) (Frankfurter, J., concurring) (quoting *Chicago, Burlington & Quincy Ry. v. Babcock*, 204 U.S. 585, 598 (1907).

33. Carolyn Nyhus, State Bar of Arizona, letter to author (1986).

34. D. Rhode, "Moral Character as a Professional Credential." Figures in parentheses are percentages of respondents in her study who conform to the statement.

35. N.Y. Comm. Report on Character and Fitness, 33 *The Record* 20, 26, 48 (1978).

36. Ibid.

37. Ibid. See also D. Rhode, "Moral Character as a Professional Credential," at 522, 565–575.

38. Ibid.

39. Interview, Member, Michigan Board of Bar Examiners (July 12, 1983). The state board rejected the local committee's recommendation. See also D. Rhode, "Moral Character as a Professional Credential," at 538.

40. Compare *In re Application of A.T.*, 286 Md. 507, 408 A.2d 1023 (1979) (drug addiction treated as mitigating condition) with *In re Monaghan*, 122 Vt. 199, 167 A.2d 81 (1961) (alcoholism) and *In re Willis v. North Carolina State Bd. of Law Examiners*, 430 U.S. 976 (1975). Green, "Procedures for Character Investigations," 35 *Bar Examiner* 10, 13 (1966) (suggests that more than one drunk-driving charge would probably prevent admission). See also D. Rhode, "Moral Character as a Professional Credential," at 538.

41. D. Rhode, "Moral Character as a Professional Credential," at 552, quoting *Halliman v. Committee of Bar Examiners*, 65 Cal.2d 447, 462; 421 P.2d 76, 89 (1966).

42. *In re Summers*, 325 U.S. 561 (1945).

43. *Application of Brooks*, 57 Wash.2d 66, 355 P.2d 840 (1960).

44. Ibid. at 68, 355 P.2d at 841.

45. *In re Anastaplo*, 366 U.S. 82 (1961).

46. Ibid. at 107 (Black dissenting).

47. D. Rhode, "Moral Character as a Professional Credential," at 544 and *Matter of Elkins*, 302 S.E. 2d 215 (1983), cert. denied, 464 U.S. 995 (1983).

48. Ibid., Rhode at 552.

49. See *Florida Bar v. Turner*, 334 So.2d 1280 (Fla. 1977) (public reprimand); *Florida Bar v. Soloman*, 338 So.2d 818 (Fla. 1976) (six-month suspension where failure to file income tax return was coupled with other instances of misconduct); *In re Schonfield*, 336 So.2d 688 (Fla. 1975) (public reprimand); *In re Snyder*, 313 So.2d 33 (Fla. 1975) (public reprimand).

50. Compare *In re Application of James G.*, 296 Md. 310, 311 (1983) with *In re GLS*, 292 Md. 378, 439 A.2d 1107 (1982).

51. D. Rhode, "Moral Character as a Professional Credential," at 565–6.

52. Thomas D. Morgan, "Thinking About Bar Examining: The Challenge of Protecting the Public," 55 *Bar Examiner* 27 (November 1986).

53. See Donald T. Weckstein, "Recent Developments in Character and Fitness: Qualifications for the Practice of Law: The Law School Role; The Political Dissident," 40 *Bar Examiner* 17, 19–21 (1971). (51 percent would exclude individuals convicted of selling hard drugs, 57 percent would exclude those with moral turpitude offenses, 56 percent would discipline students convicted of a felony, and 35–39 percent would discipline students engaged in disruptive activity); see also Maximilian W. Kempner, "Current Practices of Law Schools With Respect to Character Qualifications of Students," 34 *Bar Examiner* 106, at 107–08 (1965) (noting variety of schools' approaches to such issues). During the mid–1960s and early 1970s, a significant minority of law schools reported that they would deny admission to applicants with misdemeanor convictions, selective service offenses, or a large number of traffic violations, and would take "a hard look at sexual misbehavior or homosexuality." See D. Rhode, "Moral Character as a Professional Credential," at 525.

54. *Syllabus*, September 1982 at 1, 3 (1982). "Comments on the Subject of the Panel Discussion," 34 *Bar Examiner* 117 (1965).

55. Weckstein, "Recent Developments in Character and Fitness," at 19–21 and 25 (40.3 percent would admit such an applicant; 45.5 percent would not).

56. D. Rhode, "Moral Character as a Professional Credential," at 527, quoting the admissions director of Wayne State University Law School (August 2, 1983).

57. Ibid. at 528.

58. Ibid.

59. N. Krivosha, "The Matter of Character and Fitness," 55 *Bar Examiner* 4 (May, 1986).

60. Every jurisdiction has laws or regulations concerning the privacy, security, and accuracy of criminal history records. See *Crim. Justice Newsletter*, Aug. 16, 1982, at 7 (citing Bureau of Justice statistics, criminal justice information policies). Many states, including New York, have statutory prohibitions that ban discrimination based upon, or inquiries relating to, juvenile offenses and arrest that terminated in favor of the accused.

See N.Y. Crim. Proc. Law 160.60 (Mckinney 1981); also Note, "Criminal Procedure: Expunging the Arrest Record When There Is No Conviction," 28 *Okla. L. Rev.* 377, 386–87 (1975) (citing statutes). See also Rhode, "Moral Character as a Professional Credential," at 577.

61. Michael K. McChrystal, "Resuscitating Character and Fitness Standards," 55 *Bar Examiner* 13–14 (November, 1986).

62. *Konigsberg v. State Bar*, 353 U.S. 252, 263 (1957).

63. D. Rhode, "Moral Character as a Professional Credential," at 585.

64. D. Besharov and T. Hartle, "Here come the Mediocre Lawyers," *Wall St. J.*, Feb. 22, 1985, p. 30, col. 4.

65. See *Application of Matthews*, 94 N.J. 59, 77, 462 A.2d 165, 173 (1983).

66. Sumner T. Bernstein, "Coordinate Law Review into Law School Curriculum," 18 *Syllabus* 8 (March 1987).

67. "Law Poll: Self-Regulation, Some Lay Participation Still Are Favored," 69 *ABA J.* 154 (1983).

68. Ibid.

4

FEEDING THE COURT DINOSAUR: THE WAR OF PARTS AGAINST THE WHOLE

> When the law is against me, I pound on the facts; When the facts are against me, I pound on the law. When the law and the facts are both against me, I pound on the table.
>
> —Anonymous lawyer

> You have created a system that tries to live out the American dream; the problem is that it is killing you.
> —Michael Crozier, French author, in *The Trouble with America* (1985)

The American court system of the 1980s has become a dinosaur, lumbering toward extinction because of its rigor and complexity. Unless radical changes are made, metropolitan civil courts may well be extinct in twenty years. Their rigidity and complexity are largely due to judicial and legislative submission to our Anglo-American legal heritage and to litigator control of the courts, which has reduced them to cumbersome and arbitrary lotteries.

Three real-life examples reveal the cumbersome caprice of this dinosaur:

1. At attorney request, a judicial colleague has just employed a mammoth jury questionnaire in a murder case. It is thirty-seven pages long and asks 108 questions dealing with the personal lives and beliefs of seventy prospective jurors. There are multiple-choice answers of "Yes," "No," "Think So," "Not Sure." Personal interviews with the attorneys and judge followed the questionnaire. It took more than three weeks to empanel the jury for a trial lasting less time.

2. Just recently, the longest trial in American history ended after three-and-a-half years. *Kemner v. Monsanto*, which began February 22, 1984, concerned whether sixty-five plaintiffs were injured when one-half teaspoon of dioxin escaped in a 1979 tank car derailment in Sturgeon, Missouri. They sought $35.4 million in compensatory and $100 million in punitive damages. Monsanto's ten

examining doctors testified about each of the sixty-five plaintiffs' medical history. The plaintiffs' attorney spent fifty days cross-examining the doctors. One witness was ordered to jail for contempt for giving an unresponsive answer. After the contempt, Monsanto moved for a mistrial, one of one hundred such motions. Over the course of trial, the judge's wife began and completed a master's degree in education. Two jurors were married. One-hundred-eighty-two witnesses testified, and six thousand exhibits were used. Transcribers pecked out more than 100,000 pages of testimony, the equivalent of a thirty-three-foot stack of paper. Monsanto's court costs alone were $81,000. The three-and-one-half-year trial was originally estimated by all attorneys to last six months.[1]

One juror was dismissed only forty-five minutes before jury deliberations began. The juror cried when she heard the news. Her sadness turned to anger and disillusionment with the judicial system: "If I get called to serve on a jury again," she said, "I'm going to try to get out of it."[2]

The plaintiffs' expert doctor acknowledged that each of the plaintiffs received a thorough test for dioxin without any evidence of it in their blood. Even so, he argued, their ailments stemmed from dioxin exposure. The jury concluded that the plaintiffs suffered no ill effects from the spill. Yet it awarded the Sturgeon 65 a multimillion-dollar judgment. One of the jurors explained their inconsistent verdict: "We couldn't prove that the dioxin caused these people's illness," she said, "but they [the plaintiffs] did prove that there was dioxin in the rail car, and that Monsanto had known that there was dioxin in the tank car." The jury thus found Monsanto innocent of harming the plaintiffs but guilty of knowing that a teaspoon of dioxin was being carried on a rail car through the town of Sturgeon. Another juror complained after the trial that she was "ganged up on" by other jurors who wanted her to sign the judgment even though she sided with Monsanto. The other jurors, she said, were determined not to let the case end in a mistrial after devoting nearly four years of their lives to it.

When the wheels of justice spin pointlessly, as they did in St. Clair County Circuit Court for almost four years, the public discovers again that a courtroom is a place where lawyers and jurors toss money around like dice on a crap table.[3]

3. Caprice is also a frequent spice in this untasty pie. *Pennzoil v. Texaco* is another embarrassing case in point. In December 1983, Pennzoil made an offer to buy a 42 percent interest in Getty Oil Company at $100 a share. Before a binding contract could be signed, Texaco offered to buy 100 percent of the stock at $125 a share. What Texaco bought was a Texas-sized lawsuit. In February 1985, Pennzoil went into the 151st District Court of Harris County, Texas, and asked $15 billion in damages for breach of contract on the theory that even though no valid agreement had been executed, the parties had shaken hands on the deal, i.e., that there was no binding contract at all but only an agreement to agree. In November 1985, a lay jury agreed and awarded Pennzoil $7.5 billion in compensatory damages and another $3 billion in punitive damages.

The jury's award was wildly unrelated to whatever damages Pennzoil had suffered. The compensatory damages rested on hypothetical reckoning of Getty's future reserves. The case should have been tried exclusively under New York law, where Texaco is based, but the Texas judge conceded that he knew nothing about New York law. In Texas, judges are elected in partisan elections. They solicit campaign contributions just like any candidate for sheriff or mayor, and these contributions come from the very lawyers who practice in the candidate-judge's court. Within a month after suit, Pennzoil's lead counsel gave a $10,000 contribution to the first judge in the case—part of the $248,000 his firm contributed since 1980 to Texas judges. Months later, when this contribution became known, Texaco asked the judge to disqualify himself. The judge who heard the recusal motion said it would upset the Texas judicial system if judges had to step aside merely because they had been paid campaign contributions by attorneys or "merely" appeared to be biased or prejudiced.[4]

COURT ORIGINS

Our courts originated from a need to quiet disputes, not increase them. Courts emerged institutionally to resolve quarrels that threaten the peace of the community. As Carl J. Friedrich put it: "The settling of disputes is the primordial internal function which a political order has to perform, antedating the making of rules and the application of such rules in administrative work."[5] A single act of killing by a hot-headed individual often led to a blood feud that spread geographically over time. Except in societies whose rulers came to the fore by warding off attack by outsiders, the need to suppress this desire to repay one killing with another gave birth to the political ruler, whose first duty was to settle disputes. Studies of African tribes during the twentieth century support this view; for the express purpose of being able to settle quarrels, a Ugandan tribe without a leader recently sought out a ruler from a neighboring clan known for its chiefs.[6]

This dispute-resolving function was central to the leadership of Great Britain. Before the twelfth century, courts represented the self-interested justice of the nobles, who exercised the power to put down insurrection and to settle disputes among serfs in order to consolidate their own role as petty sovereigns. Until the kings established royal courts and substituted public sanctions and a system of compensation for blood feuds, violence and warfare were the norm. From the time of the Norman Conquest, the kings professed to be the guarantors of justice. Within two centuries, royal judicial writs had swept away the private courts that dispensed justice on the manors. One effect was to make law and justice public. In the early years, the prerogative of dispensing justice was personal to the king. By the fifteenth century the press of judicial business had become too heavy, and the monarchs quit the judicial side of Westminster Hall, leaving the administration of justice to a cadre of judges specially trained in the law.[7]

ASSUMPTIONS OF THE ADVERSARY SYSTEM

The traditional theory underlying litigation is that truth emerges from the clash of opposing points of view, i.e., that a jury or judge can best resolve a dispute when each side pits its strongest contentions against each other. This dialectical theory rests on a number of ill-supported assumptions: that each side is represented by equally skilled advocates; that each side has equal financial resources; that each side has unlimited time; that judges control litigation; that the disputants are rational people who make deliberate decisions calculated to enhance their positions; that the disputants have the resources to obtain and present pertinent information; that attorneys' interests coincide with those of their clients; and finally, that competition between roughly equal opponents will lead to the triumph of truth. With the two sides thus matched, the deserving party will win.

Each of the foregoing assumptions is ill-founded. Lawyers, resources, time, skill, money, and judicial talent are rarely distributed evenly. The adversary system that depends upon these assumptions of parity is thus undermined at its very core. The 1980s litigation world is marked by imbalance in some or all these areas to the point where imbalance is the norm rather than the exception.

The causes, in part, of imbalance relate to litigator control of litigation, delay, language abuse, excessive costs, and gamesmanship.

Litigator Control of Courts

The 1938 Rules of Federal Procedure promoted a new set of activities for lawyers. With the new procedures came new kinds of lawyers: "litigators," who do motion and discovery practice during the pretrial process, as distinguished from "trial lawyers," who conduct trials. Today's system of civil justice is largely dominated by litigators dictating to a complaint court. Much of the problem with the adversary system results from litigator control of courts.

In the civil arena, litigators control the pace of litigation; the extent and duration of discovery; setting of trial dates; their inevitable postponement because of lawyer inconvenience, like vacations; control over order and scope of witnesses, and length and nature of argument, all to the debilitation of classically passive judges, who, as in Texas, are often supported financially by the very lawyers who render them spineless. Attorneys assert that processing of litigation in public courts is their special prerogative:[8] they are the creators, designers, and producers. They only role for a public court, they assert, is to furnish a stage and decision when requested. A judge has no business meddling with any case until the litigators request it.

Pretrial civil practice was abandoned long ago to attorneys. In 1938, liberal discovery provisions promised a systemic change from trial by surprise to trials on the merits.[9] The great promise of liberal discovery, however, has not been fulfilled. Trained in the traditional adversarial system, attorneys can manipulate discovery to subvert the opposing party by economics alone. Discovery abuse has become widespread, particularly in large cases, simply by its overuse.[10]

Lawyer control of criminal courts appears in a different setting, producing the same result: plea bargaining, the prevalent practice that serves prosecutor and defense counsel but not the victim, the court, or the public. In plea bargaining, a prosecutor reduces the charges to which a defendant pleads—for example, receiving stolen property instead of burglary, or attempted DWI for DWI. Since the prosecutor surrenders something for the guilty plea, the result is that defendants are not dealt with as severely or as accurately as their original conduct. Sometimes defendants are even *punished* for exercising their right to trial. In the late sixties, federal Judge John J. Sirica of Watergate fame sentenced an eighteen-year-old man to five to fifteen years in prison for holding up a bus driver with a toy pistol, commenting: "If you had pleaded guilty to this offense, I might have been more lenient with you"—thus penalizing the exercise of a constitutional right.[11]

Plea bargaining has been around so long that it is accepted, like delay and obscene costs, as the criminal courts' standard operating procedure.[12] Plea bargaining serves the interests of prosecutors and defense lawyers but not the court or the public interest or even the criminal's need for justice. DAs throughout the country often purposely overcharge in order to get bargaining leverage to induce a plea. Defense attorneys then urge the defendant to plead guilty to a lesser charge. Prosecutors and defense counsel both want to avoid trial because trials are hard work and take time from heavy caseloads. Some defendants also want to avoid trial; the clearly guilty fear that once the judge hears the grisly details, the sentence will be more severe than if the judge merely heard a lawyer's dispassionate summary of the crime. In a typical plea, the prosecutor and defense attorney also agree on the sentence, so there is nothing for the judge to do but rubber stamp an agreement in which judicial decision making plays little to no part.

A judge's only function in a typical morning docket filled with these five-minute guilty pleas is to make sure the defendant understands there will be no trial. The ultimate message to pleading defendants is that the justice system is exactly what they attribute to the larger society: manipulation, a sanctioned con game. Prosecutors overcharge, defense counsel pressure pleas, murder becomes manslaughter, as both sides bluff and dicker while the spectator judge watches the entire charade impassively. It is a game of fox and hounds, where the foxes become foxier as they learn that even the courts can be conned.

The Abuse of Language

Litigators' foreign language—the language of the law—helps to alienate the public from the courts. Legal language is a veiled tradition involving deception and wasted energy. It too creates a rhetorical and communication imbalance.

Diversion by language is part of this abuse. Take as an example the following closing argument by Clarence Darrow on behalf of Thomas I. Kidd:

I appeal to you not for Thomas Kidd, but I appeal to you for the long line—the long, long line reaching back through the ages and forward to the years to come—the long line of despoiled and downtrodden people of the earth. I appeal to you for those men who rise in the morning before daylight comes and who go home at night when the light has faded from the sky and give their life, their strength, their toil to make others rich and great. I appeal to you in the name of those women who are offering up their lives to this modern god of gold, and I appeal to you in the name of those little children, the living and the unborn.[13]

Darrow's rhetoric invites judge and jury to throw evidence and law out the window. However cozy such rhetoric, it is fallacious to argue that diversionary tactics such as these permit any conclusion of innocence. This oratorical language indicates that much more occurs in a modern lawsuit than devotion to evidence or facts. The system at times encourages frustration of its own goals by its tolerance of oratory, theatre, pomp, and pretense. Much language in statute and court decisions, pleadings and legal documents resembles medieval casuistry and exegesis without the lofty purposes of either. The irony becomes greater when, as in Darrow's argument, a murderer provides an example for invoking traditional values of life, all the greater an irony if these traditional values acquit those who undermine them. A similar deconstruction critique applies to the deliberate proffer of confusing jury instructions by litigators trying a losing case; these instructions are intended to mislead, not enlighten. Their language becomes an elastic mask used to hide the law and promote confusion, not clarity.

A good part of legal ceremony is as much about psychological needs as about justice. Legal language is often a quasi-religious rite, an act of affirmation like going to church. The judge giving instructions to the jury or the litigator giving an opening statement before a hushed audience accepts the tradition-encrusted mind-set that justice is being worked out beneath (perhaps despite) the verbiage. One feels the gods are placated merely by participating in the ritual, much as blind babuskas dutifully light candles before crumbling altars and absent icons. While these incantations are not negligible, their purpose is rarely to convey new knowledge or address social friction but to mouth accepted dogma with little fresh thought. The participants are beatified as worthy for a ritual they legitimize with rules they alone create and understand. Such ceremonies make the actors feel that something socially worthwhile is accomplished by their lofty isolation from common language.

The linguistic imbalance is widespread, extending even to the court's sacred address to jurors. Courts throughout the country use jury instructions that provoke a comprehension problem almost everywhere. Jurors nationwide misunderstand about half the standard civil jury instructions because of legal jargon and unfamiliar words.[14] Not surprisingly, they often fail to follow them.[15]

When you use technical words, "lawyer words," or words that are outside common usage, you not only lose your own credibility and a kind of warmth and togetherness, but you also lose the jury's attention. When you use a word that is not clear to the jury, the next ten go unheard.[16]

If jurors do not understand the foreign language of the law, their verdicts necessarily ignore the law buried in the language.[17] In fact, most jurors cannot understand the pompous language thrust on them by the legal caste.[18] Confusion increases when jurors are merely read the instructions without receiving them in writing. Amiram Elwork, Bruce D. Sales, and James J. Alfini (a linguist, a lawyer-linguist, and a lawyer, respectively) reported that their experiments with oral jury instructions produced nothing but "blank stares" from jurors.[19] Experimental research based on both criminal and civil trials indicates that juries typically do not understand or follow court instructions.[20]

Communication without legalese is learned only with great difficulty. Here as an example of typical bombast is the jury instruction routinely given in many civil cases that involve contributory negligence:

The defendant claims that the plaintiff was negligent and that his negligence contributed to cause the plaintiff's injury. Whether contributory negligence is a defense is left to you. If both plaintiff and defendant were negligent, and if the negligence of each was the cause of the injury, the plaintiff should not recover. This means you must decide two things: (1) Whether the plaintiff was contributorily negligent, and (2) If the plaintiff was negligent, whether this negligence should prevent a verdict in his favor.[21]

This instruction—often the most important instruction in a negligence case— is contradictory. After stating that the defense of contributory negligence is "left to you," i.e., the jury, the instruction says that the defense is really not left to them because once the plaintiff's own negligence helps cause the plaintiff's injury, then the "plaintiff should not recover." In ordinary English that would be the end of it. However, once hearing that "the plaintiff should not recover," the jury is then told to determine two further things, the second of which is whether plaintiff's conduct "should prevent a verdict in his favor," i.e., whether the plaintiff can recover anyway. The last sentence thus flatly contradicts the earlier denial of any possibility of recovery.

State courts are not alone in this word-tossed sea. Devitt and Blackmar's authoritative *Federal Jury Instructions*, the bible for federal instructions, offers a verbal smorgasbord on nearly every page. Here is a popular instruction dealing with the acts and declarations of criminal conspirators:

Whenever it appears beyond a reasonable doubt from the evidence in the case that a conspiracy existed, and that a defendant was one of the members, then the statements thereafter knowingly made and the acts thereafter knowingly done, by the person likewise found to be a member may be considered by the jury as evidence in the case as to the defendant found to have been a member, even though the statements and acts may have occurred in the absence and without the knowledge of the defendant, provided such statements and acts were knowingly made and done during the continuance of such conspiracy, and in furtherance of some purpose of the conspiracy.

Otherwise, any admission or incriminatory statement made or act done outside of court, by one person, may not be considered as evidence against any person who was not present and did not hear the statement made or see the act done.

Therefore, statements of any conspirator, which are not in furtherance of the conspiracy, or made before its existence, or after its termination, may be considered as evidence only against the person making them.[22]

This instruction, popular in federal conspiracy cases, is often read to a jury that is not furnished written copies. Aloofly addressed in the third person, the jury must be blessed with supernatural gifts of syntax and memory. The entire first paragraph consists of one sentence with eight subordinate clauses suffocating the main idea "may be considered" in the middle of an indigestible sandwich of conditionals. Despite all the qualifications, the instruction is permissive, not mandatory. Fortunately for the federal criminal justice system, at least one court has lately concluded that this instruction is "unnecessary, confusing and more burdensome to the government than the law requires."[23]

Part of the law's language dilemma comes from a trend to believe that language cannot reach objectivity. Some courts hold that even carefully-crafted words cannot be made meaningful. In *Pacific Gas and Electric v. G. W. Thomas Drayage and Rigging*, a famous California Supreme Court held that words do not have objective or "true" meanings.[24] That case involved a clear indemnification contract, but the court said that the words used didn't settle the matter, so that the plaintiff could present other evidence so that the court could allocate risks irrespective of the contractual language fixing risks. Chief Justice Traynor rejected the common law notion that parties must be free to negotiate among themselves. This old view that individuals can use words—that is, contracts— to allocate risks and rewards, he wrote, "is a remnant of a primitive faith in the inherent potency and inherent meaning of words." To him words "do not have absolute and constant referents." Only primitives ascribe binding meanings to words, a conviction supported by one of the strangest footnotes in American jurisprudence:

E.g., "The elaborate system of taboo and verbal prohibitions in primitive groups; the ancient Egyptian myth of Khern, the apotheosis of the words, and of Thoth, the Scribe of Truth, the Giver of Words and Script, the Master of Incantations; the avoidance of the name of God in Brahmanism, Judaism, and Islam; totemistic and protective names in medieval Turkish and Finno-Ugrian languages; the misplaced verbal scruples of the 'Précieuses'; the Swedish peasant custom of curing sick cattle smitten by witchcraft by making them swallow a page torn out of the psalter and put in dough. . . . " from Ullman, *The Principles of Semantics* (1963 ed.) 43.

Here the fault is not that of lawyers or parties but of judges' reluctance to accept the meanings of words assigned by the parties at the time of a contractual transaction. Such freewheeling interpretations of words make California and other such states dangerous places to do business, for even sophisticated words and adept drafters cannot avoid semantic litigation. If the courts cannot say that businesspeople, dealing face-to-face with semantic care, can find binding words with objective meaning, how can the same courts send anyone to jail for violating statutes consisting, again, of mere words? If words have no binding meaning in civil contracts, strictly construed criminal statues have less fixed meaning. We are left to flounder in a sea of surging subjectivity. Such reasoning undermines the rule of law: decisions turn not on objective criteria but on subjective interpretations. In so doing the law succumbs to the deconstructionist critique of the critical legal studies thinkers.

Sanctity of contract remains an important, civilizing idea, embodying important ideas about the nature of human existence and about rights and responsibilities: that people have the ability to fix their legal relationship by private agreement; that the future is inherently unknowable but manageable by predictive words; that enforcement of agreements will not be held hostage to court's deconstructionist attacks on objectivity.

Delay

Delay causes further imbalance. It is the inevitable result of any system where litigators determine their own day in court. It is the most significant single problem affecting modern courts. Reformers from the time of Jethro, the father-in-law of Moses, have recognized the need to conclude disputes promptly for the sake of the community. Yet, like the common cold, delay remains an intractable problem that weighs against speed and deterrence.

In Illinois and Rhode Island, jury cases now take more than four years to resolve after filing. In Los Angeles, between the day an average complaint is filed and the day trial begins, fifty-four months pass. Progress on the Los Angeles civil docket is marked by reducing the number of *years* to trial. That city has also given the United States its longest preliminary hearing: a two-and-one-half-year-long hearing in a child molestation case now costing $8 million. In Chicago and Boston, it is not unusual for some cases to be untried for ten years. A federal suit involving Indian claims in northern California is now in its twenty-fifth year of litigation—part of the defense strategy has been "delay, delay, delay."[25]

Our system sometimes even encourages delay. Tax laws encourage litigants to prolong litigation; the deductibility of litigation expenses means that the government, in effect, subsidizes lawsuits. Many defendants find it more economical to pay deductible legal fees to defer an ultimate judgment. If a litigant can endure this dance marathon, the ravages of time and expense may cause the opponent to go away. Lawyers thus often protract cases so that witnesses die or the opposition surrenders in exhaustion. Delay is relative, not absolute, when lawyers control the pace of litigation. Yet lawyers are not able to predict how long a case should take, in part because their opponents' expectations are unknown.

No economic incentives exist to move cases speedily because a sizeable case inventory keeps income levels high. Indifference toward delay is institutionalized.[26]

Most civil rules contain no counterincentives designed to offset the delay-inducing effects of profit and insensitivity. Most were designed under the assumption that ethical duties would promote a delay-reducing strategy by the lawyer, but the new Model Rules of Professional Conduct provide such vague guidance about delay as to be of limited practical utility. Rulemakers have institutionalized delay by drafting rules that either imperfectly control the pace of litigation (deadlines only for answers to complaints and a few discovery initiatives) or actually embody a lawyer-controlled delay mechanism (the Vermont rule providing that the court cannot order the lawyers to expedite procedural filings during the first two years after case filing). Such codes encourage procrastination in cases that do not pay to be moved expeditiously.[27]

While some delay flows voluntarily from malicious litigants or attorneys, other delay occurs from the complexity of the process. Repeated discovery requests, tangential claims, and legal gamesmanship also contribute to delay. No cost-effective business would tolerate such hoop-jumping. To a business client, a claim is a frank business matter. Motions, countermotions, briefs, and the endless rabbit trails of procedure hinder arbitrating the problem. A half decade to resolve disputes is intolerable. Business ventures cannot wait that long. Most ordinary litigants cannot pay medical bills or feed their families for years while awaiting a court judgment. In a world in which airplanes connect Washington and Moscow in a matter of seven hours and astronauts travel to the moon in a few days, five years is an archaically long time for anyone to await a day in court. Because of speedy trial rules for criminal defendants, the system shows an unusual paradox: indigent criminals have ready access to courts for their innumerable trials, sentencings, appeals, and petitions, whereas the average law-abiding middle-class citizen cannot get quick judicial relief for a modest neighborhood dispute.

Our court procedures are now the most complex in the world and the most expensive, intimidating, and riddled with delay. The system resembles the health care system of fifty years ago when competent medical care was available only to the wealthy. Today, millions of middle-class persons cannot afford modest legal care. Laws that address affluent clients and large institutions generate intricate court labyrinths groomed by sophisticated practitioners who make them inaccessible to ordinary mortals. The average noncriminal middle-class citizen feels increasingly estranged. Access to this arena, open to everyone in principle, is limited in practice to those of ample pocketbook, steady nerve, and limitless patience—or to those charged with crime. Too much law exists for those who can afford it, too little for those who cannot: much law but little justice.[28]

Part of the problem is that the "enemy" lawsuit model has been our paradigm for settling differences. Other countries, notably Japan, Germany, China, and our common law ancestor England, have moved away from the adversary lawsuit to effect quick resolution of disputes in less ceremonial formats. In Germany, business differences are usually settled by the local chamber of commerce, where resolution is quicker, cheaper, and less likely to involve procedural dances. Court procedures in this country remain ideally suited to a lawsuit by General Motors and IBM; both have the resources to afford the expense, the stability to accommodate the delay, and the intestinal fortitude to suffer years of acrimonious ambush. For the masses of the citizenry not endowed with these uncommon assets, courts have ceased to be accessible resolvers of disputes.

Costs

Costs and the ability to bear them contribute to the imbalance among litigants. Often only attorneys win big in court. In the fall of 1975, fifteen-year-old Chris Thompson lay on a high school football field outside Seattle, paralyzed by a broken back. Eight litigious years later, thanks to the dedication of his lawyers and his mother (who suffered a fatal stroke during the lawsuit), Chris finally received a payment of $1 million and an annual stipend of $175,000. His lawyers got $1.2 million.

Such costs and fees are entry barriers. The Rand Corporation's Institute for Civil Justice has concluded that for every dollar received by a plaintiff, taxpayers pay another dollar to provide the judicial decision. Insurance companies pay 50–75 percent more to resolve a case three to five years after its inception than to resolve it within a year. Plaintiffs must recover 30 percent more after three years just to keep pace with litigation costs.[29]

The American consumer now pays somewhere between $2.50 and $3.00 for every dollar of benefits received through the tort system. The average cost of a civil jury trial as of 1988 in Los Angeles is $11,000, about $5,000 greater than the average amount in controversy. Rand's Institute for Civil Justice reveals the following additional costs:

- Plaintiffs received about half of the $27.7 to $34.7 billion the nation spent in 1985 on tort litigation (liability for death, personal injury, or property damage).[30]

- The remainder was consumed by the civil justice system in legal fees on both sides, court costs, and other expenses, including the value of time spent by parties to the litigation and by insurance claims staff.

- Thus, to deliver $14 to $16 billion in net compensation to the injured parties, the costs of litigation were $16 to $19 billion in transaction costs.[31]

For every dollar given to a successful plaintiff, forty-four cents is spent on legal fees and other administrative costs.[32] If the value of the time spent in litigation is considered, courts return to plaintiffs 46 percent of every dollar spent to compensate them. For middle-class plaintiffs, these legal expenses eat up much of the recovery. While contingent fees sometimes overcome the cost barrier, fees still consume a third or more of the average settlement, often rising to 40 percent in trials.

This nation, which prides itself on due process, has developed a legal system beyond the pocketbook of its middle class. The courts need a new *Brown v. Board of Education* decision to open its own courtrooms to its own citizenry of average means. We have built an ornate legal castle that, while announcing equal access, is really limited only to royal pocketbooks.

EVALUATION

For those who can afford these logistics, the system produces some modest returns: some products are safer; some wrongs can be compensated; some products and practices are eliminated. As a society, however, enormous prices for legal fees, frustration, and stress lead to the all-too-frequent result that hostilities increase and instead of a winner and loser, there are only losers—except for the litigators running this lottery.

The result of the inordinate delay, complexity, and costs of the present court system is a cruel irony: legalized extortion. Parties to lawsuits such as the *Monsanto* and *Pennzoil* cases can achieve victory regardless of legal merit by simply using expensive and embarrassing techniques: motions for mental examination, for depositions, for sanctions, or subjecting opponents to repeated interrogatories and depositions. In divorce litigation, threats of sexual abuse charges are often sufficient to coerce a spouse to drop a viable claim to child custody. In medical malpractice cases, doctors free of any liability routinely settle meritless claims merely to be rid of costs to their pocketbook and reputation. The extortionate threats that in other circumstances constitute a crime are strangely part and parcel of modern litigation, which too often is not a pursuit of justice but of victory by economic coercion.

Set against this history, the diverse cases described at the start of this chapter illustrate a counterproductive enemy system of justice that does not resolve civilian disquiet but prolongs it. Lawsuits now are not merely a means to resolve disputes but protracted acts of warfare. The purpose is not merely to win, but to "chew the other guy up," to "nail witnesses to the cross," to "destroy" the opposition, to "rearrange their anatomy." Litigation recalls Vince Lombardi: "winning isn't everything, it's the only thing." Rare is the victorious litigant who walks away from the courthouse without the hostility of the dismissed *Monsanto* juror. The nominal winner often is a real loser in fees, expenses, and waste of time. More fatal, however, is the ultimate irony: the justice system perpetuates the very extortionate demands which it seeks to deter.

ALTERNATIVE DISPUTE RESOLUTION

Inaccessible language, delay, complexity, costs, and legalized extortion in turn have generated a cleansing antithesis to the courthouse: alternative dispute resolution (ADR), which stands as a pointed criticism of the courts' failures to serve its public.

ADR is a growing movement that offers more accessible justice than most courts offer. Successful applications of ADR are many and varied. They include minitrials; information exchanges; referrals to experts; presentations of argument, evidence, live witnesses, and affidavits in some combination; various types of "neutral advisors"; binding exchanges; nonbinding exchanges; contingent exchanges; arbitration; mediation; and almost unlimited combinations of the foregoing.[33] The strength of ADR, however, is the new outlook among disputants. Once parties accept that a settlement can be achieved quickly and cheaply without the help of the courts, settlement chances increase while delay, complexity, and extortionate costs diminish. The success of ADR suggests the demise of over-burdened metropolitan civil courts within a decade or two.

A variety of factors—some psychological and some strategic—make it unlikely that ADR will divert all cases from the courts in the near future. Its greatest utility lies in familial, neighborhood, or simple business disputes among related parties. ADR is ill-suited for complex matters such as class actions, public fraud, toxic torts, antitrust, patent infringement, civil rights violations, and similar information-intensive cases. While the ADR movement goes forward, reform of traditional litigation is needed for disputes unsuited for ADR. Reform is all the more needed to acknowledge ADR's devastating critique of the existing court system.

THE PRESENT AGENDA

The present dinosaurlike court system need not become totally extinct. Present resuscitation efforts fall into three broad classes: managerial, procedural, and structural.

MANAGERIAL CHANGES

Managerial innovations involve two major changes: a new judicial role and pretrial control.

The first need is to wrest control of courts from litigators and place it in the hands of a new creation—managerial judges. This remedy contradicts the traditional vision of judges as passive diners in a restaurant waiting for food to be placed before them. The judicial role needs to expand from that of adjudicator to embrace the tasks of case manager and case settler. The classical image of the judge as a blind, passive umpire is long overdue for change. In his 1906 address to the American Bar Association, Roscoe Pound spoke out strongly against the role of the trial judge as merely an umpire. Yet, rulemakers rarely have defined the duty of the trial judge toward attorneys and litigants. Federal and most state civil rules of procedure remain silent on the role of judges. In 1938, when the federal rule model was adopted, civil dockets were manageable and judges and lawyers imbued with a spirit of cooperation. These original rulemakers could little know that discovery, the mechanism designed to eliminate trial by ambush, would lead from adjudication to extortion.[34]

Over the next thirty years, rulemakers saw the need to give judges more time to handle the burgeoning caseload, which they did by gradually eliminating judicial intervention prior to discovery, thus leaving adversaries to challenge discovery overreaching after the fact. The loss of judicial control over discovery left a vacuum in "up front" control prior to trial. As the judge was removed from discovery management, the complexity of litigation was growing. Litigation became a weapon of social and economic change as constraints against excessive discovery gave way to contrary strategic and economic interests. In response in 1970, rulemakers focused on ameliorating perceived flaws in the sanction process by amending Federal Rule of Civil Procedure 37. The appropriate managerial role of the trial judge in caseflow was still ignored.[35] That role still needs to be defined.

Judges today need management and organizational skills to process caseloads, to shape and limit discovery, to promote settlement, and to control lawyers. A disappearing judicial blindfold does not suggest loss of neutrality; knowledge of issues does not generate judicial partiality any more than institutionalizing ignorance generates neutrality. In a word, today's judge must be a managerial activist. Activism in case management differs totally from activism in judicial philosophy; an activist, competent manager is unrelated to the realists' activist social reformer.

This take-charge mentality opposes the traditional view that pretrial and discovery are self-executing phases of litigation safely left to lawyers. Pretrial hyperactivity and bluffing flourish under the blissful inattention of the classical potted plant umpire; both trial and pretrial function more efficiently when judges control discovery and trial procedures like voir dire.[36] The ideal of a cooperative pretrial process never will materialize, particularly in complex cases. Adversarial lions in courtrooms do not become lambs during pretrial.

Preventing gamesmanship means controlling pretrial hyperactivity through judicial management from the moment a case is filed. The move to managerial judges also involves administrative change. In a central assignment or master calendar system, cases are assigned piecemeal only on a given date for a given purpose. Different judges assume different responsiblities on a rotating basis for pretrial litigation. One judge hears motions; another conducts pretrial conferences; another holds settlement conferences; still another handles discovery. As a consequence, since no single judge feels responsibility for the entire case, cases progress according to the relaxed whims of rotating judges who find it easy to let the next judge in line resolve the hard questions. By contrast, an individual assignment system places a case on the calendar of a given judge responsible for it from start to finish. A managerial judge on an individual calendar feels responsibility to conclude discovery and bring litigation to an end.

Changing the classical image of the judge from an ignorant, passive spectator to an active case manager also means a radical change in the way judges are selected. As the Texaco case reveals, the popularity elected judiciary is an archaic, frozen institution—a group of potted plants—resistant to improvement.[37] Instead of elections decided on financial contributions or on claims of toughness on crime, intelligent judicial selection means picking persons by merit who are blessed not only with instincts of fairness but also with firm managerial skills capable of controlling lawyers and litigation, even to the point of imposing time and discovery limits. Case management ability ought to count for more than party affiliation or the white mantle of supposed wisdom. Partisan, popular elections with balloons, bumper stickers, baby-kissing, billboard paeans to tough-ness on crime, party endorsements, and lawyer contributions do not forge man-agerial talents; if anything they perpetuate the classical potted-plant umpire controlled by lawyers and legislators.

The ad hoc nature of managerial judging imposes some limitations, but these can be ameliorated by developing guidelines to assist judges in their managerial decisions. In the bigger picture, however, more fundamental reform can proceed only by addressing the system of incentives that creates the need for managerial judging in the first place: delays in payment, delays in execution, and peculiar cost-shifting mechanisms that make delay and complexity financially attractive to attorneys. Rather than devise additional rules propelled by sanctions and penalties, a more efficient procedural system would develop incentives and re-wards to encourage lawyers to act in harmony with the system's goals of quick and efficient resolution. For example, if defendants are encouraged to delay judgment because of rules that deny successful litigants the value of money during the pendency of litigation, restructuring the system of incentives is a more pointed remedy than granting more authority to managerial judges.

Pretrial Control

Most civil courts are organized around the assumption that every case is headed for trial and that negotiated settlements are an accidental surprise. Great effort is thus spent in ascertaining conflict-free trial dates far in advance. Calendar calls are frequent and repetitive, and pretrial conferences occur only at the last minute before trial. The real battleground in contemporary litigation, however, has become pretrial, not trial. The pretrial battleground is traditionally controlled by litigators who rarely share any interest in swift movement of cases. Indeed, in complex cases one or both sides may want to prolong the agony. Class actions stand or fall based on whether they are certified. In other situations success turns on information elicited through discovery. These decision points have little to do with the merits and less to do with speed. The adversary tradition encourages use of these pretrial weapons to frustrate the enemy early.[38]

Reform in the processing of cases requires a fundamental change in the way we view civil procedure. Judges need to stop thinking of the ''pretrial'' process as a prelude to trial and begin to see it as the ''main event.'' The vast majority of cases filed will be settled during pretrial rather than via trial. Thus the pretrial process should be viewed as a series of economic stages or pressure points encouraging parties to settle before costs and emotional pressure build to the next pressure point.

Since only 3 percent of cases are actually tried, managerial judges need to know how to facilitate nontrial dispositions. Responsibility for pretrial needs to rest squarely with a managerial judge the moment a case is filed to control the overall pace of litigation from inception. Judicial energy in managing pretrial pays off even in the minority of cases that ultimately go to trail because a well-managed case is tried more efficiently once the judge becomes familiar with it.

Lawsuits belong to the litigating parties, not their lawyers. Active judicial control over pretrial management also means that the time standards are published and monitored. Delay reduction techniques successful in trial courts in Phoenix, Dayton, and Portland need to be used: leadership by the presiding judge; judicial commitment to managerial skills; good communications between the court and the bar; published case processing time standards and goals; monitoring cases from the date of filing; management of pretrial scheduling; calendaring practices providing accountability for caseloads; and use of court-annexed alternative dispute resolution programs, such as mediation or arbitration to divert low profile disputes. All these techniques can change the local legal culture about discovery, continuances, and case processing time. Once a trial date becomes known as a fixed reckoning date that will not be routinely postponed, settlements increase and judges regain control over dockets.

The leading cause of delay is failure of judges to maintain control over the pace of pretrial litigation. Judicial control over pretrial procedures reduces delay and costs. The 1984 report of the American Bar Association Action Commission to reduce court costs and delays found three procedural devices influential in reducing court delay: (1) limitations on the amount of discovery; (2) use of telephone conferences in lieu of in-court appearances; (3) expedited appeal procedures emphasizing oral argument over written briefs.[39] A fourth need is simplified rules of procedure consisting of deadlines on the timely filing of pleadings coupled with a pretrial conference to encourage settlement.

PROCEDURAL CHANGES

In addition to the role change from passive umpires to managerial judges, there exists a compelling need to inaugurate procedural change in court policy. Specifically, courts should abolish the American rule on fees, control attorney gamesmanship with witnesses and discovery, and eliminate plea bargaining.

The American Rule

One of the first economic needs is to abolish the American rule on costs, which lets costs and attorney fees lie where they fall rather than on the losing party. The typical winning party may emerge from trial with substantially less than a full award because of attorney's fees. It is now distressingly commonplace that fees and costs *exceed* the amount of the judgment itself, thus making the winner a net loser. The American rule discourages marginal claims by imposing the risk of double costs. To recover costs from the loser is more consistent with efficiency and fairness. The price tag for whatever virtue adheres in the American rule makes it a greater vice. Eight hundred years ago the English adopted the practice of taxing attorney fees against the losing party.[40] It deserves to enter the new world. In addition, judges should monitor accumulating attorney fees and court costs against the amount in controversy, so that when the former exceeds the latter, the mandatory settlement conference is set. Under no circumstances should the sum of attorney fees and costs exceed the judgment.

Narrowing Attorney Gamesmanship

An example illustrates widespread attorney gamesmanship. During the last months of her husband's life, when he was gasping for every breath, Dollie Root rarely slept. She nursed the retired construction worker until he died of congestive heart failure and lung cancer shortly before Christmas in 1983. About a year later, she filed a lawsuit against General Cigar & Tobacco Company, whose pipe tobacco her husband had smoked, charging that General Cigar knew tobacco was far more toxic than any warning had suggested but did not alert its customers. Thus began a two-year legal battle that ended only when she dropped her lawsuit in February 1987. The seventy-three-year-old widow could no longer stand the grueling interrogations by the tobacco company lawyers on such topics as her infertility and her feelings about adopting children over forty years ago. When she withdrew her suit, she asked: "What does any of this have to do with my husband's death?"

Tactics like this unfortunately have everything to do today with defeating lawsuits.[41] Discovery techniques today constitute psychological and economic coercion against a modestly endowed opponent. Opposing attorneys often seek broad discovery as self-defense against economic coercion. Seeking massive discovery conveys an intent to make war, to get by procedural complexity what cannot come by a fair verdict. Billing practices tied to discovery create a convergence of two strong motivations: a professional urge by attorneys to leave no stone unturned and an economic interest in increasing billable hours. Discovery can become a Frankenstein monster, an end in itself irrelevant to the incremental value of discovered materials.

An effective way to respond to this baroque spiral is to reduce discovery by narrowing its scope from "relevancy" to the narrower concept of "relevant to the issues in litigation." In practice, this goal involves imposing numerical limits on interrogatories, depositions, and document requests and punishing such questions as were asked of Ms. Root. Thus, in litigation under $50,000, it may be appropriate to limit the parties to one deposition of principal parties, one set of narrowly framed interrogatories, and perhaps two or three productions of documents. More complex forms of litigation, of course, could permit more complex discovery on request.

Eliminating Plea Bargains

A further procedural change to enhance judicial control of courts involves elimination of plea bargaining in criminal cases. Plea bargaining compares with hypothetical "grade bargaining" in school between students and teachers. Instructors who do not want to read term papers, for example, might be willing to give a B to avoid reading. Students know that they would have but a slim chance for an A and that their papers would most likely pull Cs or below if graded fairly. The B compromise provides certainty to the students who accept the deal and a saving of teacher time. Since teachers do not have to read papers, they can process students more efficiently, and the school can trim the size of its faculty by grade-bargaining deals. Teachers can grade more harshly those papers they do have to read. With the possible exception of a few students who deserve an A and gamble with the conscience of the instructor and lose, all the participants would be happy with the deal; most students would get good grades, teachers' jobs would be easier, and the taxpayers would save money. Term papers would be written but never read—and grades would be meaningless.

Plea bargaining is an exact parallel: it is as deeply flawed an approach to criminal justice. The practice weakens the appearance of justice, rewards passivity, and encourages defendants to play a new kind of con game. It can be eliminated without docket disaster. Alaska and New Orleans have debunked the expediency argument. In 1980, the National Institute of Justice concluded that, despite dire predictions, the Alaska plea-bargaining ban was successful; guilty pleas continued to flow in at nearly undiminished rates. Most defendants pleaded guilty even when the state offered nothing in exchange for their plea. Contrary to expectations, the cases moved more quickly without plea bargaining than they had before abolition.

The disposition times for felonies in Anchorage fell from 192 days to just under 90. In Fairbanks, the drop was from 164 to 120, and in Juneau, from 105 to 85. Sentences were more severe for crimes that had been the subject of plea bargaining before the ban, that is, those in which prosecutors had been making concessions to get guilty pleas. Similar results occurred in New Orleans where a plea-bargaining ban runs the gamut from misdemeanors to felonies. Prosecutors process between eight and nine thousand felony arrests and four to five thousand misdemeanor arrests every year. Their key to success is careful screening of the cases referred to them by the police. In approximately half these cases no charges are filed. Defendants plead guilty to charges as filed or go to trial. No docket disasters have resulted.

Ultimately, plea bargaining needs to be eliminated as much for the appearance as the reality. Justice cannot be achieved unless its procedures convey a message of answerability for misconduct rather than bluffing, "dealing," and conning the system.[42]

RESTRUCTURING

Fundamental restructuring needs to take place in court foundations in order to categorize cases by kind and incorporate ADR.

Categorizing by Kinds

Lawsuits need to be categorized according to kind. Traditionally, taking cases through court has been like buying cake at the bakery: take a number, get in line, and wait a turn. A more realistic way of processing cases is to divide civil cases into categories or "lines" such as fast, custom, record, and standard. Simple property damage and contract cases would fall under the fast track, with limited discovery, with each side having only ten to fifteen interrogatories and pleadings completed within 180 days and trial in another 180 days. The custom track, designed to handle common law disputes, would provide custom-tailored scheduling, with one judge handling the case from start to finish. Record track, involving administrative appeals and other matters based on a transcript or tape recording, would avoid the ordinary procedural preliminaries and be heard quickly based upon the existing record. The standard track would handle all other cases.

By whatever names used, cases need to be classified and put in specialized tracks for processing unique to that track rather than simply wait a turn at a single judicial checkout lane.

Incorporating ADR

One of the principal ways to simplify the Byzantine facade of contemporary litigation is incorporation of alternative dispute techniques *within* court rules, so that the courthouse becomes a multidoor facility inviting its users to consider ADR techniques before resorting to litigation weaponry.

Many misdemeanor criminal cases and neighborhood disagreements arise out of ruptured personal relationships. A finding of the enemy's guilt rarely resolves these feelings; it often provides the successful litigant with a trophy to flaunt. Similarly, where the disputants are romantically involved or are neighbors like landlord and tenant, mandatory arbitration under court auspices is more productive than the present condemnatory process. Mediating parties are also more likely to adhere to a solution of their own making. In divorce litigation, where attorneys often intensify hostility with unrealistic promises ("I'll get you the kids"), nonadversarial mediation ought to be required well before the parties solidify their demands and hostilities. ADR techniques generally are superior to litigation as a means of resolving marital disputes because they foster communicating, compromising, and cooperating. Mediation is less damaging emotionally, involves less conflict, preserves greater individual and family autonomy, and produces arrangements that have greater support from the parties than traditional litigation.[43]

Cases like these are best managed by nonadversarial adjudication. ADR serves both interests by providing efficient, less costly, and less adversarial settlement *before* court procedures become adversarial. Some common ADR techniques can be easily built by court rule into the early steps of most low profile cases:

Arbitration, the most widely practiced form of ADR, is informal adjudication in which the parties agree to accept the early judgment of a third party to resolve their dispute. The determination is enforceable in court, and the loser has recourse to a trial by judge or jury.

Mediation involves a private agreement to use the services of a third party to assist the parties as a go-between in resolving the dispute. Before certain disputes are tried in court (divorce cases, for example), the parties must submit to mediation as a necessary prelude to any adversarial posturing.

Minitrials, a rapidly developing form of adjudication, permit parties to agree to have an abbreviated trial for an advisory judgment to be used for settlement negotiations. Parties are not bound by the decision. The process has repeatedly proved successful in corporate and governmental disputes in this country and especially in Europe. A key element is that a representative of each client with the authority to settle is present. Minitrials cost one tenth as much as a traditional lawsuit.[44]

Summary jury trial is a minitrial before a jury without the force of a binding judgment, although the jurors may not be so advised. The parties have an opportunity in a shortened time period to assess the strengths of each side by seeing what jurors think of the case. It is the technique used in some medical malpractice cases where a specialized panel presents an advisory verdict.

Special masters are a new breed of peacemakers. Federal and state courts for many years have appointed masters to handle accounting tasks and other technical matters. The role expanded in the 1970s to carry out ambitious court orders to desegregate schools and reform prisons. Masters also can settle enormous product liability suits that threaten to paralyze the courts. The use of special masters challenges the assumption that justice prevails only in free-swinging confrontation. Today, for example, the settlement process in the Ohio federal courts has become so routine that a judge, unassisted, runs hearings involving 150 claims at a time. "No depositions, no experts, no trial dates, no jurors summoned," he says. "This thing actually works and we're clearing the docket."[45]

Alternative dispute resolution deserves to become the focal point for court improvement efforts. Court-sponsored programs generally effect the settlement of cases quicker and more cheaply and with greater satisfaction to the participants.

Both judicial management and ADR trends posit a new model of litigation that deviates from the traditional pattern of two adversaries confronting each other in an interface of formalized rules as they await an official decision. They assume a diversity of lawsuits with multiple degrees and causes of conflict. Both movements believe that procedural devices can be tailored to each dispute to foster resolution in a less confrontational way. Both movements also contend that the stylized adversarial adjudication may solidify positions instead of encouraging cooperative settlement. They also share a recognition that lack of parity has become the norm—uneven resources, uneven talents, uneven patience and access. Both movements see disputes intensified by lack of trust between the parties as the process becomes formal, tricky, time-consuming, and distorting. Both systems of thought draw heavily on inquisitorial elements associated with European justice systems and cooperative skills developed in arbitration. Indeed, American civil procedure may find its future more like its European counterparts: less adversarial, less lawyer-dominated, more centered on judicial fact-gathering and less on confrontational posturing.

Each trend shares the conviction that adjudication has become a dinosaur, that settlement is preferable to it, and that the judicial role needs to move away from that of umpire-adjudicator to case manager-settler. Use of judges to assist in ADR and settlement involves a basic redefinition of judging and courts. Ultimately the message is a social one: consent is preferable to judicial compulsion because it better serves to maintain the city wall.

THE FUTURE AGENDA

For the long-winded, more can be done to effect healthy change. Here, briefly put, are some issues that deserve the persistence and originality of creative reformers.

Ever since its creation, the American judicial system has employed a unique duality of courts at state and federal levels. Unlike other federal systems such as Belgium, the Soviet Union, or the Federal German Republic, American courts exist side by side at state and federal levels, with dual general jurisdiction courts and dual appellate courts. Americans think this system is fixed in concrete. It need not be. Other systems operate expeditiously with less redundancy. In the Federal Germany Republic, there exist a local general jurisdiction court, a state appellate court, and a countrywide federal supreme court. The possibility of endless appeals is significantly reduced, as is the chance to play one system against the other. The Soviet Union exhibits the same pattern. Our state-federal duality could be coalesced into a court system of one rather than two sovereigns, with state-level trial courts and federal-level appellate courts. Admittedly the constitutional changes needed for such a massive unification are far from simple, but the economics of such a change may counterbalance those policy issues. If changing the federal-state dualism is too monumental, at least the turf of each jurisdiction could be more sharply defined, as the following procedures illustrate.

Even within the existing state and federal duality, it is possible to reduce repeated forum shopping. The side-by-side duplicity permits litigants, particularly criminal defendants, to review cases repeatedly in new forums. Many a defendant convicted in a general jurisdiction state court may appeal to a court of appeals, a state supreme court, and, if unsuccessful there, to federal district court by a writ of habeas corpus and then, if unsuccessful, to the federal circuit court of appeals and, if unsuccessful there, to the United States Supreme Court. Federal courts are overflowing with habeas corpus proceedings brought by state prisoners complaining that they were convicted in violation of federal constitutional law, and section 1983 civil rights suits brought by state prisoners complaining that their confinement violates constitutional rights or constitutes cruel and unusual punishment. Jurisdiction is premised on distrust that state courts protect the federal civil rights of criminal defendants. Because the state must prove a defendant's guilt beyond a reasonable doubt and since the reasonable doubt standard stops well short of certainty, it implies to the unknowledgeable that a significant if small fraction of innocent people are convicted, which seems to warrant additional tiers of judicial review. In reality, the possibility of such error is illusory.

Originally conceived as a narrow remedy for testing the legality of executive detention, habeas corpus has grown to the point where it permits a single federal judge to review and overturn the repeated criminal judgments of a state's trial, appellate, and supreme courts. The result has been an enormous volume of frivolous habeas corpus petitions to the federal courts, not because the first appeal was wrongly decided but because its correctness is forever testable. This layered redundancy of appeals adds to delay, frustration, and expense and spreads a message of manipulation and frivolity. The ultimate message is that there is no finality, that the courts can never be sure of themselves.

The right of a criminal defendant to appeal a final state court decision to federal court by habeas corpus could be limited. Each criminal defendant could be permitted to appeal a conviction through the highest state court once by way of routine appeal or writ of habeas corpus, plus the existing procedures of post conviction relief. After these appeals are exhausted, no further appeals could be filed.

The death penalty provides a similar instance of bravado instead of backbone. Whatever its merits—and they are debatable—an imposed death penalty becomes a laughingstock when it is delayed for years by repeated appellate nitpicking. The courts' inability to carry out such publicized sentences sends a message of impotence and spinelessness: the sentence does not really mean what it says on its face. If this ultimate penalty is thought advisable for retributive or deterrent purposes—a still questionable conclusion—it requires that it be carried out rather than shrunk from. The present appellate labyrinth makes a mockery of a legislated death sentence. For criminals, the first step in the direction of any personal rehabilitation coincides with the step needed for institutional respect: an acceptance of being properly convicted. Moral reeducation is at odds with a system that continuously suggests that someone or something else is more responsible for conviction than the criminal. The message implicit in endless habeas petitions and death penalty appeals is not of the need for personal rehabilitation but rather that someone else is to blame. This message is commonplace talk in our halls of justice and prisons. The prospects of any true reality therapy are thereby constrained; the system teaches the opposite of what it stands for.

Tort liability is no longer a matter of just deserts; it has become the junk food section of the courts, a veritable smorgasbord of theatrics, coercion, bombast, tears, and legal indigestion.

Initially envisioned as a mechanism for enforcing a public standard of care, the tort system has increasingly become a game of chance, a legal "wheel of fortune." Factors other than law and evidence influence the outcome of most personal injury cases, and thereby significantly diminish the ability to punish fault and deter dangerous behavior. Haphazard verdicts have undercut fair compensation; some victims recover far more than their economic losses while others, similarly injured, do not recover at all. Much depends on sympathy, appeals to likability or its opposite, oratory, nice guy vs. bad guy polarities, and magnification or minimization of tragedy. These personal factors count for more to a jury than the objective facts and law.

Tort law is today a *ménage à trois* of rhetoric, theatrics, and chance. It involves shin-kicking motion and discovery practice. It operates to the detriment of claimants, defendants, and society as a whole. It often permits lotterylike litigation in addition to an administrative remedy.[46] The injuries that find their way into court result, mainly, from accidents rather than from intentional wrongdoing. A victim recovers not from the individual but from a corporation or government entity, and sometimes recovers twice. Recovery is connected not to desert but to lawyer's talents, the tenacity of the defendant, and the physical attributes of the claimant.

The uncertainty of liability and the generous compensation of lawyers constitute massive incentives both to prosecute and to protract tort actions. Plaintiffs' lawyers typically handle tort litigation on a contingent fee basis; the losing plaintiff loses nothing but the costs. The system is monetarily risk-free for plaintiffs, aside from the sometimes substantial nonfee costs of litigation. The plaintiff's lawyer is handsomely compensated with a large proportion of a successful recovery. These factors often lead defendants to settle claims of marginal liability. Many plaintiffs' lawyers thus file frivolous suits because of the slight economic risk and high prospect of settlement.

Defendants' lawyers, by no means without complicity, are paid on the basis of a predetermined rate. They function with virtually unrestrained discretion. Insurance companies usually prefer to have claims resolved in the distant future rather than the present because a one hundred dollar judgment paid a year from now equates with a present liability of about ninety dollars. Hence, delay qua delay is beneficial both to the insurer and to the billing lawyer. For both sides, motion and discovery practice provides opportunities to turn almost any claim into a paper battle with harvests of thick files and fat bills.[47]

This flawed tort system could profit from a sense of uniformity either in a renewed fault system without pain and suffering or from the no-fault worker's compensation model. In the latter system, any defendant could be given the opinion of offering to a claimant, within 180 days of injury, periodic payment of the net economic loss, medical expenses, and wage loss beyond any disability insurance. Prompt offers to pay these amounts would preclude a tort claim. Offers could be refused when the defendant had acted intentionally, when the victim's economic losses are minimal or where the offer is below out-of-pocket losses. Such a system, despite its conceptual modification of the fault principle, would be more cost-effective than the present roulette and would constitute a gain in uniformity and breadth.

Civil juries could profitably be eliminated in most cases. Despite the late Irving Younger's soothing reassurance that when the twelve people of the jury gather together, the Holy Spirit descends upon them, the brutal fact is that juries make mistakes, as the *Pennzoil* and *Monsanto* cases illustrate.[48] That they make mistakes should be no surprise. The inexpert member of the public called upon to make choices in the jury box is the same person already judged incompetent to make these choices in the marketplace. Their mistakes result in small part because of gullibility for lawyer theatrics and in greater part from ignorance of the subject matter being litigated. Complex cases such as medical and engineer malpractice, antitrust, toxic torts, and similar high tech issues are beyond the understanding of the average juror and cannot be taught by partisan counsel during trial.

Abilities of lay juries cannot keep pace with high tech litigation. A number of federal courts, faced with complex cases on their civil dockets, have concluded that some such cases may be beyond the capabilities of the ordinary jury.[49] A nonjury expert tribunal of a judge, lawyer, and specialist could contribute more expertise to many technical contests. Such a body would have a better chance of understanding factual materials bearing on the issues, as well as being able to see below the surface for specialized inferences. Even where private parties are the sole litigants, Congress and courts have the authority to dispose of complex matters unsuitable for jury determination in a forum structured to provide the necessary ingredients for rational adjudication.[50]

Despite the Seventh Amendment guarantee of jury trial, the institution of lay jurors finds its best role as a buffer between government and criminal defendants and its least effective function as arbiter of high tech commercial issues. These matters require cognitive expertise, not a sense of moral outrage. The solution is not wholesale abandonment but modification of the jury concept to permit the infusion of reliable expertise into decision making.

CONCLUSION

Burdened with delay, cost, complexity, and theatrics, the present U.S. court system offers legalized extortion instead of its historic promise of true conflict resolution based on merit. A good part of its extortionate character stems from manipulation and economically oppressive tactics that have nothing to do with legal merit. Much of it involves shinkicking even before the ball is snapped. Like football, our courts emphasize strategy, tactics, and low blows. They suffer from litigants' lack of parity and a pursuit of victory rather than truth—attributes perfectly acceptable for a mere game of force. Today's justice system has become Levi-Strauss's "hot" society whose pursuit of complexity exhausts its original *raison d'être*. It exemplifies Heidegger's forgetfulness of justice as litigants devour themselves in a no-win cockfight. In many cases its harm exceeds its good, for it dismantles rather than builds the city wall by increasing rather than reducing civilian rancor.

Some solutions are at arm's reach. Comprehension tests can easily strip legalese from court language and legislation. An ADR-oriented option can be built within the existing system by rule changes to resolve pedestrian disputes before graduating to formal adjudication. The selection of managerial judges on the basis of merit is the best alternative to potted-plant umpires fed by politicians and obsequious litigators.

The great need is for parity of standing before the law for all social classes. In practice, our courts' sense of equality today resembles Anatole France's memorable example of the just law that equally forbids rich and poor to sleep under bridges. We need a new way to assure that courthouse doors swing wide enough to admit easy entry by the poor and middle class, who, after all, help pay for them. These groups feel unwelcome to enter—and when they do, they often wish they had not. People in the middle-income bracket face a difficult situation. On one hand, they are not eligible for government-subsidized or other free legal services; on the other hand, they are unable to pay the going rate for lawyers to handle serious legal problems. Meeting the middle-income consumers' needs is aggravated by the fact that the group is large in number.

It is an ironic measure of our fall from a sense of parity that we tell the masses their access to courts is guaranteed by numerous Supreme Court decisions affirming equality before the law. That mentality smacks of Roman Emperor Caligula who wrote the criminal laws on pillars too high to be seen. The task is not to cite court decisions but to develop flexible, inexpensive nonlawyer routes analogous to small claims procedures to permit citizens to walk into courthouses and be assisted in mundane resolution of disputes by court personnel, paralegals, or even relatives, without the need to hire lawyers to strap on shinguards.

Such remedies are a necessary corrective for a court system increasingly dinosaurlike in its rigidity, baroque in its complexity, and counterproductive to its historic role as peacemaker. As Learned Hand said in 1921, urging a kind of Husserlian *epoché* to divest mine-numbing allegiance to tradition: "No rules [of procedure] in the end will help us. We shall succeed in making our results conform with our professions only by a change of heart in ourselves."[51] In Learned Hand's word, there is but one commandment: "Thou shalt not ration justice."

NOTES

1. "The Longest Trial Is Over," 73 *ABA J.*, Nov. 1, 1987, at 14.

2. Ibid.

3. Ibid.

4. See J. Kilpatrick, "Soap Opera," *The Arizona Republic*, August 3, 1987, p. A13, and *The Arizona Republic*, November 15, 1987, p. 1 AA. Mr. Jamail, Pennzoil's lead counsel, reportedly received a legal fee of $600 million for his services in the case. *Wall Street Journal*, Dec. 23, 1987, p. 14.

5. C. Friedrich, *Man and His Government, An Empirical Theory of Politics*, 423 (New York: McGraw-Hill, 1963).

6. L. Mair, *Primitive Government*, 58 (Bloomington: Indiana University Press, 1970).

7. J. Lieberman, ed., *The Role of Courts in American Society*, 72 (St. Paul, Minn.: West Publishing, 1984).

8. This actually is embodied in statute or rule in some jurisdictions where, for example, the prosecutor provisionally schedules the cases for trial. See, e.g., La. R. Civ. P. (First Judicial Dist.) 17; Mass. R. Crim. P. 36(c). See also M. Solomon and D. Sumerlot, *Caseflow Management in the Trial Court*, 49 (Chicago: American Bar Association, 1987).

9. For a discussion of the purposes of liberal discovery, see *Hickman v. Taylor*, 329 U.S. 495, 507 (1947) ("Mutual knowledge of all the relevant facts gathered by both parties is essential to proper litigation.").

10. See A. Miller, *The August 1983 Amendments to the Federal Rules of Civil Procedure: Promoting Effective Case Management and Lawyer Responsibility*, 7–9 (Federal Judicial Center, 1984).

11. Quoted in R. Fine, *Escape of the Guilty*, 34 (New York: Dodd, Mead, 1986).

12. Ibid.

13. As quoted in Irving Stone, *Clarence Darrow for the Defense*, 23 (1941).

14. A. Elwork, *Making Jury Instructions Understandable*, 177 (Charlottesville, Va.: Michie Company, 1982).

15. Hager, *The Tulsa Tribune*, Oct. 6, 1959, p. 74.

16. Ibid.

17. Rand U. Charrow, "Psycholinguistic Study of Jury Instructions," 79 *Colum. L. Rev.* 1306, 1359 (1979).

18. Hager, *The Tulsa Tribune*, Oct. 6, 1959, pp. 74, 80.

19. Elwork, *Making Jury Instructions Understandable*, at 178.

20. A 1981 study found that as the trial length increases, jurors are more likely to rate the judge's instructions "difficult" or "very difficult" to understand (*Market Facts* 1981, p. 27). See also Reid Hastie, Steven D. Penrod, and Nancy Pennington, *Inside the Jury* (Cambridge: Harvard Univ. Press, 1983).

21. Revised Arizona Jury Instructions, "Negligence 5-Contributory Negligence," State Bar of Arizona (1980).

22. Devitt and Blackmar, 2 *Federal Jury Practice and Instructions*, § 27.06, 3rd. ed. (1978).

23. *United States v. Enright*, 579 F.2d 980 at 986, (6th Cir. 1978).

24. 69 Cal.2d 33, 69 Cal. Rptr 561, 442 P.2d 641 (1968).

25. *People v. McMartin and Buckey* went to trial December 1, 1987, in Los Angeles

Superior Court. On December 11, 1987, after intensive interrogation on the witness stand, the chief defense investigator committed suicide. The trial was preceded by the years-long investigative phase, eighteen months of pretrial hearings (a state record), and three months of jury selection.

Children who were enrolled at the McMartin nursery school when the molestations were alleged to have occurred are now junior high age. Charges against five of the original seven defendants were dropped when the district attorney decided the evidence against them was "incredibly weak." Raymond Buckey, on trial with Peggy McMartin Buckey, at the end of 1987 had spent more than three and a half years in jail on charges of abusing young children at the McMartin Preschool. During that time he had not been allowed his freedom on bond, at the same time undergoing extended arraignment proceedings and preliminary hearings. Finally, late in 1987, the trial judge decided to grant him bail of $3 million.

Richard Ramirez was arrested on charges of a series of heinous murders and has become known as the "Night Stalker." Ramirez has been in court for so many hearings covered by television cameras that his appearance is better known than a number of the soap opera stars.

It is hard to escape the feeling that the passage of years before such unusual criminal cases can be brought to trial does not serve the basic purpose of law enforcement or protection of the public. Public costs in the McMartin Preschool molestation case have nearly reached the $10 million mark, according to a report from Los Angeles County Auditor-Controller Mark H. Bloodgood. Bloodgood also reported that costs in the Richard Ramirez "Night Stalker" murder case have exceeded $1 million.

For the federal Indian litigation, see the *San Francisco Banner Daily Journal*, March 15, 1988 at II, p. 1.

26. *Attacking Litigation Costs and Delay*, 75 (A.B.A., 1986).

27. Ibid.

28. See D. Bok, *A Flawed System*, *N.Y.S. Bar J.*, 8–16 (Oct. 1983).

29. J. Kakalik and N. Pace, *Costs and Compensation Paid in Tort Litigation*, 76 ("Rand") (1986). See also "Annual Report," Institute for Civil Justice, Rand Corp., Los Angeles, 1989.

30. Ibid. at 70 and 76.

31. *National Symposium on Civil Justice Issues, Conference Report*, April 30 to May 1, 1986 (New York: Fordham) (1986), and Rand, *Costs and Compensation Paid in Tort Litigation*, Los Angeles (1986) at 69–70.

32. Rand, *Costs and Compensation Paid in Tort Litigation*, Los Angeles (1986) at X and 70.

33. These various approaches are discussed more fully in *Corporate Dispute Management*, Center for Public Resources (Ann Arbor, Mich., 1982).

34. "The Causes of Popular Dissatisfaction with the Courts" (A.B.A., Chicago, 1906).

35. *Attacking Litigation Costs and Delay*, 8 (Chicago: A.B.A., 1986).

36. "Jurists Told to Wield Firmer Judicial Hand," *National Law Journal*, April 18, 1988, pp. 5–10 ("justice is swifter when judges exercise more control over all trial phases including voir dire").

37. It also means increasing judicial salaries. "We cannot have judges who view their service on the bench as a stepping stone to earning big bucks in private practice. Yet when law clerks can go out and immediately earn more than their judges, what can we

expect?'' Mortimer B. Zuckerman, chairman and editor-in-chief of *U.S. News & World Report*, quoted in 73 *A.B.A. J.*, March 1, 1987, 31.

38. *Attacking Litigation Costs and Delay*, 8.

39. *Attacking Litigation Costs and Delay*, at 130.

40. See text discussion of fees exceeding judgments under ''costs.''

41. ''Tobacco Goes on Trial,'' *Reader's Digest*, October 1987, p. 225.

42. R. Fine, *Escape of the Guilty*, 110 (New York: Dodd, Mead, 1986) to whom the grade analogy is indebted.

43. R. Cochran, ''Mediation of Marital Disputes,'' 15 *Pepperdine L. Rev.* 51 (1987).

44. ''Minitrials Called Boon to Business Litigation,'' *Daily Journal*, Nov. 27, 1987, p. 5.

45. Ibid. Here is some suggested reading for mediation and special masters:

1. American Arbitration Association, ''Mediation Procedures and Techniques,'' AAA, Department of Education and Training, 3033 N. Central Avenue, #608, Phoenix, AZ 85012–2803.

2. T. Christian and M. Volpe, eds. *Problem Solving Through Mediation*, ABA Special Committee On Dispute Resolution, Washington, D.C., 1984.

3. Richard W. Evarts, James L. Greenstone, and Gary J. Kirkpatrick, *Winning Through Accommodation; The Mediator's Handbook* (Dubuque, Iowa: Kendall Hunt Publishing Company, 1983).

46. See Jeffrey O'Connell, ''Ending Insult to Injury,'' passim, *U. of Va. Alumni Magazine*, II, 24 (1987); Stephen Sugarman, ''Serious Tort Law Reform,'' 24 *San Diego L. R.*795–849 (1987); Alfred W. Cortese, Jr., and Yosef J. Riemer, ''Defining the Agenda for Serious Tort Reform,'' 24 *San Diego L. Rev.* 903–916 (1987), and D. Hensler et al., *Trends in Tort Litigation*, 30 Rand (1987).

47. J. Little, ''Up with Torts,'' 24 *San Diego L. Rev.* 861 (1987).

48. It was a Houston jury that decided that Texaco owed $10.53 billion in damages to Pennzoil for improperly luring Getty Oil from a merger with Pennzoil. Mr. Joe Jamail (a flamboyant Houston personal injury lawyer who had won more than forty verdicts of over one million dollars) repeatedly goaded Mr. McKinley (of Texaco) to speak up, an old trial lawyer's trick to plant suspicion among the jurors over credibility. Although Mr. McKinley overall didn't leave an unfavorable impression, he couldn't match the populist appeal of Mr. Liedtke (of Pennzoil), who had preceded him on the stand. The garrulous Pennzoil founder regaled the jury with a romantic account of his career, beginning with a partnership in the 1950s with George Bush. The ultimate irony is that the jury appeared to be influenced by the theatrics rather than by the evidence.

For discussion of this ''lottery'' type of justice, see J. O'Connell, ''Bhopal, the Good Lawyer, and the American Law School: A Torts (and Insurance) Professor's Perspective'' 36 *Journal of Legal Ed.* 311, 312 (1986).

49. *Zenith Radio Corp. v. Matsushita Elec. Indus. Co.*, 478 F. Supp. 889, 892 (E.D. Pa. 1979), vacated sub nom. *In re Japanese Elec. Prods. Antitrust Litigation*, 631 F.2d 1069 (3d Cir. 1980). The case involved an alleged worldwide antitrust conspiracy that had lasted for thirty years. See also *Curtis v. Loether*, 415 U.S. 189 (1974).

50. *Atlas Roofing v. Occupational Safety Comm.*, 430 U.S. 442 (1977). For articles dealing with *Atlas*, see Kirst, ''Administrative Penalties and the Civil Jury: The Supreme Court's Assault on the Seventh Amendment,'' 126 *U. Pa. L. Rev.* 1281 (1978); Note, ''The Seventh Amendment and Employee Safety—Conflicting Values?'' 2 *Indus. Rel. L. J.* 632 (1978).

51. L. Hand, ''Address Before the New York Bar,'' November 17, 1921, reprinted in 3 *Ass'n Bar City of New York, Lectures on Legal Topics* (1926).

5

VICTORY V. TRUTH: LITIGATION ETHICS

I don't see why we should not come out roundly and say that one of the functions of the lawyer is to lie for his client; and on rare occasions, as I think I have shown, I believe it is.

—Charles Curtis[1]

The greatest thrill is to win when you're wrong!

—Wall Street lawyer

I saw that the litigation, if it were persisted in, would ruin the plaintiff and the defendant, who were relatives and both belonged to the same city. . . . [I]t might go on indefinitely and to no advantage of either party. . . . In the meantime, mutual ill-will was steadily increasing. I became disgusted with the profession.

—Mahatma Gandhi[2]

INTRODUCTION

Lawyers lately have been feeling a good deal of self-pity for being bashed about in public. Much as one would like to believe the legal profession is undeserving of its low image, and that the image is correctable simply by doing charitable deeds, ample reason remains for incisive examination of whatever professional conscience still exists. Though unethical behavior runs well beyond the courthouse, some practices of the average courtroom litigator offer more than enough pangs of compunction, especially in light of the Model Rules of Professional Conduct.[3] Somehow our adversary system elicits a kind of ethics at once both commonplace and uncommonly out of place in a profession priding itself on the pursuit of justice.

The problem goes beyond mere image. Lawyers and judges were indicted, and some convicted, in Chicago for accepting bribes in the Operation Greylord investigation of corruption in the Cook County Circuit Court, the nation's largest court system. Lawyers who descended on Bhopal, India, in the wake of a toxic gas leak that killed more than two thousand, reeked of ambulance-chasing at its worst.

Enough scandals involving corporate lawyers exist to make it doubtful that members of the bar always act in the public interest or even in the interest of justice. The system may be as much the problem as the people greasing its wheels. When Judge Sirica opened the Watergate trial,[4] he is reported to have announced that he would relax the rules of evidence ''in the interest of finding the truth.''[5] This unusual judicial comment implies that the rules of evidence stand somehow in the way of truth. If that is so, one wonders if many other conventional courtroom procedures make litigation, for some lawyers, more a game of technique than a pursuit of truth. Our adversary method, notwithstanding its benefits, is at times a cumbersome giant that, to some, may exalt trickery and victory over ethics and truth. Its contentious nature fosters a hired gun or mercenary role of the lawyer. At the same time, the system's rules encourage casuistry. Litigating also offers recurring temptations to lie, to cheat, to mislead. Because of valued client confidences and too-trusting judiciary, a litigator can engage in deception without great risk of being caught. In playing the adversary role, the litigator may become an amoral technician committed to winning the adversary battle by any means at hand.[6] Ironically, perhaps the adversary system's penchant for rules elicits unruly behavior; perhaps its postulates of integrity and candor elicit their opposites.

Unlike the Continental inquisitional system where judges investigate the facts and question witnesses at trial, the Anglo-American adversary method pits parties against each other before a usually passive judge or jury. Lawyers are active; judges passively watch the lawyers' combat. The origins of this adversity reach far back in English history. When William the Conqueror introduced trial by combat to England in the eleventh century, the combat was initially a personal battle between the injured and the accused.[7] In a dispute over land, for example, the plaintiff did not need to offer battle personally. Instead, he could send a surrogate, one of his men, to do battle for him. The person sent was supposed to be a witness; in practice he was a hired professional who made his living fighting litigation battles, seeking to make the opposing party cry ''craven,'' that is, confess to being a liar.[8]

These seminal analogies to our adversary system are troubling. Wigmore said that the common law originated in a community of sports and games, which he saw as ''legalized gambling.''[9] James Marshall spoke of trial as an occasion where parties engage in a ''sporting'' duel.[10] Even today, part of the academic legal community at times disparages truth as the goal of the adversary process and instead emphasizes the rituals of the ''game,'' the winner being the more skilled, the loser the less so, neither having any expectation of truth.[11]

Today's adversary trial still resembles these earlier battles of blood and joust. It often is a ritualistic duel via surrogate warriors who use weapons of examination, cross-examination, verbal disputation, and sometimes sleight of hand to benefit clients. Sometimes the weapons are blunt and conventional; at times they are lethal and unconventional, like deceit, trickery, bluffing, and harassment.[12] As in physical combat, legal victory does not necessarily follow virtue; it sometimes goes to the wily warrior.

Whether the system and its participants encourage game playing or truth seeking is open to debate. They may well serve both. If so, it may be provocative to consider some litigation tactics that serve victory but not truth. These common practices illustrate the gaming litigator's mixture of wily tricks, which turn the courthouse into a lawyer's playpen, generate apt questions about professionalism, and ultimately raise the issue whether integrity is consonant with adversarial shin kicking.

TRICKS OF THE LITIGATION TRADE

Frivolous Lawsuits

A good part of the practice of some hungry lawyers involves frivolous lawsuits. Frivolity does not mean a sheer volume of suits; the term concerns the quality, not the quantity, of litigation. Both plaintiffs and defendants file frivolous claims. They appear not only as complaints but also as defensive counterclaims and crossclaims. They involve every conceivable area of the law but cluster about the deepest wells. Frivolous suits are filed for all sorts of reasons—to forestall a problem, to punish an opponent, to harass, and, at times, to line a lawyer's pocket.

Bizarre examples of frivolous lawsuits abound. A classic example is the attempted takeover of the Erie Railroad by the New York Central Railroad in the 1860s.[13] The attorneys involved, including David Dudley Field, filed twenty-six lawsuits throughout the State of New York, all involving the same parties and issues.[14] Field, author of the New York Code of Ethics,[15] defended his tactics by stating, "I have done not only what I have a right to do but what I was bound to do."[16]

More modern examples are prevalent: a woman files a half-million-dollar suit against community officials who forbade her to breast-feed her child at the community pool;[17] a child sues his parents for "malparenting";[18] a disappointed suitor brings suit for being stood up by a date;[19] an irate sports fan sues to overturn a referee's call.[20] Sports officials have been advised on how to protect their rights.[21] Even the clergy have been advised to take out malpractice insurance.[22]

While frivolous suits are not limited to medical malpractice, that area of litigation offers enough well-documented increases in filings to suggest deep-pocket frivolity:

Americans are filing three times as many malpractice claims as they did when the crisis began a decade ago. Today 20 out of every 100 physicians face a suit, compared with

12 per 100 in 1979. In 1982, there were more than 250 jury verdicts of over \$1 million, and in some states awards average \$100,000. An alarmed AMA is urging tougher peer-review procedures to weed out incompetent doctors, but its larger concern is capricious lawsuits.[23]

In 1981 3.2 malpractice claims were filed for every 100 physicians; by 1985 the figure had grown to 10.1. In Cook County (Chicago), Illinois, alone, more than 1,800 medical malpractice suits were filed in 1983, more than twice the number filed in 1975.[24] Nationwide, to at least one admittedly partial observer, more than 90 percent of those suits are "totally" without merit.[25] Even allowing for overstatement, the medical field is witness to a burgeoning trend of reckless filings against deep-pocket defendants.

Frivolous litigation also appears in other garb. Twenty-five years ago, punitive damages were sought and awarded only in rare instances. Today it is common-place for some plaintiff's counsel to toss in a paragraph demanding punitive damages even where there is no evidence beyond ordinary negligence. Routine negligence pleadings regularly seek compensatory damages so inflated that they are usually ignored as nothing more than puffing and intimidation.

One corollary of this paper artillery is that many complaint pleadings do not really mean what they say. Instead of telling the truth, they serve goals of power, intimidation, and bravado.

The Shotgun Complaint

The shotgun complaint names as defendants every entity having the slightest connection to the heart of the litigation, regardless of fault. For example, in the medical malpractice field, plaintiff's lawyer may sue not only the doctor who performed a faulty operation, but also nurses, orderlies, the chief of staff, the entire hospital, the board of directors, its insurer, and the local hospital association.[26] Shotgunning frequently appears in personal injury cases where a plaintiff sees an opportunity to draft innocent defendants into litigation to force them to exonerate themselves by incriminating the truly culpable parties. For such a plaintiff, shotgunning can be a vicarious and inexpensive way to conduct discovery by watching, vulturelike, the internecine struggle of defendants developing the plaintiff's case by incriminating each other.

The economic cost of most litigation today is enormous, but the cost to shotgunning attorneys is comparatively small as innocent defendants exonerate themselves by satisfying the plaintiff's discovery needs. Shotgun tactics some-times—but rarely—result in a boomerang effect.[27]

The Tactical Counterclaim

Improper claims are not limited to the plaintiff's bar. Some defense litigators engage in a companion sort of rebound frivolity. In contract litigation, for example, once a plaintiff has filed suit, it is commonplace for the defendant to counterclaim. Some of these counterclaims have merit; most, however, are filed only to achieve litigation leverage. Sometimes counterclaims intend to convey to a judge that the sides are equally balanced. In fact, they rarely are. When counterclaims are groundless, they cause results similar to the shotgun complaint: increased confusion and costs.[28] Often their purpose is to put pressure on the plaintiff to drop or settle the original claim. Whatever the result, false counterclaims serve goals of intimidation and confusion rather than truth.

The Sexual Abuse Claim

Equally popular, and equally suspect ethically, is today's penchant in divorce litigation to file false claims of sexual misconduct against a spouse seeking child custody.[29] The claim is easily made; it is difficult to refute, especially when children are coached to embellish the story. Nationwide, the false claim of sexual abuse has become a leading offensive strategy, "a nuclear weapon" in custody disputes.[30] Even when it is rankly false it offers tactical advantages; it raises prospects of criminal prosecution and embarrassment, each of which pressures an innocent spouse to abandon a viable custody claim.

More than leverage, this sort of intimidation should be called what it is: a form of extortion, actively aided by lawyers and tolerated by potted-plant judges.

Pettifoggery and Stalling

In both civil and criminal litigation, a widespread belief exists that delay benefits the defendant because incriminating witnesses disappear, die, or forget as a case ages. Delay is neither new nor creative. In the hands of a game-playing litigator, it takes many ingenious forms advantageous to the client and detrimental to justice.

The late Bruce Bromley, a judge on the New York Court of Appeals and thereafter a senior litigator in a private law firm, managed to make one antitrust case last fourteen years and another eighteen years.[31] To Bromley, litigation was a game, the playing of which was not a cause for shame. In a 1958 speech to a conference of judges wrestling with the vexatious (to them) problem of litigation delay, Bromley trumpeted that he could take the simplest antitrust case and protract it for the defense almost to infinity.[32] As a young attorney, he resolved to make a "stupendous production" out of a government antimonopoly case against Paramount Pictures.[33] He insisted that the court sit in each of sixty-two cities so that the government would have to prove separately in each city the claimed block-booking practice.[34] If a judge had asked, Bromley would have admitted "readily" that his client was using the all-or-nothing booking scheme, but because no judge shortened the proceedings, Bromley felt no compunction about putting on a road show production lasting fourteen years.[35]

That fourteen-year delay was not Bromley's crowning achievement. In that same 1958 speech, he described with relish his eighteen years of foot-dragging in a price-fixing case against the American gypsum industry.[36] He unashamedly told his audience that if he had been asked to admit price-fixing agreements did in fact exist, "we would have done so," and the case "certainly would not have lasted eighteen years."[37] He confessed that during the last part of the eighteen years, "I stirred up a fight among the co-defendants just to keep the case going a little longer."[38]

The same bar that now anxiously seeks to mend its poor public image has admired this sort of gamesmanship. On January 3, 1963, the Bar of the City of New York dedicated its annual Twelfth Night party to "Bruce Bromley, Esq., Michigan's Gift to the New York Trial Bar" with a poster depicting Bromley as a barefoot country bumpkin, under a scroll bearing this verse:

> BUST IF YOU MUST
> THIS GIANT TRUST,
> BUT LET'S TAKE
> DEPOSITIONS FUST.[39]

Steeped in this Bromley tradition of jockeying, the warrior litigator invents excuses to prevent the opponent's day in court. Criminal defense attorneys, for example, often maintain that they are so unprepared that, if forced to trial, they would be unable to give competent representation to their client.[40] This too-frequent ululation puts the trial judge in the dilemma of either allowing delay or denying a continuance, with certain appellate reversal of any guilty verdict for ineffective assistance of counsel.[41]

Today, the road to delay is paved with stipulated extensions of time to answer, stipulated continuances, motions to continue on the inactive calendar, controverting certificates filed to avoid a trial date, strategic changes of judge, and spurious discovery disputes. All these modes of delay line lawyers' pockets while delaying justice and clients' return to normalcy. Few courts have the gumption to describe delay for what it really is: a vexing and expensive sport, oriented to victory, not truth.

We cannot overlook the conduct of defense counsel, which deserves our strongest censure as being dilatory, obstructive and harassing. Altogether the record shows some 135 filings in the case, almost 100 of them before trial. Many are routine but far too many are petitions, applications, motions—endlessly repeated—and frequently without any semblance of merit. At the same time counsel was trumpeting for a speedy trial and claiming denial of constitutional rights because the case was so long delayed. We agree with the trial judge—one of six who became the object of defendant's carping during the course of the case—who said defendant was using delay and hindrance as a ploy to set up a basis for appeal. . . .

Lawyers are officers of the court, too, and actions which can most charitably be described as pettifoggery have no place in the representation of a client.[42]

The Expert Witness

The civil adversary system relies to a great extent on the expert witness. The expert is someone who has extensive knowledge or expertise beyond layfolk.[43] In practice, it often means scouting around for someone with credible credentials to testify in support of partisan views. Civil litigators regularly shop around for experts to support a partisan theory rather than accept a neutral expert who speaks with objectivity. Some experts become professional testifiers, advertising their availability and pliability in legal journals.[44] Lawyers on both sides commonly call them "whores."

The primary job of an expert is to help jurors understand the issues. Experts receive fees ranging anywhere from $50 per hour—for some social scientists— to thousands of dollars a day for preeminent medical specialists. They evaluate the potential worth of lawsuits, assist in developing evidence, and present testimony by deposition or at trial. A few charge fees contingent on the outcome of the case, a controversial practice that most authorities decry. The variety of available experts is astounding. Legal periodicals abound with ads touting those claiming expert knowledge of everything from artificial turf to the weather.

In addition to the ads of individuals, national clearinghouses offer witness referral services to attorneys. Most charge a flat service fee tacked on to the hourly fee set by the expert. Some attorneys and experts have secret understandings regarding bonus compensation after a successful verdict, though, of course, such a bonus is not called a contingent fee. Attorneys are forbidden by Rule 6–101 of the Code of Professional Responsibility to compensate a witness based on the outcome of the case. Perhaps nowhere has the use of the expert been abused more than in psychology and psychiatry, where mercenary psychiatry rules the halls: experts are bought and sold, and their testimony occurs under a tarnished halo. A recent study suggests that flipping a coin is more accurate than relying on the testimony of psychologists and psychiatrists.[45]

Witness Rehearsal, aka "Sandpapering"

Attorneys regularly rehearse witness testimony. Rehearsal occurs at all levels from depositions to trials. Attorney General Edwin Meese reportedly was rehearsed for thirty hours by Justice Department attorneys before his testimony at the 1987 Iran-Contra hearings. Line-drawing is the name of the game. The line between refreshing memory and planting creative fiction is thin to nonexistent. Lawyers supposedly use rehearsal only to help their witness remember. Much more is regularly done. Witnesses are advised how to handle questions and even how to give selective information.

Party witnesses present grave temptations to fabricate. It is not unusual in a criminal case for a defense lawyer to say things like: "You've got no defense to the charge of murder unless, of course, there's evidence of self-defense. Think about it overnight and we'll talk tomorrow." Such rehearsal is an open invitation to perjury. Rehearsal of any kind destroys witness open-mindedness and spontaneity. Rehearsal regularly leads at least to obstructionism and evasion, as witnessed in this 1987 deposition exchange with a client advised by his Dallas law firm (later fined $15,000) to evade questions:

Attorney: "When did you review those documents?"

Witness: "What do you mean by when?"

Attorney: "The documents that were reviewed, where were they located?"

Witness: "They were located . . . what do you mean by 'where?' "

Discovery Abuse

The richest area in which the adversary system encourages sport and games is discovery. Supposedly, discovery is the cooperative exchange by opposing lawyers of factual data in order to get the truth. Particularly in large jurisdictions, legitimate efforts to obtain authorized information from an adversary are sometimes met with a variety of strategies ranging from outright lying, to flat refusals to comply, to overkill.[46]

Under our jousting rules of discovery, each side may obtain all the unprivileged, relevant evidence that the other side has uncovered.[47] However, you get what the discovery rules entitle you to only if you ask the right questions; if you don't ask, you don't get. A lazy or less than brilliant lawyer gets less than an ingenious one. Continuing legal education programs teach techniques of ingenuity. These programs have such titles as "The Art of Discovery," where finding the truth, or, more aptly, the most appealing "face" of the truth, becomes an art remote from the administration of justice.

When overuse of discovery serves client interests, hyperactive discovery results. Discovery rules envision few limitations; they offer incentives to keep seemingly endless discovery music playing without reaching a crescendo. Discovery tangos come to resemble the dance marathons of yesteryear: get on the dance floor, hang onto a client, and drift about endlessly to the music until someone collapses from financial exhaustion.[48] Where the object is to beat every plowshare into a sword, attorneys can employ excessive discovery as crushing weaponry to avoid reaching the merits.[49]

Gaming litigators know well these common tactics for circumventing legitimate discovery:

1. Construe all inquiries as narrowly as possible to limit the useful information that must be divulged;
2. Refuse to respond to written requests that have the slightest ambiguity;
3. Construe the desired materials as shielded by attorney-client confidentiality;
4. Bury significant documents in mounds of irrelevant material;
5. Refuse to respond to interrogatories or production requests until compelled by a court.[50]

These tactics are graphically illustrated in a recent federal case, *Carlucci v. Piper Aircraft.*[51] In *Carlucci*, the defendant obstructed discovery in bad faith for five years by destroying documents, lying, and disobeying repeated court orders.[52] The defendant's attorney was personally fined $10,000 for discovery abuse.[53]

Most average litigants today are overdiscovered, overinterrogated, overdeposed, and underqualified financially for all this attention. Discovery marathons readily induce the parties to buy out of litigation because discovery may well cost more than the value of the claim. Many medical and legal malpractice cases succumb to settlement where no real liability exists simply because innocent parties must buy out rather than suffer the enormous costs involved to win on the merits. Well-to-do parties, therefore, can overwhelm less resourceful opponents with burdensome discovery requests having no relation to the merits. Again, the goal is victory, not truth; money defeats justice.

Destroying Witnesses

Although cross-examination may be the most powerful engine for eliciting truth, cross-examination by harassment is one of the greatest impediments to truth. An all-too-frequent occurrence in sporting litigation is the use of insult and innuendo to obscure the truth by obstructing its mouthpiece—the witness. Consider the following exchange between a witness and an attorney conducting a cross-examination:

Q. Have you ever done any flying? (asked of a confused witness)

A. No.

Q. I recommend that you don't.[54]

Embarrassing a witness also obscures the truth. In a case in which a defendant was charged with murder in the shooting of his father-in-law, on cross-examination a prosecutor asked the defendant:

[I]sn't it a fact that the only time you have sought psychiatric counseling or have used insanity as a defense are the two times criminal charges were brought against you, once in December of 1975 and another time in February of 1972, isn't that a fact, sir?[55]

In fact, the 1975 charge was a civil commitment proceeding the defendant's wife instituted, and the state dismissed the 1972 charge.[56] No factual basis whatsoever existed for asking the intimidating question.[57]

Harassment may also involve body language. Opposing counsel advances menacingly and, in a lenient court, winds up nose-to-nose with the witness. Witnesses are jousted about on trivia by innuendo and tone of voice: "Well, Mr. Witness, is it a fact in your deposition you said the light was red, not 'bright' red?" Documents are tossed at witnesses, books slammed shut, depositions quoted in a tone of preening triumph. Harassing objections are used to interrupt and to distract the flow of testimony.

Some litigators adopt this rule of thumb: destroy a witness telling harmful truth and rehabilitate a witness who tells favorable stories, whether true or not. A common query to discredit an adverse witness is: "To whom have you talked about this case?" Of course, the witness has usually talked at least with the attorney who called him. The witness may believe that talking to others about the case is forbidden. Or the witness may assume that the question excludes the calling attorney. Even so, a "no one" answer permits the cross-examiner to pounce. The witness has been caught in a lie, the lawyer shouts, so the entire testimony must be discounted.

Another rank device capitalizes upon the myth of perfect recall. For instance, in questioning a witness about an event that occurred years before, an attorney might ask: "In what month was that?—Well, which was it, then?—Ah, you're not sure? Your testimony is, then, you don't remember?" According to one commentator, the purpose behind such questioning is that "the more times . . . [the lawyer] can make the witness say 'I don't remember,' . . . the better will be the psychological effect."[58] Another commentator explains, "[i]t is impossible in a court of law to place confidence in the evidence of a witness who can be reduced in cross-examination to saying 'I do not remember.' "[59]

Wigmore called the witness stand "the slaughterhouse of reputations."[60] The decimation of a witness still remains a favorite trial tactic. "The attorney is obligated," says Monroe Freedman, "to attack, if he can, the reliability or credibility of an opposing witness whom he knows to be truthful."[61] Lewis Lake, in *How to Cross-Examine Successfully*,[62] urges the maxim: "No matter how clear, how logical, how concise, or how honest a witness may be or make his testimony appear, there is always some way, if you are ingenious enough, to cast suspicion on it, to weaken its effect."[63]

Extolled in law school and in professional workshops on trial advocacy, court-room theatrics serve the cause of victory but not always the cause of truth. At times, they fall short of the rudimentary civility one citizen shows another on the sidewalk. Our courts tolerate a lesser degree of civility toward witnesses than absolute strangers show each other on the street.

Dumb Shows

Some lawyers adopt wily silent ploys to distract judge and jury from important matters. Clarence Darrow employed one of the original "dumb" shows: he would insert a small wire into a lit cigar so that the jury's attention during his opponent's closing argument would be on the lengthening ashes that would almost, but never quite, fall.[64]

Darrow's dumb show is by no means the most distracting or offensive. A criminal defense attorney appeals to jury sympathy by arranging to have the defendant's small child crawl to him during closing argument. Here is the way the attorney describes this ploy:

If the kid's a crawler, the best time to let him loose is during final argument. Imagine that little tyke crawling right up to you (make sure he comes to you and not the DA or, worse yet, the judge; a smear of Gerber's peaches around the cuff worked for me) while you're saying: "Don't strike down this good man, father to little Jimmy. Why Jimmy!" Pick the child up and give him to Daddy. If the DA objects and gets them separated, so much the better. Moses himself couldn't part a father and a son without earning disfavor in the eyes of the jury. Babies are truly miracles of life; they've saved many a father years of long-distance parenting. If your client is childless, rent a kid for the trial.[65]

There are infinite variations to this silent plea. In my own experience, I have seen a defendant approach the judge for sentencing while carrying a child to suggest that no one else is available to care for the child, who will be abandoned if a prison sentence is imposed.

Some lawyers plant silent jury messages outside the evidence. In a suit against an insurance company alleging a failure to settle in good faith, plaintiff's counsel placed a photocopy of a legal newspaper on the edge of his desk nearest the jury box.[66] Its headline read: "Didn't Settle in Policy Limits; OK Mental Suffering Award."[67] Questioned by the judge, the lawyer responded that the article was reference material needed during trial, even though it was three years old and available in the reports (in smaller print, of course).[68] In reversing a substantial verdict favorable to plaintiff, the appellate court observed:

[C]ounsel for plaintiffs stated he had the article on the table for use in discussing jury instructions "and other leading points." This excuse is incredible. . . . We cannot help but conclude that the article with prominent headlines was exposed for the purpose of influencing the jury. No one knows whether any jurors saw the headlines, and if so, what, if any effect they had on the jury in its deliberations. It would appear from the size of the verdicts that the headlines might have influenced the jury. Under such circumstances we hold that the trial court abused its discretion in not granting defendant's motion for mistrial.[69]

Coaching Witnesses via Objection

Sporting lawyers commonly make "speaking" objections. Instead of simply citing the appropriate rule of evidence, the objecting lawyer launches into a curmudgeonly speech approaching closing argument. Sometimes the objection seeks to remind the witness how to answer the pending question: "The witness couldn't possibly answer that question, Your Honor, because she was out of town at the time." When questioning resumes, the witness responds that she cannot answer the pending question because, as she now recalls, she was out of town.[70]

By far the most common in-court abuse is over-objecting. Trained in law school and advocacy workshops to sniff out any and all evidence violations, young lawyers leap (if polite) to their feet and object to innocent, harmless testimony to demonstrate to the galleries their evidentiary prowess. To cooler heads with more common sense, these jumping jacks exhibit an opposite penchant for obstruction and theatrics. The good lawyer objects only to those few bits of evidence that truly may hurt the case and ignores other violations.

Bushwhacking

"Bushwhacking" refers to legal arguments on matters beyond the evidence, misstatements of the evidence, and wholly unsupported arguments.[71] Bushwhacking occurs inadvertently where a lawyer forgets testimony or inaccurately summarizes it. It may also reflect a deliberate effort to bring extraneous matters before a jury.[72] In a civil case, a lawyer may argue in summation that a defendant manufacturer had removed the offending product from the marketplace after injury, when there normally would have been no evidence of such removal because of the remedial measure rule.[73] Alternatively, in a capital criminal case in which the jury may not consider punishment, a lawyer may argue, as many do, that a defendant presents a "life or death" choice to the jury.

One of the most frequently violated rules of argument is the prohibition against expressing personal opinions. The following real-life example occurred in my court: "And you can believe Mr. Jones, my witness: I've known him for thirty years and wouldn't have put him on the stand if I didn't believe him." Closing arguments may also offer uninvited endorsements of one's own sainted witnesses and the low virtue of all opposing witnesses. For example, one lawyer commented, "I tell you, ladies and gentlemen, that she is an incredible witness, and she is not worthy of your belief. She is a liar, clear and simple."[74]

Bushwhacking also occurs in improper attempts to poison a jury during voir dire selection. Entrusted to litigators, voir dire questioning becomes an undisguised effort to shape and imbed favorable attitudes—in a word, to secure a biased jury. Here is a defense lawyer's account of the purpose of voir dire:

The fundamental purpose of voir dire is to select a jury which has no prejudice, notions, or thoughts that will adversely affect your case. It is probably naive to talk about "a trial by a fair and impartial jury of peers"; what we really want, as advocates, is a jury of people who are attracted to our cause. The plaintiff, of course, wants the same. We will also accept a jury which appears to disfavor the plaintiff. If we can't get a jury which is biased in our favor, or at least a jury which is biased against plaintiff's case, we will accept an impartial jury.[75]

In this mind-warp, litigators in a lenient court regularly ask potential jurors questions such as:

"What bumper stickers do you have on your car?"

"If you were sitting where my client is, would you want a jury comprised of twelve Mr. Smiths?"

"You understand, don't you, that all we're trying to do here is pick a fair, impartial jury?"

"You won't hold it against me if I aggressively cross-examine my opponent's witnesses?"

"You wouldn't be opposed, would you, to awarding a substantial verdict, say up to a million dollars?"

Lying

One of the surprises to persons outside the adversary system is the fact that some attorneys lie. It should be a greater surprise to those within the system. Unfortunately, deceit is one of the weapons in some war chests. As one lawyer put it:

You would lie for your wife. You would lie for your child. There are others with whom you are intimate enough, close enough, to lie for them when you would not lie for yourself. At what point do you stop lying for them? I don't know and you are not sure.[76]

Recently Monroe Freedman, former dean of Hofstra Law School and author of a well-known book on legal ethics, proposed that deception be allowed in the courtroom:

The criminal defense attorney, however unwillingly in terms of personal morality, has a professional responsibility as an advocate in the adversary system to examine the perjurious client in the ordinary way and to argue to the jury, as evidence in the case, the testimony presented by the defendant.[77]

Under this approach, the lawyer faced with a lying client has a professional duty to ask questions that do not reveal the falsehood, and a further duty to adopt the false testimony in closing argument. More recently, another law professor has acknowledged calmly that lawyers' pleadings lie.[78]

For some litigators, the "story" is more crucial than the truth. Few lawyers actually believe their clients: clients only tell a story for court consumption. The lawyer's state of mind is one of suspended belief. After all, one may argue, truth is not for the lawyer to determine; that's why there is a jury or judge. The sporting lawyer's concern is whether the story is convincing, whether it adequately meets the opposing story, not whether it is true or false. Thus it is not at all unusual to hear a courtroom story unfold like a novel, changing as the trial proceeds. Sometimes the story becomes clearer, sometimes fuzzier, sometimes contradicted as it is orchestrated by the lawyer-maestros. As one side crafts a story, the other side expresses outrage at the opponent's fiction and responds by fictionalizing its own story. The story is not as dismaying as the attorneys' acquiescence in it. In this sort of liar's paradise, truth ceases to be a Heideggerian revelation; instead, trial evidence becomes a progressive sedimentation, with new layers of lies overlaying the original ones. When this story telling occurs in court, the trial degenerates into secondary issues. Courts thus try the defendant's pedigree, the etiquette of the police, discovery compliance, police niceties, and experts' hourly rates.

For years, the same legal profession that now gropes for professionalism has winked at lying in pleadings, negotiations, oral argument, and fee requests, treating the adversary system as a creative paper lottery instead of a pursuit of truth. Fee requests still are frequent exercises in creative arithmetic. A must-read opinion is one by U.S. District Judge Charles Hardy:[79]

> Some of the times logged . . . call into question the accuracy of the time records. For example, in one instance a lawyer logged 0.20 hour, while his counterpart logged one hour. . . . [One lawyer claimed] to have logged 18.9 hours in one day. To have accomplished this, he would have had to have been in his office from 5:06 in the morning until midnight, without taking any time for meals, to relieve himself or to do anything else. . . . A law clerk logged 3.2 hours of "research re: procedural requirements for Answer and Counterclaim," for which $144 is claimed. A lawyer who finds it necessary to assign a law clerk to research that question probably should not be involved in litigation.[80]

Unfortunately, lying is a kind of daily fare that is rarely condemned. In the eyes of some observers,[81] trials have ceased being a search for truth and have degenerated into gigantic lying contests,[82] a crime scene in themselves.[83]

EVALUATION

The preceding observations from the trenches prompt some diverse comments. First, on lying. Some law professors might argue that there is no lying where there is no reliance. Lying is only in the ears of the listener; therefore, if the listener believes that lawyers lie, there can be no lie. As Sissela Bok has observed in her book on *Lying*, this kind of reasoning is casuistry, if not pure nonsense, because it means we would trust people more if we accepted that they always lie.[84]

The slope here is very slippery. If some lies are all right, why not others? If the lawyer is sole judge of what constitutes a tolerable lie, what criteria will be used? Obviously none could be devised. Should juries be instructed that a number of lawyers believe it is their right to lie? Even lawyers willing to support the right to lie for themselves would not wish such an instruction. Once forewarned, even a naive juror would become suspicious about other deceptions by these same lawyers.

If the adversary system is nothing more than a liars' convention, nothing is amiss here. However, if the adversary system seeks goals of truth and justice, lying constitutes a sufficient affront to those goals to deserve unqualified condemnation.

In the ethical arena, the solution—at least in theory—is as obvious as it is troubling: with the exception of the discussion on experts, all the foregoing conduct appears unethical under the Rules of Professional Conduct. Rule 3.1[85] and new Civil Procedure Rule 11[86] both prohibit filing frivolous and otherwise unsupported claims. Model Rule 1.2 prohibits fraudulent conduct.[87] Rule 1.3 requires an attorney to diligently process cases without delay.[88] Disruptive cross-examination via intimidation seemingly runs counter to Rules 3.3 and 3.5 requiring both candor and nondisruptive conduct.[89] Rule 3.4 ("fairness to opposing party") prohibits discovery games and witness rehearsal going beyond mere memory aid.[90] Dumb shows and bushwhacking are largely at odds with Rules 3.4 and 3.5[91] Rules 1.2 and 3.3, requiring candor to the court in both written and oral presentations, totally prohibit lying.[92]

The ethical observation prompts a question: If the shinkicking described in this chapter is so commonplace and also unethical, why does it continue so unabashedly as part and parcel of modern litigation? Part of the answer is that the system and its participants seek victory, not truth. Litigation tactics are means to the only goal that counts: a successful outcome, which, needless to say, is unrelated to the right outcome.

One cannot but wonder at the propriety of law school and bar advocacy programs that instill in fledgling litigators a predilection for victory over truth, and in the process bestow on each pupil a bursting bag of trial tricks more like that of vaudeville actors than officers of the court. Euphemistically disguised as "techniques of cross-examination" or "the art of discovery," these programs too often emphasize not candor, careful preparation, honesty, and fair dealing, but excessive client loyalty and sleight-of-hand devices. The programs often suggest using these devices when virtue alone is not enough to win. In the courtroom, these tactics are defended as "zeal." Zealous advocacy has become the buzzword squeezing decency and civility out of the profession. Zealous advocacy is the modern day plague that weakens the truth-finding process and makes a mockery of the lawyer claim to be an officer of the court.

Part of the prevalence of lawyers' unprofessionalism lies squarely at the feet of a too-passive judiciary. The Anglo-American adversary system has strongly encouraged the role model judge as a smiling, passive ticket holder at a lawyers' nightclub act. Judicial evaluation polls have encouraged popularity via timidity. Judicial spectatorship breeds an intolerable patience where holy anger would be appropriate. Trial and appellate judges, typically drawn from the litigation bar, rarely have the spleen to control or denounce the tactics described here. Judges have the greatest opportunity to mitigate misbehavior, delay, and economic extortion. The blame belongs with us for surrendering to gamesmanship and thereby debilitating our public trust. We have cast our lot with our litigation peers rather than with the public. Despite their obligation in the Canons of Judicial ethics to refer misbehaving attorneys for discipline, the obligation continues to be evaded. "I would feel very uncomfortable doing it," says Los Angeles County

Superior Court Judge Robert Weil, a former president of the California Judges Association. "It's strange to get judges to snoop on lawyers. It's not a tradition."[93] A judge's duty in an arena of frivolity and unprofessionalism is to be an active member in moving cases and monitoring compliance with rules of ethics and procedure. Such an attitude, admittedly, does not play up to a judicial evaluation poll nor to lawyer campaign contributions. It might, however, have more to do with justice.

Careful thought also needs to focus on the provocative correlation between some lawyer misconduct and the adversary system. Undoubtedly, the causes of popular dissatisfaction with the profession go well beyond the courtroom. However, the adversary system's penchant for conflict and drama, coupled with high stakes and behind-the-scenes confidences, put even greater temptations on trial lawyers than on desk lawyers to use questionable tactics to secure victory. The examples here include heroes. The ABA's Winter 1984 *Litigation* magazine contains an article written by Gerry Spence.[94] This is the same Gerry Spence who was the foe of Kerr-McGee in the Silkwood case,[95] and the foe of *Hustler* in the Miss Wyoming case.[96] Spence reasons that if the attorney adequately prejudices the jury in this manner, he need not worry about the facts or the law—the jury will decide the case in his favor.[97]

Our adversary system at present expresses a number of discordant ironies. One fraternal belief is that justice should be free: the loser often should not have to pay the winner's expenses. From this belief follows a contingent fee system and lack of inhibitions on running up an opposing party's costs. Entry into the profession should be democratic: admission is relatively easy, levels of training uneven, professional *esprit de corps* weak, and self-policing low. One result is differing levels of professionalism. Still another fraternal belief is that militancy to the point of obduracy is an efficacious barometer of social conscience: the relentless prosecutor, the fearless vindicator of the oppressed, the wily strategist for the phone company—these are all heroes. These heroes instill a belief that litigation is theatre, the privileged stage for social change. It would be far better if courts and litigators understood, with Learned Hand, that being in litigation, whatever its outcome, is akin to sickness and death.[98]

More philosophically, the adversary system raises the question whether the litigator really exists as a moral agent under the hired gun mask. The public becomes hostile to lawyers when it views personality as constituted merely by a series of staged performances or masks.[99] Sartre makes this point in his analysis of the grocer in *Being and Nothingness*:

A grocer who dreams is offensive to the buyer, because such a grocer is not wholly a grocer. Society demands that he limit himself to his function as a grocer, just as the soldier at attention makes himself into a soldier-thing with a direct regard which does not see at all. . . . There are indeed many precautions to imprison a man in what he is, as if we lived in perpetual fear that he might escape from it, that he might break away and suddenly elude his condition.[100]

Part of the lawyer's public opprobrium is precisely this moral ambiguity. Litigators embody the theatrical masked self. For that very reason, Rousseau thought actors dishonorable because their talent lies in the art of counterfeit, of putting on "another character than his own," of appearing "different than he is, of "forgetting his own place by dint of taking another's."[101] Rousseau contrasted the actor and the orator as the counterfeit and the genuine:

When the orator appears in public, it is to speak and not to show himself off; he represents only himself; he fills only his own role, speaks only in his own name, says, or ought to say, only what he thinks; the man and the role being the same, he is in his place; he is in the situation of any citizen who fulfills the functions of his estate. But an actor on the stage, displaying other sentiments than his own, saying only what he is made to say, often representing a chimerical being, annihilates himself, as it were, and is lost in his hero.[102]

Against that scenario, the litigator making an argument to the jury or negotiating with the opponent advocates only the interests of his client. His speech does not represent a personal view, nor even necessarily the standards of the law. To distinguish between personal views and those of a client would make the client suffer. The correct lawyer thus can only appear sincere. Like the actor, the litigator must conceal personality and values, yet must also appear as an orator exercising the highest function as an eloquent citizen, while in the adversary guise being an actor swallowed up in a client. "A good lawyer must be a great liar," we say—all the greater, indeed, because it is often hard to see a moral agent under the mask.[103]

Part of the problem, of course, is the theatre analogy. A courtroom should be more than good theatre. To be sure, actors in a play take on roles and say things that the characters, not the actors, believe. The audience knows it is a play and that they are actors; there is no expectation of factual accuracy. Courts are not theatres; if they indulge in fictions, they do so only reluctantly. When a litigator's words are totally for sale to the client, the public hostility to litigator roles and morals appears well-founded.

The legal observer with a sense of history would expect to find an "officer of the court" under the litigator's theatrical mask. Though that label persists, its role has disappeared or been subordinated to client goals. Instances of misconduct of these officers is everywhere. To add to those already mentioned, on January 31, 1985, in a published opinion, the Eleventh Circuit Court of Appeals affirmed a fine of $50,000 imposed upon two attorneys in a respected law firm in Atlanta, Georgia. They had advised their client how to violate a direct order of the U.S. district court. In 1985, a Wall Street law firm was fined $50,000 for violating Rule 11 by making baseless allegations in court pleadings. In West Palm Beach, Florida, a district judge struck the pleadings of Piper Aircraft for deliberate violations of discovery orders by counsel in a multimillion-dollar death case. In the Dalkon Shield case, there is sworn testimony given by an attorney concerning the deliberate destruction and withholding of records upon the advice of senior house counsel. All these miscreants served as "officers" of the courts and betrayed that trust.[104]

The term "officer of the court" was once an integral part of the English system when lawyers were directly amenable to the king as parts of the royal judicial system. The first licensed practitioners were called "Servants at law of our lord, the King." In 1275, a statute regulating the practice of law provided that

[I]f any Sergeant, Pleader [Attorney] or other, do any manner of Deceit or Collusion in the King's Court or consent (unto it) in deceit of the Court (or) to beguile the Court or the Party and thereof be attained, he shall be imprisoned for a Year and a Day, and from thenceforth shall not be heard to plead . . . in (that) court for any Man.[105]

Notably, this first attempt to regulate an attorney's professional conduct prohibited deceit upon the court. The role of a lawyer as an officer of the court became firmly embedded in the legal tradition to describe a whole host of duties owed by the lawyer to the court prior to duties to the client.

The bar's fall from grace parallels its fall from the status of an officer of the court. The *Model Rules of Professional Conduct* reflect a continuing decline in a lawyer's obligations both to the court and to the public's city wall. Nowhere is there an ethical reference to "officers of the court." Rule 3.3, entitled "Candor to the Tribunal," is the only remnant of this early philosophy. It prohibits false statements of material fact or law, proffer of false evidence, and failure to disclose a material fact when necessary to avoid criminal or fraudulent conduct. All of these duties are based upon a "knowing" act. There is no duty whatsoever to aggressively ascertain objective truth. The litigator is protected by ignorance; indeed, ignorance is encouraged. The litigator obviates the rule by simply not asking the client too many questions and by learning only the client's "story."

This professional ethic mandates that lawyers owe complete allegiance to their clients, very little to the system or to the law, and none at all to the adversary. If lawyers ever hope to regain public trust, their first and overriding loyalty must be to the law. The role as an officer of the court is not merely a restriction on fouling judicial process but also a challenge to serve as a magistrate in the first instance, a justice of peace in the trenches, Langdell's jurisconsult to the common man. The client is entitled to sound, honest legal advice—and nothing more—and ultimately this is in the best interest of both the client and the citizenry at large.

Thanks in good part to the codified ignorance encouraged in the rules of ethics, the officer of the court role of the litigator is hidden. The client mask obliterates the distinction between the performing self and the moral self. The litigator becomes composed only of clients, constituted by performances, consumed by theatre. Animosity comes from the suggestion of empty integrity under the mask. Effacement of the moral self reappears in the typical litigator's indifference to the justice system and to reforms such as those proposed here. When litigators discuss such justice issues as in this book, they appear to have come from another planet—like a visiting foreign law professor—to observe justice as a theoretical exercise without any responsibility for its problems. Their investment in the status quo is first priority.

THE AGENDA

The preceding introspections prompt a number of diverse observations. Some problems suggest their own solutions. "Sandpapering" could be addressed by rules requiring tape recordings of interviews from start to finish and by affidavits regarding coaching. An alternative to the partisan expert is also easily available: the greater or even exclusive use of experts by the judiciary so that experts report objectively on behalf of neither party, a concept no stranger to the legal profession, whose members are wont, at convenient times, to laud themselves as officers of the court. Neutral experts would be less costly to the parties than partisan experts. Expertise would be made more available to the poor who now have difficulty hiring partisan experts. Neutral experts would also lessen the prostituting of opinions in a Ping-Pong volley.

Solutions in the tradition-immobilized area of "officer of the court" are hard to find and harder to sell. One of the first is to replace the exhausted "officer of the court" label with a new label like "minister of justice," redefined in a new Code of Ethics making the barrister's first duty to the law and to the court, the second to full knowledge about client conduct, and the third, the last, to the client.

The theatrics, gamesmanship, and ineptness of some litigators could well be remedied by an adaptation of the English barrister system to require bar certification, by examination, as a trial specialist as a prelude to court practice. In the present system, no special training is the prerequisite to the courtroom. Theatre beckons all aspiring actors. The result is often either gross ignorance of the complexities of trial work or, at the other extreme, gross abuse of these procedures by manipulative litigators. Both kinds of abuse could be lessened by requiring what universities require before giving tenure or what surgeons require of medical novices: a period of internship where the candidate with a general license works closely with a tenured, reputable trial specialist to be supervised and evaluated before being specially licensed for trial work. Such a certification program would fit comfortably with existing programs of specialization in criminal law, tax, and worker's compensation. More importantly, it would inculcate more than rhetoric and theatrics for the delicate process of litigation.

Like the great auk, lawyers render their effectiveness extinct through aberrant behavior in the courtroom. The judge is not the trial lawyer's only—or even most important—audience. Juries, and the public at large, are starved for a look at competent trial lawyers. As in a Disney true-life adventure, in which the humor of the gooney bird trying to take off only makes the majesty of the eagle more impressive, the difficulty of litigation makes all who see a true master of it humble in the face of mastery.

In the same vein, precisely because of the abuses described above, there is compelling need for a periodic ethical review of the litigation bar, not by re-passing another memorized code of ethics, but via peer review by opponents whose report card would, in effect, have the power to revoke the specialty license and revest only a general license requiring work under supervision.

The theatre and game models of litigation need to yield to truth-oriented models. Theatre connotes acting and *persona*; games connote gamesmanship. Neither is what the courts are about. The courtroom pursuit is a detective quest with resonance in a religious calling, like the quest for the Holy Grail, the sense of desert that explains why cases are decided by courts instead of by cards.

Perhaps, in the end, we must change the adversary system. The adversary system could in part adopt the Continental inquisitorial system's emphasis on cooperation, truth seeking, a more managerial judiciary, and a more passive barrister. At least in lower profile cases we would benefit from replacing ad-versarial shin kicking with a participatory system based on cooperation and mutual shaping of the result.

Finally, the arctic winter of the dogged litigator needs warming by more than fires of zealous advocacy. Old-timers remember lawyers who once were learned in the law. The leaders of the bar once read in the classical languages for pleasure and quoted the Bible and Shakespeare in their briefs as a matter of course. History, politics, ethics, physics, oratory, poetry, and criticism are as necessary as law to form an accomplished lawyer. One recalls Felix Frankfurter's urgings that "no one can be a truly competent lawyer unless he is a cultivated man. . . . The best way to prepare for the law is to come to the study of law as a well-read person." This literate portrait would do any litigator an honor appropriate for a newly inspired minister of justice who realizes that putting victory ahead of truth is a Pyrrhic victory at best.

NOTES

1. Curtis, "The Ethics of Advocacy," 4 *Stan. L. Rev.* 3, 9 (1951–52).

2. M. Katsh, *Taking Sides: Clashing Views on Controversial Legal Issues* 14, 2nd. ed. (Guilford, Conn.: Dushlein Pub. Group, 1986) (quoting Mahatma Gandhi's auto-biography).

3. 17A Ariz. Rev. Stat. Ann., Sup. Ct. Rules, Rules of Professional Conduct, Rule 42 (1986) [hereinafter Ariz. Rules of Professional Conduct].

4. The Watergate trial is the case nickname of *Senate Select Comm. on Pres. Campaign Activities v. Nixon*, 366 F. Supp. 51 (D.D.C. 1973); *In re Nixon*, 360 F. Supp. 1 (D.D.C. 1973).

5. For Judge Sirica's impressions of Watergate, see J. Sirica, *To Set the Record Straight* (New York: W. W. Norton, 1979).

6. See J. O'Connell, *Ending Insult to Injury* 7 (Urbana: University of Illinois Press, 1975); See also Will, "Law-Civilized and Savage," *Arizona Republic*, September 26,

1986, p. A15. The frequency of the conduct discussed in these pages is as uncertain to me as it is likely to be troubling to the conscientious litigator-reader. I have no statistics. My intuition is that while the vast majority of lawyers in my experience are ethically admirable, a significant minority engage in at least some of the practices discussed here. My respect for my profession remains undaunted; as Holmes said, one may criticize even what one reveres.

7. Neef and Nagel, "The Adversarial Nature of the American Legal System: A Historical Perspective," in A. Gerson, ed., *Lawyer Ethics* 73, 76 (1980).

8. Ibid.

9. Ibid. at 86 (quoting 6 J. Wigmore, *Evidence* § 1845, at 374–75 [McNaughton rev. ed. 1961]).

10. Ibid. (quoting J. Marshall, *Law and Psychology* 106 [1966]).

11. O'Connell, *Ending Insult to Injury* 7 (1975); Irving Younger, Remarks at Discovery Seminar in Phoenix, Ariz. (February 6, 1987) (repeatedly referring to the adversary system as a "game of chess").

12. O'Connell, *Ending Insult to Injury* 7 (1975); see also J. Sigler, *An Introduction to the Legal System* 121, 190–93 (Homewood, Ill.: Dorsey Press, 1968).

13. Covey, "Lawyer's Duty of Loyalty," 16 *Loyola University of Chicago L. J.*, 471, 473 (1985).

14. Ibid.

15. Ibid.

16. Ibid.

17. *Buffalo Courier Express*, January 21, 1979, p. E–1.

18. "Why Everybody Is Suing Everybody," *U.S. News & World Report*, December 4, 1978, p. 50.

19. Ibid.

20. *Georgia High School Ass'n. v. Waddell*, 248 Ga. 542, 292 S.E.2d 7 (1981).

21. See, e.g., Narol, "Protecting the Rights of Sports Officials," *Trial*, January 1987, p. 64; Narol, "Refereeing Athletic Officials' Calls is Ruled Out of Bounds for Courts," *National Law Journal*, September 23, 1986, p. 24; Narol, "Courts May Soon Be Asked to Be Monday Morning Quarterbacks," *National Law Journal*, March 19, 1984, p. 22.

22. See Thomasen, "Clergy Malpractice Goes to Court," *Liberty*, November–December 1985, p. 13.

23. *Newsweek*, January 28, 1985, p. 62.

24. Miles J. Zaremski, "Doctors and Lawyers as Adversaries: Stemming the Tide of Malpractice Litigation," *For the Defense*, October 1984, Vol. 26, No. 10, p. 22.

25. The 90 percent figure comes from Dr. James Sammons, Executive Vice President of the American Medical Association. "Malpractice Crisis," 71 *J. A.M.A.* 18 (June 1985) (quoting Dr. Sammons); see Zaremski, "Doctors and Lawyers as Adversaries," p. 22.

26. Of course, many times it is prudent to sue several potentially responsible parties. These instances are distinguishable from those in which defendants are named for the improper purposes discussed in this section.

27. In *Kinee v. Abraham Lincoln Fed. Sav. & Loan Ass'n.*, 365 F. Supp. 975 (E.D. Pa. 1973), plaintiff's counsel filed a shotgun complaint against 177 mortgage and thrift associations. He did not know which of the 177 collected taxes via escrow, so he sued every lending institution listed in the Philadelphia phone book. The *Kinee* court forced

plaintiff's counsel to pay all costs personally. Similarly, in *Textor v. Board of Regents*, 87 F.R.D. 751 (N.D. Ill. 1980), the woman's athletic director sued all members of the Mid-America Athletic Conference—nine different universities—even though it was clear she could not obtain personal jurisdiction over any defendant other than Northern Illinois University. The *Textor* court again assessed plaintiff's counsel the costs the innocent defendants incurred. See also Underwood, "Curbing Litigation Abuses," 56 *St. John's L. Rev.* 625, 640–41 (1981).

28. See Underwood, "Curbing Litigation Abuses," at 649. *In re National Student Marketing*, 445 F. Supp. 157 (D.C. Cir. 1978) provides a good example of frivolous counterclaims. In that multidistrict litigation, one group of defendants filed a counterclaim against the plaintiffs and their counsel, alleging fraud and professional misconduct in connection with a prior settlement. These charges were accompanied by defense counsel's request to the SEC to initiate disciplinary proceedings against the opposing attorney. There was not evidence of any fault on the plaintiff's part. After the plaintiffs won summary judgment, the trial judge awarded them attorneys fees under the then-existing "bad faith" standard. Defendants objected to being assessed fees on the ground that their counterclaim was not frivolous. In rejecting defendant's argument, the court noted that the timing of the counterclaims and other dilatory conduct by the defendants demonstrated that the counterclaim was motivated by a vindictive attitude and for the purpose of delay.

29. See "Dads Subject to False Molest Claims," *San Francisco Examiner*, October 9, 1986, p. B–1; "Sexual Abuse Charges Levied More Often in Custody Fights," *Arizona Business Gazette*, December 29, 1986, p. C–1; see also L. Spiegel, *A Question of Innocence: A True Story of False Accusation* (1986).

30. Ibid.

31. P. Stern, *Lawyers on Trial*, 152–54 (New York: Time Books, 1980).

32. Ibid. (quoting Bromley, "Judicial Control of Antitrust Cases," 23 F.R.D. 417 [1950]).

33. Ibid. at 152.

34. Ibid.

35. Ibid.

36. Ibid. at 153 (citing Bromley, "Judicial Control of Antitrust Cases," at 418–20).

37. Ibid.

38. Ibid. (quoting Bromley, "Judicial Control of Antitrust Cases").

39. Ibid.

40. Of course, criticism of lawyers who seek continuances for delay should not adversely reflect on those defense lawyers who are so overworked that they truly need continuances in order to effectively represent their clients.

41. The judge's only real alternative is to grant the requested continuance for a short time, and in a proper circumstance assess fees against the attorney.

42. *State v. Hansen*, 215 N.W.2d 249–50 (Iowa 1974).

43. J. Wigmore, *Evidence* §556 (Chadbourn rev. ed. 1979).

44. See, e.g., *Trial*, January 1987, p. 95.

45. Study found in *Science* (July 1988) and summarized in *Los Angeles Daily Journal* (July 4, 1988, Sec. I, p. 3).

46. M. Frankel, *Partisan Justice* 18 (New York: Hill and Wang, 1978); see also Symposium, "Discovery Abuse," 2 *Rev. of Litigation* 1 (1981).

47. See Ariz. R. Civ. P. 26.

48. Wayne Brazil, "The Adversary Character of Civil Discovery: A Critique and Proposals for Change," 31 *Vand. L. Rev.* 1295, 1323–25 (1978). Methods of concealment are legion. There are multiple techniques to shadowbox interrogatories. The thrust is evasion and incompleteness. Any lawyer who can't answer interrogatories without giving an opponent useful information is not worth his salt. As one Chicago lawyer put it: "In the adversary system it's one group's job to get information and the other's not to give it," for discovery is "a game to see how much you can hide." Marvin E. Frankel, formerly a federal judge, drawing on thirteen years on the bench, has written:

The discovery process itself, with rules that frequently are (or are made to be) intricate and abstruse, becomes the occasion for expensive contests, producing libraries full of opinions. Where the object always is to beat every plowshare into a sword, the discovery procedure is employed variously as weaponry. A powerful litigant, in a complex case, may impose costly, even crushing, burdens by demands for files, pretrial testimony of witnesses, and other forms of discovery. (M. Frankel, *Partisan Justice*, at 18.)

49. Ibid.

50. Ibid.

51. 102 F.R.D. 472 (S.D. Fla. 1984).

52. Ibid.

53. Ibid. at 488. See also the similar 1987 conduct of the attorneys in note 80.

54. *Hawk v. Superior Court*, 42 Cal. App. 3d 108, 125, 116 Cal. Rptr. 713, 724 (1974) (counsel was held in contempt).

55. *Marsh v. State*, 180 Ind. App. 175, 387 N.E.2d 1346, 1347 (1979).

56. Ibid. at 1348.

57. Ibid.

58. 3 S. Goldstein, *Trial Techniques* §19.58 (1984).

59. J. Ehrlich, *The Lost Art of Cross-Examination* 100 (New York: Putnam, 1970).

60. 3A J. Wigmore, *Evidence* §983, at 841 (Chadbourn rev. ed. 1970).

61. M. Freedman, *Lawyers' Ethics in the Adversary System*, 40–41 (Indianapolis: Bobbs-Merrill, 1975).

62. L. Lake, *How to Cross-Examine Witnesses Successfully* (Englewood Cliffs, N.J.: Prentice-Hall, 1957).

63. Ibid. at 3.

64. James W. McElhaney, "Dealing with Dirty Tricks," 7 *Litigation* 45, 46 (Winter 1981).

65. John Wilkes, "Life in the Fast Lane: The Adversary Ethics of an Ex-Lawyer," 7 *Criminal Defense* 11–12 (March–April 1980).

66. *Richardson v. Employers Liab. Assurance Corp.*, 25 Cal. App. 3d 232, 242, 102 Cal. Rptr. 547, 554 (1972).

67. Ibid.

68. Ibid. at 244, 102 Cal. Rptr. at 554–55.

69. Ibid. at 244, 102 Cal. Rptr. at 555.

70. The example comes from A. Morrill, *Trial Diplomacy* 58 (2d ed., Chicago: Court Practice Institute, 1972).

71. The term comes from *Smith v. Wright*, 512 S.W.2d 943, 947 (Ky. Ct. App. 1974).

72. Ibid.

73. *Edwards v. Sears, Roebuck & Co.*, 512 F.2d 276, 283–84 (1975).

74. *Dukes v. State*, 356 So.2d 873, 875 (Fla. Ct. App. 1978). See also F. Celebrezze, "Prosecutorial Misconduct," *Trial*, September, 1987, p. 55.

75. *For the Defense*, January 1988, at 14.

76. Curtis, supra note 1 at 9.

77. M. Freedman, *Lawyers' Ethics in the Adversary System* 53.

78. See Philip Shuchman, "The Question of Lawyer's Deceit," 53 *Conn. B.J.* 101, 106–18 (1979): accord, Shuchman, "Relations Between Lawyers," in *Ethics and Advocacy* (1978).

79. *Metro Data Systems, Inc. v. Durango Sys. Inc.*, 597 F. Supp. 244 (D. Ariz. 1984).

80. Ibid. at 246–47. The circumstances of the fee request in this case arguably can also be construed as nothing worse than clerical carelessness. A 1987 federal case dealing with copyright infringement illustrates the extent to which some lawyers go in misleading courts and opponents. That court found that

the two lawyers, Voortman and Spiller began with the relatively minor, but nonetheless seminal, failure to disclose material facts by failing to "seasonably" amend material interrogatory answers, as required by Fed. R. Civ. P. 26(e). They then misled the court by omitting material facts in statements they made to the court and to others. They continued by contemptuously disobeying this court's orders. Finally, and most shockingly, Spiller and Voortman fabricated false evidence in an admitted but ill-fated attempt to defeat this court's power to compel DeMunbrun's deposition in Chicago.

Virtually all of Voortman's and Spiller's improper conduct furthered a scheme to keep DeMunbrun from being called as a witness in the trial of Case No. 82 C 4585. Voortman and Spiller acted because Voortman believed that DeMunbrun would not be a good trial witness for LPM. In order to keep DeMunbrun from testifying, LPM's and Echlin's counsel concealed from Clark and the court the facts that DeMunbrun was no longer LPM's president and would be physically outside the subpoena power of the court at the time of the trial. It is clear that both Voortman and Spiller concealed the change in DeMunbrun's position and the location of his domicile in the hope that Clark would not serve DeMunbrun with a trial subpoena before DeMunbrun left the Chicago area. Their scheme, however, was frustrated by the fact that DeMunbrun continued as director of LPM. Voortman and Spiller tried to rectify this glitch in their artifice by falsifying minutes of the 1985 LPM annual meeting. (See *Clark Equipment Co. v. Lift Parts Manufacturing*, No. 82 C 4585, N.D. Illinois (memorandum decision, October 26, 1987.)

81. See Richard Burke, "An Essay on Lying and Deceit in the Practice of Law," 38 *Ark. L. Rev.* 1, 20–21 (1984).

82. Thurman, "Limits to the Adversary System: Interests That Outweigh Confidentiality," 5 *J. Legal Prof.* 5, 19 (1980).

83. See note 81, supra.

84. *Lying: Moral Choice in Public and Private Life* (New York: Pantheon Books, 1978).

85. Ariz. Rules of Professional Conduct ER 3.1. This rule states that

[a] lawyer shall not bring or defend a proceeding, or assert or controvert an issue therein, unless there is a basis for doing so that is not frivolous, which includes a good faith argument for an extension, modification or reversal of existing law. . . .

Comment 2 to Rule 3.1 states that an action is frivolous if the client desires to have the action taken (1) primarily for the purpose of harassing or maliciously injuring a person, (2) the lawyer is unable either to make a good faith argument on the merits of the action taken or (3) the lawyer is unable to support the action taken by a good faith argument for an extension, modification, or reversal of existing law.

86. Fed. R. Civ. P. 11. Rule 11 provides in part:

Every pleading, motion, and other paper of a party represented by an attorney shall be signed by at least one attorney of record, in his individual name. . . . The signature of an attorney . . . constitutes a certificate by him that he has read the pleading, motion or other paper: that to the best of his knowledge, information, and belief formed after reasonable inquiry it is well grounded in fact and is warranted by existing law or a good faith argument for the extension, modification, or reversal of existing law, and that it is not interposed for any improper purpose, such as to harass or to cause unnecessary delay or needless increase in the cost of litigation.

87. Ariz. Rules of Professional Conduct ER 1.2. ER 1.2(d) provides that

(d) A lawyer shall not counsel a client to engage, or assist a client, in conduct that the lawyer knows is criminal or fraudulent, but a lawyer may discuss the legal consequences of any proposed course of conduct with a client and may counsel or assist a client to make a good faith effort to determine the validity, scope, meaning or application of the law.

88. Ariz. Rules of Professional Conduct ER 1.3. The rule provides that "a lawyer shall act with reasonable diligence and promptness in representing a client."

89. Ariz. Rules of Professional Conduct ER 3.3, ER 3.5. ER 3.3 provides, in part:

A lawyer shall not knowingly:

1. make a false statement of material fact or law to a tribunal;
2. fail to disclose a material fact to a tribunal when disclosure is necessary to avoid assisting a criminal or fraudulent act by the client;
3. fail to disclose to the tribunal legal authority in the controlling jurisdiction known to the lawyer to be directly adverse to the position of the client and not disclosed by opposing counsel; or
4. offer evidence that the lawyer knows to be false. If a lawyer has offered material evidence and comes to know of its falsity, the lawyer shall take reasonable remedial measures. . . .

c. a lawyer may refuse to offer evidence that the lawyer reasonably believes is false.

Comment 3 to ER 3.3 states that "the underlying concept is that legal argument is a discussion seeking to determine the legal premises properly applicable to the case."

ER 3.5 states that

A lawyer shall not:

a. seek to influence a judge, juror, prospective juror or other official by means prohibited by law;
b. communicate ex parte with such a person except as permitted by law; or
c. engage in conduct intended to disrupt a tribunal.

The comment makes clear that disruptive conduct may be considered improper influence upon a tribunal.

90. Ariz. Rules of Professional Conduct ER 3.4. This rules provides, in part:

A lawyer shall not:

a. unlawfully obstruct another party's access to evidence or unlawfully alter, destroy or conceal a document or other material having potential evidentiary value. A lawyer shall not counsel or assist another person to do any such act;

b. falsify evidence, counsel or assist a witness to testify falsely, or offer an inducement to a witness that is prohibited by law;

c. knowingly disobey any obligation under the rules of a tribunal except for an open refusal based on an assertion that no valid obligation exists;

d. in pretrial procedure, make a frivolous discovery request or fail to make reasonably diligent effort to comply with a legally proper discovery request by an opposing party;

. . .

f. request a person other than a client to refrain from voluntarily giving relevant information to another party unless; (1) the person is a relative or an employee or other agent of a client; and (2) the lawyer reasonably believes that the person's interests will not be adversely affected by refraining from giving such information.

Note that discovery games may not only subject an attorney to disciplinary action under the *Model Rules of Professional Responsibility*, but may also result in financial penalties and contempt citation. See, e.g., Fed. R. Civ. P. 37.

91. Ariz. Rules of Professional Conduct ER 3.4 and 3.5.

92. Ariz. Rules of Professional Conduct ER 1.2 and 3.3.

93. *California Lawyer*, November 1988, p. 26.

94. G. Spence, "Questioning the Adverse Witness," 10 *Litigation* 13 (Winter 1984).

95. See, e.g., *Silkwood v. Kerr-McGee Corp.*, 769 F.2d 1451 (10th Cir. 1985), cert. denied, 106 S.Ct. 1947 (1986).

96. Spence, "Questioning the Adverse Witness," at 13.

97. Ibid.

98. J. Frank, *Courts on Trial: Myth and Reality in American Justice* 40 (Princeton, N.J.: Princeton Univ. Press, 1950) (quoting Judge Learned Hand).

99. For a criticism of "the 'dramaturgic approach' to social experience," see S. Messinger, "Life as Theater: Some Notes on the Dramaturgic Approach to Social Reality," 25 *Sociometry* 98 (1962).

100. J. Sartre, *Being and Nothingness* 59 (H. Barnes trans. 1956).

101. J. Rousseau, *Politics and the Arts: Letter to M. D'Alembert on the Theater* 79 (A. Bloom trans. 1960). In language that may be applied directly to lawyers, Rousseau condemned the actor's profession as

a trade in which he performs for money, submits himself to the disgrace and the affronts that others buy the right to give him, and puts his person publicly on sale. I beg every sincere man to tell if he does not feel in the depths of his soul that there is something servile and base in this traffic of oneself. (Ibid.)

Rousseau's complaint echoes earlier Puritan attacks on the acting profession, which were couched in specifically theologial terms. Consider William Prynne, *Histrio-Mastix. The Player's Scourge or Actor's Tragedie* (London, 1633), p. 159.

William Prynne's diatribe against actors:
God requires truth in inward parts; in the soule, the affections yea, in the habits, speeches, gestures, in the whole intire man. Now this counterfeiting of persons, affections, manners, vices, sexes, and the like, which is inseparably incident to the acting of Playes, as it transforms the Actors into what they are not; so it infuseth falshood into every part of soule and body, as all hyprocrisie doth; in causing them to seeme that in outward appearance which they are not in truth; therefore it must needs bee odious to the God of truth. . . .

102. J. Rousseau, *Politics and the Arts: Letter to M. D'Alembert on the Theatre* at 80–81.

103. *Dictionary of Proverbs*. See also R. Post, "On the Popular Image of the Lawyer: Reflections in a Dark Glass," 75 *Cal. L. Rev.* 379 and following (1987).

104. P. Fay, "Attorneys as Officers of the Court," *33 Fed. Bar Journal* No. 6, 235 (July–August, 1986).

105. G. Sharwood, *Professional Ethics* 168 (1876).

Conclusion: Waiting for Justice

> The system! I am told on all hands, it's the system. I mustn't look to individuals. It's the system.... I musn't go to Mr. Tulkinghorn, the solicitor in Lincoln's Inn Fields, and say to him when he makes me furious by being so cool and satisfied—as they all do, for I know they gain by it while I lose, don't I?—I musn't say to him, "I will have something out of someone for my ruin, by fair means or foul!" He is not responsible. It's the system. But, if I do no violence to any of them...I will accuse the individual workers of that system against me, face to face, before the great eternal bar!
> —Charles Dickens, *Bleak House*

> The old order changeth, yielding place to new.
> —Tennyson, *King Arthur*

The preceding chapters illustrate contradictory behavior in the legal establishment. Like the seven deadly sins of the Middle Ages, these problems illustrate ironic self-deception in a profession that prides itself on unmasking deception:

- The same bar that claims to be a profession to a growing extent abdicates public service for the pursuit of money.

- Legal education prepares its graduates to enter an increasingly statutory and administrative world with the mind-set of nineteenth century, common law combat litigation.

- The bar exam that professes to measure ethics and competency tests primarily memory and logic; it determines competency, ethics, and character and fitness on a largely standardless, once-in-a-lifetime basis.

- Our halls of justice that otherwise punish extortion often subordinate justice to victory because of extortionate court costs, delays, and manipulation.

- Officers of the court—lawyers—sworn to give first allegiance to the courts often twist litigation procedures to serve their clients' purposes but not that of the law or the courts.

Thus the irony: the group claiming anxiously to be a profession becomes increasingly nonprofessional. The establishment dedicated to the rule of law becomes lawless, its skills to reveal others' deception unable to reveal its own, its pursuit of justice weakened by its own injustice. Like lax medieval monasteries, which they historically resemble, the bar and bench have fallen short of their calling to the point where one can question what they really do "profess." They need reform today as much as in Bentham's day. No abbot, pope, Martin Luther, or Bentham appears to lead the reformation. The best-placed leaders— the Supreme Court's chief justice and the president of the American Bar Association—have often been content with calming platitudes, putting layers of clean diapers over ones needing to be changed. What is most needed is a renaissance of moral soul to inspire pursuit of justice rather than victory or money.

In the absence of other leadership, the front-line responsibility to shepherd justice lies with the judiciary. It must bear much of the blame for feeding the dinosaur now mired in the mud. Much of the judicial soul has dissolved into paper. Roberto Unger's comments appear to fit the collective judiciary:

When we came, they were like a priesthood that had lost their faith and kept their jobs. They stood in tedious embarrassment before cold altars. But we turned away from those altars, and found the mind's opportunity in the heart's revenge.[1]

We judges have failed to prescribe restrained rules for damages, to control attorney fees, to discourage gamesmanship, to eliminate delay and costs, to pursue, above all, a sense of justice. So much power and tradition clings to our robes that it is difficult to see the centuries of custom, pretense, and boilerplate that cling underneath them. The Texas judge who took the $10,000 campaign contribution from the Pennzoil lawyer in the Texaco case discussed in chapter 4 saw no impropriety. What was offered him had been offered to and accepted by his colleagues from the dawn of judicial time and repeatedly approved by his appellate brethren. To lay eyes, the contribution, of course, is a bribe. In the rationalizing judicial tradition, however, the contribution is nothing but the time-honored, broad ranging "cooperation" between bench and bar.

Tradition can be a curse as well as a blessing, for it brings its own blinders. Here Husserl's *epoché* reveals in the ancient bench-bar fraternity a strange role reversal: in order to play a leadership role a judge must please the people to be led, and must seek their support to the extreme of accepting their plaudits and money. We judges thereby become lawyers' mistresses. Tradition has made us a school of umpires who find it hard to make difficult calls without reference to judicial evaluation polls, elections, popularity, and the popular demagoguery of being tough on crime. For decades, if not longer, we have abdicated responsibility to "tradition" for this role reversal and have therein lost control of courtrooms, dockets, litigation tactics, discovery abuse, extortionate demands, and excessive verdicts. As a body, we have failed to keep the courthouse open to the general public and to sustain public confidence to enter it proudly. We justify Heidegger's criticism in *Sein und Zeit* of having fallen into an everydayness of custom that has caused forgetfulness of the justice whose place we are.

To the extent they exist at all, remedies here include special judicial preparation, managerial training, leadership skills, a creative divorce from attorney or legislative control, selection by nonpoliticians on a nonpartisan, nonpolicy basis—and, not least of all, a renaissance in the judiciary of the quest for the absent guest of the courthouse, justice itself.

WHERE IS JUSTICE?

This need for a renewed sense of calling invites the following brief search into larger, less resolvable values of jurisprudence. Judges characteristically do not have articulated theories of jurisprudence. They do not keep copies of Kant or Bentham under their robes for ready reference. What follows here is no replacement for Kant or Bentham but a modest aperçu to suggest that both judging and lawyering involve in their best moments a pursuit of justice itself. The jurisprudential slices offered here are neither whole nor definitive but only passing cafeteria offerings, admittedly subjective, for thinking about where to look for justice.

Law and Economics

According to the law and economics school popularized, among others, by Coase and Posner, every legal decision bears economic freight. A judicial decision is a bargaining chip in a poker game played by those upon whom these decisions fall. These decisions, of whatever kind, seek to maximize options toward wealth, the best target for legal decisions, or at least the best proxy for utility because most conducive to happiness. Wealth maximization either increases happiness or promotes an attractive mix of happiness and protection of rights.

Judge Posner has called the principle of wealth maximizing the "capitalist conception of justice." According to this conception, the ethical basis for determining whether a particular state of affairs is "just" is determined by the single criterion of whether it promotes wealth maximization. Applied to judicial decisions, Posner's principle of wealth maximization means that the decision maker should decide in a manner that will bring about an increase in social wealth measured in dollars. For example, judges should resolve conflicting claims to common resources so that resources are shifted to most productive uses as determined by consumers' willingness to pay.[2]

Economists see this wealth model as a definitive account of decision making. It finds its roots in nineteenth-century utilitarianism, the industrial revolution, and the common law origins of property, torts, contracts, and corporations. Even today these areas of the law reflect laissez-faire attitudes of enhancing, or at least conserving, wealth apart from those who threaten its accumulation.

The law and economics movement raises value assumptions disquieting from both a judicial and philosophical perspective. Human perfection in this view seems spent in the pursuit of wealth for its own sake. Wealth, the assumed greatest human good, comes via calculating costs and benefits as an economist does. Whether it is to create one's own wealth or to distribute it equally, the result appears the same: wealth is the goal rational people should care most about.

One may question whether the true motivation of legislatures and judges is really the maximization of wealth or, instead, a variety of competing motivations, some of which seem inconsistent with wealth. To pose the question differently, would legislators interested in maximizing their own wealth enact laws that maximize the wealth of society as a whole? Both legislators and judges at the front end of the legal decision could easily make larger short-run profits through conduct financially negative to the larger society. The motivation of honest legislators and judges does not seem consciously wealth-oriented; in fact, they seem often explicitly oriented to the public good in such welfare decisions as funding public defenders, increasing health services, legal aid, and a whole panoply of civil rights decisions that drain the public treasury to provide benefits to persons unlikely ever to reimburse that treasury or their own. Some public decisions simply do not maximize options toward wealth but actually decrease wealth in preference to other goals: a sentence of life imprisonment; a death sentence; an executive order emancipating slaves or reimbursing Asian-Americans for unjust imprisonment.

A painful decision of my own several years ago invalidated a $4.3-million computer contract with the state lottery for violation of the open meeting law. The state lost the contract and the computer companies lost hardware and programs approaching that sum, and even the betting public lost its game for a year. The goal of that judicial decision was hardly wealth maximization but, instead, the economically inefficient principle that the public has a right of access to public agency decisions. Such a wealth-wasting decision can be squared with the wealth maximization generalization only by saying that one or the other is wrong.

Psychological problems arise with any view of human nature as primarily wealth-oriented. Wealth does not seem what we humans always act toward. At times we make conscious decisions toward goods that involve poverty but promote desirable goals that make the poverty unimportant: service with the poor, a career in the Peace Corps, public service, or working as a teacher, artist, or social activist. Persons who make these kinds of decisions see wealth as arbitrary and instrumental only, at best a mere means to ends more enriching than wealth.

From a social perspective, a society composed of people obsessed with wealth may be an entrepreneurial society but not one that nurtures humane interests such as the arts or altruistic service to others. Such a society seems to need police agencies or rules to restrain competing demands for wealth. If wealth is the ultimate good, these police agencies may well be subverted by bribes— much, as an ironic footnote, as today's legal profession loses professionalism in its raging pursuit of wealth rather than service. What the law and economics movement inadvertently may explain best is the very demise of professionalism in its own ranks when wealth outstrips higher ends such as justice.

Law and economics seem to explain wealth-intensive decisions in wealth-intensive areas of the law such as corporate law and antitrust. Its extension across the judicial landscape seems too elastic. If justice equates with wealth, injustice equates with poverty. Is the just society compared only to Holmes' "bad man" restrained by police and courts, or rather composed of persons seeking virtue for its own sake regardless of wealth? What is missing in the capitalist conception of justice is the notion of distribution. Instead of being a matter of accumulation of wealth, justice is a matter of proper distribution of wealth *and* rights. By ignoring choices of distribution, ethical issues concerning disparities in economic power—as well as reasonable expectations of security—become largely irrelevant for legal analysis, which in turn devolves into market analysis, just as legal education shrinks to a variant of Langdell's "science of fundamental principles," albeit economic ones.[3]

An important task for an a priori legal psychology is not to derive legal rules from a principle of wealth maximization but to first determine the human qualities furthered by such an economics. For the courts and the bar, as with human nature, neither professionalism nor virtue seems for sale for money.

Critical Legal Studies

This book finds some superficial affinity with the scholars loosely called the critical legal studies group, or "crits." Deconstructionism shows some affinity insofar as the crits find fundamental dualities such as objective/subjective that underlie the development of legal values and cause indeterminancy. The crits show a leftist tilt in arguments that the legal system perpetuates hierarchies of power and wealth—oddly, the very position that economics scholars praise. To deconstructionist crits, the present legal system achieves unfair results because it places form over substance and tradition over equality by using polar doctrines that reflect continuing feudal master-slave polarities. The crits' larger complaint is that the epistemological project of finding a foundation for rationalism has been in retreat for one hundred years in all fields of knowledge except for a few ideologically petrified areas such as law, which still resists the relativizing spirit. In order to get the maximum support for this story, crits depict all legal theory as rigid, rationalist, and ideological.

Vulgar Marxism, containing theories of class conspiracy or a psychoanalytic analysis of semantic legal reasoning might support the crits. One wonders, however, if our legal institutions, with their real shortcomings, readily reveal either rationalism or foreordained Marxism. One of the ironies is that *both* the middle class and the poor are denied realistic access to our civil courts, while the criminal poor are afforded repeated, free access to trial and appellate courts, and endless petitions for review. Delay, extortion, and complexity cut across all social classes, including rich litigants. Psychological coercion in settling lawsuits may well support the crits' view of manipulation, but not the crits' conclusion about rationalization or about the class-justice of rich against poor. The imbalance does not seem primarily class-oriented or rationalist but caused instead by simpler things such as lack of parity in legal skill and lack of court access. Marxist ideological dialectics of master-slave, in sum, poorly equates with the plaintiff/defendant, subjective/objective or in-court/out-of-court polarity.

The collateral strain in some crits, particularly Unger and Kennedy, to trash judicial decisions seems to rest on the assertion that all such decisions are necessarily explainable by political criteria outside the judge's stated rationale. Legal decisions therefore show policy and nothing more; though the decision is embedded in rules and procedures, these details really do not count for as much in the eventual decision as the judge's personal policy. Some crits go on to deny the rational determinancy of all legal reasoning: judges merely mouth rules as a cover for totally arbitrary policy. These crits exhibit a general intellectual cynicism that teaches the emptiness of the ideal of truth and the pointlessness of efforts to attain it, not to mention broadly impugning all judicial integrity.

Lurking throughout the crits' legal landscape is the bramble of deconstruction, whose fruit is both sweet and sour. The critique of rigid rationalism in the legal tradition of the West has the benefit of suggesting legitimate gray areas between the traditional black-white polarities of right/wrong, win/lose. In making this valid point, however, critical scholars go on to trash a rationalist theory of language to the point where, as in the *Pacific Gas and Electric* case discussed in chapter 4, even carefully crafted words lose reliable, constant meaning. The result of this deconstruction attack is that words—the very skin of the law—become so ambiguous as to be meaningless. In the end, law as communication becomes an impossible human project and yields its place to law as rank coercion. In the process, justice ceases to involve moral persuasion and becomes equated with political might.

Conscientious judges of flesh and blood likely find the crits' cynical description of political decision making hard to recognize, if not degrading. Apart from rank political appointees with a campaign platform, few judges decide cases the way social engineers eradicate slums, with a goal in mind first and then an effort to chop a path to get there. This kind of agenda is foreign to the judicial oath. This kind of activism belongs to politicians, not judges. That judicial decisions illustrate policy and nothing more seems generally true only if "policy" means interpreting legislative purpose. Unlike the common law era, judicial decisions today are almost all based on interpretation of conflicting statutes or cases. Rare is an issue posed without statutory or case guidance; a question of first impression is a novelty like a hole in one.

The scope of honest judicial policy is really severely limited. Statutory and case interpretation is policy only in the sense that a conscientious judge tries to find and follow the purpose of the statutes and cases involved. When these purposes conflict, weighing of the scope of each comes into play, but this weighing is hardly an activist creation of policy *ex nihilo*. The "tabula rasa" world where judges, in Nietzsche's words, become "walking legislators" seems a remnant of New Deal activism. It is only the activist social reformer promoted by Arthur Miller whose judicial decisions embody explicit social policy; most judges are not activist in this social engineering model. The true issue reverts to whence and how legislative policy is found in statute and cases: what interpretive tools should guide and shape exegetical "policy" (e.g., original intent?) remains the harder, unexplored question.

To the extent that the crits' attribution of rank personal policy to judicial decisions is true, it constitutes a damning indictment of the antediluvian election of judges on popular, partisan, or "platform" bases. These judges subordinate their impartiality to "policy"—a policy that, like all agendas, is as much closed minded as it is open.

POSITIVISM

The heirs of Thomas Hobbes and John Austin see law and morals as totally separate. Law consists only of the enacted law that derives its coercive effect from external enforcement mechanisms such as police and prison. Laws thus are valid without regard to moral goodness or badness. Law is neutral and value-free; it becomes confused when mixed with social, political, and moral values, and so it must be "purified"—to use Kelsen's terminology—by being stripped of ethical, social, scientific, or historical considerations. Positivism thus involves a commitment to obedience to law as an end in itself, not simply as a means to an end.

In a judicial context, positivism leads to a mechanical application of written law, a kind of legal formalism, where the judge makes no value choices but acts only as a calculation machine or phonograph repeating exactly what the written law declares. In Blackstone's metaphor, the positivist judge becomes the "living oracle of the law" in the non-Blackstone sense of being a passive transmitter rather than interpreter. It is not that the positivist is unconcerned with justice and law's relation to it; rather, the positivist refuses to accept that value is more than an adjective and part of the law's very essence. The supposed neutrality of positivism seems merely a device to legitimate an internal ideology. Positivism is an essentially formal doctrine of obedience by coercion to any authority having enforcement power.

Former Supreme Court nominee Robert Bork eloquently epitomizes positivism. Bork identifies a court's role in terms not of restraint but of moral neutrality: "the judiciary has no role to play other than that of applying the statutes in a fair and impartial manner."[4] Legislatures make value judgments, not courts, and it is the duty of the courts to "accept any value choice . . . made in the framing of the Constitution."[5] He rejects both substantive due process and substantive equal protection, stating that courts are inferior to the will of legislatures whenever the Constitution is silent. In his words:

> There is no principled way in which anyone can define the spheres in which liberty is required and the spheres in which equality is required. These are matters of morality, or judgment, or prudence. They belong, therefore, to the political community.[6]

That no particular values are implied in positivism seems specious; its apparent neutrality masks the desire to achieve through obedience the political goals embodied in any given regime's written law. Since positivism operates a pedigree test in order to determine valid law, the source of these rules must be historical, be it custom, case law, or legislation. Present and future conduct is thus regulated by the past statement of original intent, which imposes a straitjacket on adaptation.

In order for jurisprudence to be more than a conjunction of lexicographies conjoined with local histories, positivism must decide what is to count as law for purposes of description. For example, the law of the international community like the United Nations, Common Market, or World Court can look to no sovereign for its enforcement. Similarly, there are no sanctions to our Constitution or its amendments. The enactments of these bodies represent law without enforceability and hence, to the positivist, no law at all—a conclusion most governments, unlike H.L.A. Hart, would likely reject.

Despite its claim of value neutrality, positivism seems unable to escape implicit value judgments. H.L.A. Hart himself is illustrative. In viewing the working of the legal system through the eyes of its functionaries, he, like Bork, suggests that it be seen from the top down rather than from the bottom up—an explicit "authority-power" model. To adopt this model carries with it a suggestion of dominance and submission. A "subjects" model, by contrast, would focus on how authority depends on what it does and not merely on its formal pedigree (e.g., whether it stems from a constitution). Such a model carries with it an entirely different, more artificial value, but in either model, the hierarchy alone implies value.[7]

It would seem that whenever the value preferences of the theorist insinuate themselves in positivism, the latter enters the normative field and loses its professed purity. If the entry of valuations is inevitable, positivism is an alloy of both positive and normative elements, for added to the positivist task of pedigree analysis is the normative task of justifying the implicit valuations of command, obedience, and order intertwined in the hierarchy.

In the end, there is no neutral matrix for positive law; valuation and participatory roles are built into any pecking order. Whatever else positivism contributes, it generates a rhetoric that functions to forward particular policies of unthinking submission to power, yet it would deny to those subject to that power the opportunity to evaluate the acts of the sovereign or even to replace the sovereign.

If law and morals are separate, judgment on the merits of a judicial decision becomes impossible, or at least univocal. In positivism, we are left unable to condemn or revolt from laws such as slavery, genocide, racism, or even disproportionate sentences for crimes, such as wholesale vehicle forfeitures for small amounts of drugs carried by a passenger. If the Nuremberg trials mean anything, it is that the judicial vocation, like the human vocation, involves, at rare times, more than merely following orders.

History teaches a recurring Januslike discomfort with the positivist view of law. The assumption that justice can be attained through the written law carries an equally powerful counterbelief, contrary to positivism, that positive law often perverts justice. The West's legal history shows the need to critique the written law by a standard outside itself. The consequence is an ambivalent love/hate, Scylla/Charybdis relationship between law and justice: one part of the tradition—positivism—urges blind commitment to law as the sole route to justice, and another part of the tradition glorifies the critique of written law via efforts to improve it. This tendency to reduce justice exclusively to positive law, thereby cheapening the ideal, is the dark side of the commitment to justice through law. Positivism deserves our oaths of allegiance to the written law as long as that law is morally good; it deserves no allegiance when it puts blinders around our eyes to urge mindless following of immoral orders for their own sake.

Sociological Jurisprudence of "Interests"

One of the reigning dogmas of our Gallup poll era, sociological jurisprudence, claims that legislative and judicial decisions reflect and accommodate competing interests of adverse segments of society. Much of the theory comes from Roscoe Pound and through him from earlier German writers, especially Rudolf von Jhering, Josepf Kohler, and Friedrich Nietzsche. The ideas of "promotion" and "balancing" of interests belong largely to him, as do such modern developments as the creation of political action committees. "Social engineering" sees justice as an adjustment of social demands with the least waste, achieved via a weighing and balancing of competing cultural interests.

One cannot exaggerate the influence of Nietzsche both on Pound and indirectly on sociological jurisprudence. His writings are a kind of Rubicon for sociological jurisprudence. More than a hundred years ago he laid down what is now publicly accepted: culture cannot be reconciled with justice and truth. Nietzsche's ridicule falls on those who want to maintain any content to justice or truth. Justice does not exist apart from cultural values. As a cultural relativist, he saw that culture means competition rather than peace, cruelty rather than compassion. Cultures fight wars with each other because values can be asserted only by overcoming others, not by reasoning with them. There is no communication about the highest values. Culture means war against chaos and against other cultures. The cultural relativist cares for culture, not truth. Nietzsche formulated the new jurisprudence when he said, "A good war makes sacred almost any cause." Causes are values simply because they are asserted. Self-assertion, not justice or a clear view of rectitude, is the crucial element in evaluation. Like the language that accompanies and expresses it, a culture is a set of mere accidents that add up to a coherent meaning. Nature is banished from the study of humankind, for it can only be understood as a myth, even though the very notion of culture is inconceivable without the prior elaboration of the state of nature.

A culture generates its own principles, particularly its highest ones, with no authority above it. If there were such an authority, the unique way of life born of its Dionysian principle would be undermined. Human inequality is proved by the fact that there is no common experience accessible in principle to all except the culture which replaces nature. Such dualities as authentic/inauthentic, profound/superficial, creator/created replace true/false or right/wrong distinctions.

Profoundly influenced by Nietzsche, Max Weber becomes the lantern-bearer for societal interests. Societies need myths, not legal science, for they succeed, as do our political candidates, by charisma and self-assertion, not by merit. Weber's three forms of legitimacy—tradition, reason, and charisma—mean that all societies require persona-type domination to make order emerge from the chaos of competing cultures, each of which, of course, is equally valid in the absence of a normative nature.

Like Nietzsche, Weber denies the rationality or objectivity of values. There are only "decisions," not "deliberations," imposed on a chaotic world by powerful personalities like politicians and judges. Values that make the world are acts primarily of the will. Such acts are unreasonable because they are based on nothing but will assertion, i.e., organized social pressure. Lack of will, not lack of understanding, becomes the crucial human defect. Commitment is *the* moral virtue because it indicates the seriousness of the agent. It is Pascal's wager, no longer on God's existence but on belief in oneself and one's chosen social goals. Commitment itself values the values. Not love of truth but intellectual sincerity characterizes the authentic state of mind.

Nietzsche and Weber prepared sociological jurisprudence by helping to jettison good and evil without offering judgmental alternatives other than culture. Talcott Parsons makes Weber and Nietzsche routine; he sanctifies the replacement of right/wrong with degrees of social pressure. Thus, in the United States as in the Germany of the turn of the century, a new generation is now educated "beyond good and evil" to get legal rights by the exercise of *will* in conflict with other wills, with social strength or aggression, not rationality, as the barometer of the rectitude of their cause. This ideology is squarely in our legal roots.

As early as 1892, Professor Christopher G. Tiedeman underscored the limitations of the right/wrong dogma. What he argued has become the common wisdom. *Roe v. Wade* is a triumph, of sorts, of this sociological jurisprudence. The majority opinion argues that under the Constitution the allocation of rights is prior to any account of the good. Rights have no foundation other than the positive law, which, in turn, has no task other than to arbitrate competing social interests. The law's continued existence depends upon force alone, which, in the case of abortion, is exercised under the charismatic doctrines of privacy and health. Thus the decision's fascination with divisions into threes, a novel Caesarean approach to abortion. As Caesar divided Gaul into three parts, so too is fetal development divided. Each competing interest gets a part of the baby: the prochoice activist gets the first trimester, prolife activists the last, with the state in the elastic middle. This tripart division finds its roots neither in legal precedent nor in medicine, and certainly not in King Solomon, but instead in the willingness to placate competing social interests without making any hard "true/false" or "right/wrong" judgments.

Contrary to Pound, there may be social demands that are not good to satisfy. Social engineering needs to be supplemented with protection against the hurricane of social demands. In his "jural postulates of civilization," Pound is forced in the end to concede some basic precepts: we must assume that others will not commit intentional aggressions; that one may control one's own discoveries, the product of one's labor, and what is acquired under the existing economic order; that others will deal in good faith; that people will not cause unreasonable injury.

These postulates reveal a covert appeal to natural law precepts to govern the hurricane of social interests. Sociological jurisprudence is thus upended by the realization that Nietzsche's chaos of cultures must be judged by normative principles beyond mere mass demand. Even cultural differences ultimately imply real differences in fundamental beliefs about good and evil.

Sociological jurisprudence has subtle lessons for the judiciary. What emphatically does *not* work in a judicial context, contrary to Justice Richard Neely,[8] is deciding cases on the basis of mass demand, popularity among constituents, Gallup polls, or reelection prospects. Sociological jurisprudence reaches its logical but self-defeating epitome in a passive, populist, elected judiciary that panders to the cultural barometer of the Gallup poll, trying to be all things to all social groups, giving part of the baby to each contender, and in the end succumbing to the crits' view that judging is merely distributing "policy" to the masses.

The Rights School

Rights theorists like Rawls and Dworkin conceive of law as the implementation of inherent moral principles seen as rights. The notion of inalienable natural rights prior to any civil society and apart from nature, plus the view that civil societies exist to ensure those rights, is an invention of modern legal philosophy, not ancient natural law philosophy. Rights now are founded not in nature but in social contract. The traditional human rights are political and civil rights such as the right to life, liberty, and a fair trial. What are now being put forward as universal human rights are economic and social rights, such as the right to unemployment insurance, old age pensions, medical services, and holidays with pay.

When in the eighteenth century nature was removed as the source of moral law, social contract theory was introduced to legitimate coercion by virtue of an assumed mass consent given in a hypothetical primitive state. This social contract becomes the keystone for modern rights analysis. Like all social contract theories, Rawls's theory thus rests on an imaginary situation: a group of men and women with ordinary tastes and convictions, temporarily ignorant of differing aspects of their personalities, meet in a pregovernment setting to seek agreement upon a governing contract before self-awareness develops.

These citizens choose two basic principles: (1) that every person must have the largest political liberty compatible with a like liberty for others, and (2) inequalities in power, wealth, income, and other resources must not exist except insofar as they benefit the worst-off members of the society. Contract theory presupposes this enthusiasm for shared value through the temporary suspension of awareness of individual differences. Consent gives this primitive community the right to impose judgments and demands upon individuals contrary to their well-being. This contract brings the community into being and allows it to coerce. Contract thus becomes the source of rights; there are no rights before or apart from it.

Critical questions abound for rights theory. In the first place, the social contract is hypothetical rather than historical fact. It has never happened and never will. Furthermore, even assuming its existence, it is doubtful that descendents ever buy into such an amorphous exchange by their ancestors. More crucially, the contract can hardly spell out all rights (to privacy, to one's own body, to have food stamps) nor can it mediate unforeseen conflicting rights (the government's need for tax revenues versus my right to the fruits of my labor).

Most importantly, this sort of social contract involves confusion between equality in nature and equality in ability: that all are equal as human beings does not mean equality in aptitude. Insensitivity to individual differences creates a false equality. Dworkin, like Rawls, thus gives the least productive persons important rights against society as a whole, even to the extent of suggesting that anyone may claim that "the world owes me a living." The obligation to pay runs against no one in particular. Rights exist apart from duty, even duty to oneself.[9] A Theory of Justice thus maintains that the physicist or the poet should not look down on the person who spends life performing frivolous activity like counting blades of grass; this person should be esteemed, since esteem is a basic need. This exaggerated view of equality seems to mean that we are not permitted to seek for the natural human good and be praised for it, nor, for example, is a teacher permitted to condemn sloth nor a court to condemn crime, for condemnation runs counter to the need for esteem from others.[10]

Unfortunately, no consensus exists in Rawls, Dworkin, or others as to the nature and source of these fundamental rights apart from the social contract. Presumably there are no natural rights until the contract is negotiated; thus there are none if the contract is abrogated, say by revolt. Ultimately, much of rights theory seems rooted in a psychology of need rather than in a philosophy of ought. One challenge for the rights theorists is to identify a neutral source of rights apart from contract. But common moral sentiment and norms seem just as historically fickle as the hypothetical contract. How can people have agreed to something—custom or contract—they have not really thought about and often reject when they do?

Theories that ground individual rights in social contract provide no standard to evaluate the rightness or wrongness or presocial natural liberty or to justify duty to perform the promises that constitute the social compact. A sound rights theory must explain why a particular action ought to be performed or avoided independently of need for a common denominator equality in every respect. In short, a "desire ethic" that derives obligation exclusively from a commitment to ends that different individuals may choose to seek is not an ethic at all because these ends can be arbitrarily chosen—e.g., men shall hunt and women shall cook. These "rights" could just as arbitrarily be reversed, and thus have no coercion against the woman who decides to hunt or the man who decides to cook. The social contract, like certain governments, could also seek evil rather than good, and when revolt invariably comes against such a contract, citizens exist in a rights vacuum until a new contract is negotiated by a new governing body, which necessarily will define rights differently from the prior contract. In short, contract theory has only "positive," not natural rights, and thus seems exposed to the flaws of the very positivism it seeks to overthrow.

To speak of a universal right is to speak of a universal duty; to say that all have a right to life is to impose on all the duty of respecting human life, to put all under the same prohibition against attacking, injuring, or endangering the life of any other human being. If this universal duty were not imposed, no sense could be made of the concept of a universal right.

The so-called economic and social rights popularized by former President Carter and the Helsinki Accords, insofar as they are intelligible at all, impose no such universal duty. They are rights to be given things such as a decent income, schools, and social services. But who is called upon to do the giving? Rights theory thus fits into our comfortable modernism by offering rights without duties, equality without effort, an egalitarianism blind to individual differences in talent.

NATURAL LAW

An earlier time showed a general consensus of the existence of "law" as the law of yesterday, today, and tomorrow, rooted in the historical soil of morality. Today law is becoming more fragmented, more subjective, geared more to expediency and less to morality, concerned more with immediate consequences and less with consistency or continuity. This trend has reached the point where the timeless normative character underlying written law is obscured.

Jurisprudence theories continue to vie with one another, and the competition is encouraged in the name of pluralism, our era's euphemism for relativism. None of the foregoing theories has managed to win the support of a majority of the legal world, and we are invited by default to go back to our roots in natural law. Hesitation over natural law theory seems based on the view that it is ethereal, other-worldly, a numinous presence in the sky so remote as to be unsuited to found human obligation. This suspicion seems not a problem of substantive natural law as much as of its discredited historical and metaphysical underpinnings.

Hence this modest support of a natural law theory partly by the default of those discussed above, and partly by the belief that natural law is not a brooding presence in the sky but the working of human thought in history and in legal experience. Let me take three indicia: the search for parity, the recognition of criminal law interests, and the experience of revolution.

The Search for Parity

In *The Morality of Law*, Lon Fuller located an "internal natural law" in the procedures embodied in constitution and rule that seek to ensure equal standing. He sees the due process clause of the fourteenth amendment, along with liberty of contract, as such procedural conditions.[11] The principle, for example, that no one shall profit from his own wrong, which denies inheritance rights to a murderer, is also a purely procedural rule that seeks a fair result apart from probate doctrine. Such norms are not laws as much as ways in which laws are to be applied. These procedures are inseparably connected with morality and as such are axiomatic, deducible only from a source of fairness.

In building on Fuller's analysis one can find a whole panoply of devices beyond procedural rules that seek to correct the imbalances discussed in preceding pages to provide parity to litigants: access to a jury of peers, the effort in voir dire to strip jurors of biases, the admonition to decide cases based only on evidence, devices allowing reconsideration of erroneous rulings, devices limiting discovery, techniques to shift costs, and appellate review to correct lower court error.

Parity implies both procedural and substantive rights: no guilt without a hearing, no taking of property without compensation, no convictions based on lying, no taxation without representation. These rights are not merely the procedural rights of the Fourteenth Amendment but broad substantive demands of equal treatment.

Similarly, and less codified, the use of judges and juries to administer rules reflects the belief that written rules need a human rather than mechanical application to tailor law to individual circumstances. Equity courts reflect a similar awareness that the rigidity of the written law needs, at times, to be corrected because of individual injustices—hence England to this day, and the United States in a merged format, maintain equity courts to temper the dumb hammer of the positive law. The institutional history of judge, jury, and equity courts, and even movements like alternative dispute resolution, illustrate the instinct to inculcate a higher, partly unwritten law of parity that seeks humane treatment before an impassive law.

These devices also show an effort to give each side parity of resources and equality of standing before the substantive law. Though they do not constitute substantive doctrines as such, these efforts at parity constitute a *removens prohibens*, a removal of obstacles that could inhibit consideration of substance. The pursuit of parity exemplifies that doctrine is to be applied in the absence of bias and prejudice, with an opportunity for each side to have an equal voice even before application of the substantive law.

In exercising judicial review, judges thus should be concerned not only with how the framers of the equal protection clause constructed equality, or even with how the average citizen understands equality, but rather with the true meaning of equality in the sense of parity, i.e., equal access and equal posture before the written law.

Parity refers to a metaphysical equality of human nature, not an equality of legal merit. It means among other things that like cases should be treated alike. Some thinkers believe that the maxim "like cases should be treated alike" is circular, that any two cases are similar in some respects and different in others. This circular view is a radical logical positivism that seeks to defeat the concept of equality by the same rationalism the crits deplore. This attack on equality presupposes that legal reasoning is deductive in form; it also presupposes that legal rules have a precisely defined scope of application. Both of these presuppositions are implausible. Although deductive argument may play a part in legal reasoning, it hardly constitutes the whole of legal reasoning. The scope of application of common law rules and constitutional provisions is notoriously difficult to establish. Whether two cases are alike depends on the rule under which they are judged. There is no circularity in looking to the purpose of a rule to see whether two fact situations should be treated similarly. It is commonplace legal analysis that to apply a rule to a new factual situation, one must look to the rule's purpose.

Substantive Natural Law of Interests

While the terminology of natural law may define only the roughest characterization of moral judgment, the term still makes explicit that there is a "natural" way of pursuing human ends as opposed to the purely conventional order defined by social contract or cultural will. The natural order is not the chemical or physical order but the moral order that underlies reflective human thought. The irreducible minimum of substantive natural law is the proposition that nature is significant in the evaluation of human conduct and that right/wrong determinations flow from a basis in reflective human nature other than from arbitrary will assertion.

The problems with such a substantive natural law theory seem to have been twofold: natural lawyers seem to require a human nature that is both (1) a timeless, fixed metaphysical entity, and (2) totally knowable. Darwinism is a chief obstacle to the first, and cultural anthropology, among others, an obstacle to the second. These obstacles need not be fatal. Even if evolution is fact rather than theory, homo sapiens have over five thousand years of recorded history with enough continuous teleology to suggest a regular and fixed orientation to ends. As to the second obstacle, critics of the intelligibility of human nature maintain that natural law requires a knowledge of human nature that must itself be a fixed, timeless state of mind. This argument demands too much. If human nature is totally unknowable, then so is human good, and it becomes impossible to talk about humanity as such, since persons could never be identified apart from physical description. If knowledge of humanity is impossible, the word "human" would not distinguish humans from other beings. Anything we might say would be meaningless—even including the statement that human nature is unknowable. Some historical knowledge of our natural goals must exist, and, however modest, it seems enough to recognize recurring goals.

Natural law substantively is the *determinatio*, as John Finnis puts it, by which human beings discover the goals of their nature—not *all* the goals, and not with *perfect* knowledge, to be sure, but well enough to reach seminal conclusions about what being human is about. What is understood is no less an essence of human good than are the basic rules of geometry, biology, chemistry, or physics. We come to know this nature by coming to know our capacities, which we come to know from what we in fact do regularly. These actions we understand by the goals these actions regularly seek. Because these goals are good for us as humans, there is an obligation to pursue them. This obligation is the root for all subsequent legal obligation, which at its best helps rationality flourish. Natural law in this view is the pursuit of rational life, a self-evident a priori principle not deduced from something else.

The positive law's task is to pursue the goals of human nature. It tends to achieve these goals when it brings definition and clarity by a system of rules and institutions that work toward what is best for human beings qua human. Thought, not Nietzsche's will, is primary. Once we discover that our lives are communal, our thoughts and interests become shared enterprises, with each individual demand limited by another's. We thus create a criminal law to define the limits of demand. When turned inside out to focus on protected interests rather than prohibitions, the body of penal law reveals basic interests common to humans—and indeed almost all societies: the interest in self-preservation (hence assault and murder are prohibited); the interest in self-propagation (hence crimes interfering with reproduction); the interest in resources needed to sustain and enhance life (hence theft); the interest in free movement (hence kidnapping); the interest in truth (hence fraud, perjury, and free speech statutes).

These interests protected generally by penal law and occasionally by civil law are not the arbitrary interests of competing cultures but the governmentally protected ends of individual and collective human nature. These interests exist even if not codified. Their discovery in human nature requires reflective thought precedent to will. Freedom in this view depends on reflective thought. This, in effect, is Aristotle's reply to Nietzsche and to sociological jurisprudence: human nature is not pure freedom of will but is thought. Aristotle's answer to the Marxist view of the dominance of the social and its history is similar: we are, historically, creatures of thought, subject to social formation, and to change over time only because we transcend in thought varying social or political ideas.

If social self-creation is what human nature points to, and if such a condition is a condition of thought, Aristotle's answer to the question about the good life is also clear: it is the thoughtful life, with intellect ruling will by proposing the goods to be chosen and evils to be avoided, with law protecting these interests— interests that are in our nature prior to any codification or contract, and which receive a natural law elaboration in the United Nations Declaration of Human Rights.[12]

Revolution

There is a third, albeit amorphous, index of natural law. Unlike positivism, natural law can free one from repressive political ideology. Its validity does not depend on enforcement nor on allegiance to any sovereign apart from human nature. It may be the Magna Carta of England, the *liberté, égalité, et fraternité* of revolutionary France, or the natural rights of the Declaration of Independence. It may be broader inspiration for the great national outcries against an unjust positive law, as occurred in Russia in 1917, France in 1776, America in 1789, England in 1640, and Germany in 1517. Each of these revolutions involved a violent upheaval in which the existing political, legal, religious, and cultural relations were overthrown, purified, and replaced by a new one. Each revolution shares common elements, particularly an apocalyptic vision of a future regeneration of written law to free whatever had been suppressed in human nature. These five great national revolutions each transform the written law by overhauling it to attune it to the wellsprings of human nature. These revolutions are not simply limited protests for bread or against taxes, but for the deeply human interests discussed above: liberty, equality, right to speak, right to worship, and other natural law principles existing beneath any written law, social contract, or reigning culture.

What these revolutions show is at least twofold: (1) that at times the written law becomes unbalanced in its intent, application, or both, and that (2) the human instinct for congruence to its own nature looks beyond the existing written law for a measure to determine its congruence, and hence a standard of right and wrong, true and false comes into existence to found such derivative sociological and psychological distinctions as authentic/inauthentic and sincere/insincere.

CONCLUSION

Law is a many-splendored thing with its own hierarchy. It is an instrument of domination, a means of effectuating the will of the lawmaker. But this positivist school of jurisprudence tells only part of the story. Law is also an expression of moral standards understood by reason. This natural law theory is also true. Finally, law is an outgrowth of custom, a product of historically rooted values and norms. This third view, identified with the historical schools of legal philosophy, can also claim—like the other two schools—part of the truth. This tripartite division is not equal. Natural law acts as a law for all seasons, a critique of the other theories as well as of itself in its pursuit of an infused teleology. Amid all the protests and cries of dismay at the written law, our faith as humans is not simply in the platonic ideal of justice or in the written law but in the conviction that our law, indeed any law, can be made to better approach the ends of our nature and that we as individuals, judges, courts, and governments can pressure to make it so.

Put in confrontation with positivism and sociological jurisprudence, natural law thus carries with it an implicit philosophy of human nature which, while constituted with a metaphysically fixed nature, is historically flexible. This flexibility shows up in our historical satisfaction in fighting back, individually and collectively, against the established injustices in our lives. In this sense we are both context-bound and context-breaking: we relate to each other by developing constraining social contexts, and we enrich ourselves and others by replacing these structures with new ones. Our task in such a condition is to construct social worlds of laws that more fully embody the creative power necessarily restrained to some degree in any set of laws. In this way we emancipate, over time, the richness of potentialities imbedded in our given nature.

With Fuller, natural law is thus the Eighth and Fourteenth Amendments and more: the historical search for the "X" of fairness that when added to the written law makes justice, the unending critique of the written law, the measuring rod for human law and the invitation to pursue the divine. Chesterton remarked in *What I Saw in America*:

Men will more and more realize that there is no meaning in democracy if there is no meaning in any thing, and that there is no meaning in any thing if the universe has not a center of significance and an authority that is the anchor of our rights.[13]

The nature that founds natural law thus may invite further inquiry about an author. Even a critical scholar like Unger is thus led, in *Knowledge and Politics*, to state:

Desirous of faith, touched by hope, and moved by love, men look unceasingly for God. Their search for Him continues even where thinking must stop and action fail. And in their vision of Him they find the beginning and the end of their knowledge of the world and of their sympathy for others.[14]

NOTES

1. Roberto Unger, *Knowledge and Politics* (New York: Free Press, 1975).

2. See R. Posner, "Strict Liability: A Comment," 2 *J. Legal Stud.* 205 (1973).

3. R. Posner, *Economic Analysis of Law* (3rd ed., New York: Little, Brown, 1986).

4. Robert Bork, "Neutral Principles and Some First Amendment Problems," 47 *Ind. L. J.* 1 (1971) at 10.

5. Ibid. at 10–11.

6. Ibid. at 12.

7. H.L.A. Hart, *The Concept of Law* (Oxford: Clarendon Press, 1961), pp. 188–195.

8. Richard Neely, *The Product Liability Mess* (New York: Free Press; London: Collier, Macmillan, 1988).

9. Ronald Dworkin, *Taking Rights Seriously* (London: Duckworth, 1978).

10. John Rawls, *A Theory of Justice* (Cambridge: Belknap Press, 1971).

11. Lon Fuller, *The Morality of Law* (New Haven: Yale University Press, 1977).

12. *Human Rights*, Comments and Interpretations, UNESCO (New York: Columbia University Press, 1949).

13. G. K. Chesterton, *What I Saw in America* (2nd ed. New York: Da Capo Press, 1968), p. 302.

14. Unger, *Knowledge and Politics*, p. 295.

SELECTED BIBLIOGRAPHY

ALTERNATIVE DISPUTE RESOLUTION

Christian, T., and M. Volpe, eds. *Problem Solving Through Mediation*, ABA Special Committee on Dispute Resolution, Washington, D.C. (1984).

Goldberg, Stephen B., Eric Green, and Frank E. A. Sander. *Dispute Resolution*, Little, Brown and Company, Boston (1985).

"Protecting Confidentiality in Mediation," *Harvard Law Review*, Vol. 98, #1 (Dec. 1984), pp. 441–459.

CASE MANAGEMENT

Brazil, Wayne D. "Improving Judicial Control over the Pretrial Development of Civil Actions: Model Rules for Case Management and Sanctions 1981," *American Bar Foundation Research Journal* (1981), pp. 875–965.

Connolly, Paul R. J., and Patricia A. Lombard. *Judicial Controls and the Civil Litigative Process: Motions*, Federal Judicial Center, Washington D.C. (1980).

Elliott, E. Donald. *Managerial Judging and the Evolution of Procedure*, Working Paper #35, Yale Law School Program in Civil Liability, New Haven, Connecticut (Sept. 1985), p. 33.

CIVIL JUSTICE AND LITIGATION ISSUES

Feinberg, Kenneth R., et al. *The Legal System Assault on the Economy; Vol. 1: The High Cost and Effect of Litigation*, National Legal Center for the Public Interest, Washington, D.C. (1986), p. 65.

Galanter, Marc. "Reading the Landscape for Disputes: What We Know and Don't Know (And Think We Know) About Our Allegedly Contentious and Litigious Society," reprinted from *UCLA Law Review,*, Vol. 31, Oct. 1983, pp. 4–72.

Institute for Civil Justice, *An Overview of the First Five Program Years, April 1980–March 1985*, Rand Corporation, Santa Monica, California (1985), p. 68.

Lieberman, Jethro K. *The Litigious Society*, Basic Books, New York (1983), p. 212.

COSTS OF LITIGATION

Feinberg, Kenneth R., et al. *The Legal System Assault on the Economy; Vol. 1: The High Cost and Effect of Litigation*, National Legal Center for the Public Interest, Washington, D.C. (1986), p. 65.

COURT COSTS AND DELAY

American Bar Association Action Commission to Reduce Court Costs and Delay. *Attacking Litigation Costs and Delay: Executive Summary*, [pamphlet] American Bar Association, Washington, D.C. (1984), p. 84.
Harvard Law School Program on the Legal Profession. *Recommendations to the American Bar Association Action Commission to Reduce Court Costs and Delay*, Cambridge, Massachusetts (1983), p. 168.

DISCOVERY AND CIVIL PROCEDURE

Segal, Daniel. *Survey of the Literature on Discovery from 1970 to the Present: Expressed Dissatisfactions and Proposed Reforms*, Federal Judicial Center, Washington, D.C. (1978), p. 200.
Willging, Thomas E. *Court Appointed Experts*, Federal Judicial Center, Washington, D.C. (1986), p. 25.

FRIVOLOUS LAWSUITS AND SANCTIONS

Chin, Audrey, and Mark A. Peterson. *Deep Pockets, Empty Pockets: Who Wins in Cook County Jury Trials*, Institute for Civil Justice, Rand Corporation, Santa Monica, California (1985), p. 100.
Comment, "Courts Are No Place for Fun and Frivolity: A Warning to Vexatious Litigants and Over-Zealous Attorneys," *Willamette Law Review*, Vol. 20 (1984), pp. 441–493.
Klevornick, Alvin, et al. *Information Processing and Jury Decisionmaking*, Working paper #10, Yale Law School Program in Civil Liability, New Haven, Connecticut (1983), p. 62.
Note, "The Case for Special Juries in Complex Civil Litigation," *Yale Law Journal*, Vol. 89 (1980), pp. 1155–1176.

NO FAULT LITIGATION

O'Connell, J. *Ending Insult to Injury: No-Fault Insurance for Products and Services*, University of Illinois Press, Urbana, Illinois (1975).
Posner, Richard A. *Economic Analysis of Law*, Little, Brown and Company (1977) (2nd edition).

INDEX

About the Author

RUDOLPH J. GERBER is a Judge on the Court of Appeals of Arizona. His previously published books include *Contemporary Punishment* (1972), and *The Insanity Defense* (1984), and articles in such journals as *American Journal of Jurisprudence* and *Arizona Law Journal.*